Pra

Items should be returned on or before the date shown below. Items not already requested by other borrowers may be renewed in person, in writing or by telephone. To renew, please quote the number on the barcode label. To renew online a PIN is required. This can be requested at your local library.
Renew online @ **www.dublincitypubliclibraries.ie**
Fines charged for overdue items will include postage incurred in recovery.
Damage to or loss of items will be charged to the borrower.

i............................g.

Charles Dunstone, Founder and Chairman, The Carphone Warehouse

'Congratulations on pulling together such a comprehensive list of essential learnings.'

Cli................................ esident USA
                              ., Starbucks

D1462864

Smart Retail

Pearson

At Pearson, we have a simple mission: to help people
make more of their lives through learning.

We combine innovative learning technology with trusted
content and educational expertise to provide engaging
and effective learning experiences that serve people
wherever and whenever they are learning.

From classroom to boardroom, our curriculum materials, digital
learning tools and testing programmes help to educate millions
of people worldwide – more than any other private enterprise.

Every day our work helps learning flourish, and
wherever learning flourishes, so do people.

To learn more, please visit us at **www.pearson.com/uk**

Smart Retail

Winning ideas and strategies from the
most successful retailers in the world

Fourth edition

Richard Hammond

 **Pearson**

Harlow, England • London • New York • Boston • San Francisco • Toronto • Sydney
Auckland • Singapore • Hong Kong • Tokyo • Seoul • Taipei • New Delhi
Cape Town • São Paulo • Mexico City • Madrid • Amsterdam • Munich • Paris • Milan

PEARSON EDUCATION LIMITED
Edinburgh Gate
Harlow CM20 2JE
United Kingdom
Tel: +44 (0)1279 623623
Web: www.pearson.com/uk

First published 2003 (print)
Second edition 2007 (print)
Third edition 2011 (print and electronic)
Fourth edition published 2017 (print and electronic)

© Pearson Education Limited 2003, 2007 (print and electronic)
© Pearson Education Limited 2011, 2017 (print and electronic)

ISBN: 978-1-292-08220-2 (print)
        978-1-292-08221-9 (PDF)
        978-1-292-08223-3 (ePub)

British Library Cataloguing-in-Publication Data
A catalogue record for the print edition is available from the British Library

Library of Congress Cataloging-in-Publication Data
Names: Hammond, Richard (Retail management consultant), author.

Title: Smart retail : winning ideas and strategies from the most successful
  retailers in the world/Richard Hammond.
Description: Fourth edition. | Harlow, England, UK: Pearson Education,
  [2016] | Includes index.
Identifiers: LCCN 2016042270 (print) | LCCN 2016051606 (ebook) | ISBN
  9781292082202 (pbk.) | ISBN 9781292082233
Subjects: LCSH: Retail trade—Management.
Classification: LCC HF5429 .H2824 2016 (print) | LCC HF5429 (ebook) | DDC
  658.8/7—dc23
LC record available at https://lccn.loc.gov/2016042270

10 9 8 7 6 5 4 3 2
21 20 19 18 17

Cover design by Two Associates
Cover image © calvindexter/iStock

Print edition typeset in 9.5/13, ITC Giovanni Std by iEnergizer, Aptara® Ltd.
Print edition printed and bound in Malaysia by CTP-PJB

NOTE THAT ANY PAGE CROSS REFERENCES REFER TO THE PRINT EDITION

Smart Retail will always be dedicated to customers; without whom...

Contents

CONTENTS

About the author

Source: Koworld

With more than 30 years of retail experience, **Richard Hammond** believes there never has been such an exciting time to be a retailer. Everywhere in this industry there is innovation, buzz and excitement. Richard plays his part as a retail problem-solver, from format development to customer experience and service-model design to operational review. Inevitably, as he closes in on 50, with so much to look back on, he is also looking forward as a retail futurologist.

He misses the early days with customers in-store but technology and opportunity have brought that thrill right back as he helps retailers and brands tackle the new reality that everywhere can be a store and that now location might even just be a state of mind . . .

Acknowledgements

Thanks once again for all the generous support and suggestions you brilliant retailers and my lovely friends have so kindly given. Thanks especially on this edition for the help and direct support of Emily, Rocky, Graeme, Kevin, Hugo and Helen. Thanks for the inspiration provided by my incredible retail undergraduates at the University of Westminster. And thanks for the distractions and beer regularly provided by Jim, John, Jason and again Rocky and Graeme.

A career in retail has taken me away from family and friends for big chunks of time, so to be a retailer would be impossible without the patience of the people we love. I have been so lucky to have a wonderful family to support me in the twists and turns of my life in retail. To my children Rosy, Isabella, Arthur and to our new baby Ezra, to my amazing partner and editor Emily and to my inspirational boy Ptolemy – thanks for being the best, kindest people I know.

Special thanks are due to those retailers who were there at the start – the people from whom I have learnt the most important early lessons: Umesh Vadodaria, Mahendra Patel, Steve Smith and Glyn Moser – all who put people first and proved that great retail is about fun and passion, creativity and teamwork, and that customers are the beginning and end of everything.

Thanks to Rachael Stock at Pearson for making the original edition better than I imagined it ever could be. Thanks to Eloise Cook, my current publisher, who has proven to be the most patient client I've ever had, for which I am incredibly grateful. I'm also grateful for the insight, challenge and knowledge she has applied to making this the best edition so far.

Thanks also to the dozens of retailers who gave up time, advice and ideas for *Smart Retail* – you know who you are and you are all superstars.

Finally, all the effort, sacrifice, setbacks and challenges have been worth it. Retail is the best life in the world.

Publisher's acknowledgements

We are grateful to the following for permission to reproduce copyright material:

Photos on pp xi, 2, 82, 104, 119, 138, 179 and 303 © Koworld; photo on p 123 reprinted courtesy of Wanzl; sketch on p 168 reprinted courtesy of the US Patent Office; photo on p 278 from the Royal Institute of British Architects Picture Archives.

Extract on pp 54–5 and 254 from 'The aggressive, outrageous, infuriating (and ingenious) rise of BrewDog', *The Guardian* (Henley, J.), 24 March 2016, copyright Guardian News & Media Ltd 2016; extract on p 178 from 'How Boots went rogue', *The Guardian* (Chakrabortty, A.), 13 April 2016, copyright Guardian News & Media Ltd 2016; extract on p 247 from 'Reality bytes back', *The Guardian* (Brooker, C.), November 2006, copyright Guardian News and Media Ltd 2006.

Introduction to the fourth edition

As I write this fourth edition of *Smart Retail*, I'm 13 years further along from the first. So much has changed in those years, not just in retail terms but also in my own confidence in a career and my understanding of the world in which I operate. It happens to us all and is one of the positive benefits that come from doing a thing long enough that you get really good at it. I'm sure it's happening to you too.

Some ideas I included in previous editions were originally informed hunches based on observing the world's best retailers, and most of these hunches have gone on to be proven correct many times over. During that time I've had the opportunity to refine my ideas and my professional practice with many great clients, an opportunity that came from the original *Smart Retail*'s big success. Lots of readers have told me how useful the book has been for them. I love hearing that feedback; knowing that something you've slaved over is actually of benefit to another person feels great. Subsequent editions have outsold the previous ones, which is apparently unusual in business publishing. New editions normally serve to squeeze the stone till the last drop of revenue reluctantly slithers out of it until some tastier flavour of the month comes along.

Why does this book sell more copies each time? I believe that is in part a function of retailing in general. We retailers are hungry for ideas and inspiration but our market changes not just in time with product and technology but also with changes in social norms and human behaviours. As our customers change and grow and the societies we operate in transform, the opportunities to feed retail consumption also change and fold and morph. The fundamentals are consistent: find ways to put stuff in front of people to whom it is of interest and work out how best to engage them in that stuff and to swap it for a commercial benefit. What changes is the way in which we can do those things, and the attitudes and needs of the people we hope to engage.

Who is *Smart Retail* for?

Over the previous three editions, I firmly placed *Smart Retail* in the sphere of an enterprising store manager or owner. This time I need to adjust that positioning. The rate of retail change has developed over the last half decade at an unprecedented pace. I will explain the impact of this in more detail in the Secrets section, but that change has produced one development so fundamental to what we do, that it overwhelms almost everything.

It is the word "almost" that is one of the biggest benefits of reading this new edition. I promise to help you avoid throwing the baby out with the bath water and identify the right relationship for your business between technology and emotion, such that you keep the critical things and develop the right solutions to the new realities around those.

This massive rocking of our retail boat has meant that I've needed to bring to the surface some significant chunks of the supporting theory. Times are more complex for us now as there are lots more balls to juggle, but there are also many more opportunities to put our formats in front of the right customers at exactly the right moments.

So for the first half of the book I have moved the emphasis to retail leadership, to those developing new formats, running sparky new independents, integrating new technologies and those whose livelihood depends on them backing the right horses. I am presenting a collection of new fundamentals that have never before been put together in the way I have: this is your headstart, right here in this book.

Despite this, *Smart Retail* remains a holistic book on retailing. I want as many of the answers to be in here as possible, so as well as exploring, for example, the psychology of choice, you'll look at motivating a retail store team on a tough Saturday morning. But if you're not a CEO or keen commercial director but are an enterprising store manager, I believe it is critical that you too should also be aware of the theories that will have such a profound impact on what you do day in and day out. You are the future of this industry, always have been and always will be. You and your teams continue to be the most efficient and productive interfaces with customers: you are the ones who *know* customers.

So why shouldn't you also be in on the future? Understanding the tools that come your way, in a fundamental machine-under-the-hood fashion, will make you better able to get the most from those tools as you make your way along a retail career.

Scribbles and coffee stains

When all is said and done, this is still a working book. I invite you to flick through, to cherry-pick the bits that suit you best, scribble on the pages, tear stuff out, and share it. If I ever came into your office or store, I would love to see that your copy has a broken spine, page corners turned down, a forest of Post-it Notes sticking out the top, and coffee stains on the cover. Some readers send me photos of their dog-eared, well-used copies of the book, which I love seeing. They make my mum proud.

Why retailing?

One thing that hasn't changed is that retail is still physically and mentally hard work. The pressure is always on, we're only ever as good as our last trading day, and sometimes even making a big profit isn't good enough for the City! *Make More*! Every time we open our stores or flick on the servers*, what follows could be a disaster or a triumph.

And that's the answer to the question "Why retail?" because, despite the constant pressure to get things right, make difficult decisions, inspire the team to pull together, try new things and make customers happy and take some money . . . Ahh wow, those are the days that keep us all coming back for more.

Doing retail right – prompting a person we don't know to make a free choice to spend money with us, to type our name in a browser, to walk past competitors' stores – it's thrilling, it really is.

And now, we're able to put our stores exactly where and when customers are thinking about the kinds of things we can do for them. We can do it physically, virtually and a hundred hybrids in between. That's inspiring and exciting and it's today.

So, are physical and internet retailing different things?

Nope. Next question.

---

* I know you don't actually do that to the servers but I couldn't think of a better expression for going online. Perhaps that's a point in itself: virtual stores tend to open once and then stay open no matter the time of day or day of the year.

Really?

One of the biggest mistakes retailers make right now is to define bricks and mortar and online as completely different animals. They are not. All retailing is about customers, engaging people, creating experiences that make them want to shop, supporting these experiences after the sale, and putting ourselves into the customers' consideration.

All retailing is about the simplest question: Why would a person want to shop this way, in this location, with this system and for this experience?

In the section The seven secrets of modern retail I will provide all the evidence you could want because this is the new reality: customers are now in charge and we must do things their way, no matter the transaction.

Retailers are brilliant

As I write this, I'm wearing a pair of Bose noise-cancelling headphones. Yes, I'm in a café in Berlin with a laptop like a wannabe writer idiot. But I bought these headphones in a branch of Target in Philadelphia. I hadn't intended to buy them. I was researching Target for the book but there was a fantastic display of headphones and it got me engaged.

Target had installed a Bose demo unit that asked you to put on the headphones and then watch a video. The video featured a chap on an aeroplane enjoying a quiet and relaxed flight because of his Bose noise-cancelling headphones and it explained how much this model deadens tiring aircraft noise.

Then the video asked you to take off the headphones, which I did, revealing, to my absolute surprise, that the display unit itself was blaring out aircraft noise. But I hadn't been able to hear that noise because I'd been wearing the Bose noise-cancelling headphones.

I bought a pair immediately. It was that impressive a demo.

But what had Bose sold me? Silence. An absence of something. It might be a manufacturer's demo kit but I experienced it in a store. We retailers can perform miracles! We can sell people silence. Retail is incredible.

Asking the questions

That brilliance is practised across this awesome industry and that's where the impetus for this book came from. It was written as an interpretation of three simple questions that I asked, and continue to ask, of as many of the world's best retailers as would talk to me, which rather wonderfully was pretty much everyone I targeted.

That question was simple: "What makes you so good?" Which I would then follow up with: "What do you do that your competitors don't?" And finally, "Why do your customers go past other people's stores to come to yours?"

Since then, I've asked those same questions of every retailer I meet and have noticed that, no matter what their formats, physical, virtual or a combination, all of the world's best retailers do a small number of critical things in very similar ways. Those things are all here in *Smart Retail*, so let's do it!

What's in *Smart Retail*?

Part 1: The seven secrets of modern retail is a must-read for anyone developing retail strategy, considering operational change or developing on and offline formats, and is vital reading for all retailers who want to know what modern customers need.

Part 2: A bit of doing it is the practical part of the book that serves up tried and trusted consistencies of retailing in a modern connected context. If you manage a store, run an independent web store or operate a small chain, then this is essential reading. There's plenty of important comment on fundamental principles for those of you operating inside big retailers too.

Appendices: I've thrown some useful bits in here that don't fit anywhere else or that might interrupt the flow. You'll find such things as a tool for reading stores and a recommended further reading list.

www.Smart-Circle.com: I've put some extras on my website, including free-to-read bonus chapters, such as one-on-one lessons from the history of retail. This is also where you'll find new case studies and any updates that might emerge between editions.

Part

1

The seven secrets
of modern retail

Technology is changing everything, or is it?

Source: Koworld

We could once dictate to customers that this is a store, you shop at it how we want, pay how we want at a cash desk where we choose to place it and have it staffed by people trained to our standard not yours. But that era is over, finished. Gone forever. The customer dictates now and you must rise to meet them.

Introduction: how customers have taken charge

Part 1 of *Smart Retail* is for:

- **Retail leaders:** you'll find here in one place seven critical tools for analysing customer experience, improving format engagement and uncovering performance improvement opportunities. There is the potential to drive major change projects as a result and my team are always happy to help shape those, so do get in touch.

- **Owners and entrepreneurs:** follow the ideas and advice here and you will either sharpen your current offer or find a stronger and better one. All independent retail businesses will benefit from running through this material.

- **Store managers:** give yourself a head start by absorbing and learning the theory and ideas set out here. You will also uncover opportunities to improve the business that are worth sharing with your senior team.

- **Students and early career retailers:** you are our industry's future, so absorb and add the following to your melting pot of ideas and inspiration. Please feel free to challenge and shape the material and, as is the case for all readers, do get in touch and let me have your perspectives on it.

The seven secrets

I have deliberately avoided too much concentration on theory in previous editions of this book, preferring to work on the here and now of what is effective and practical. But things have moved so fast in our industry since the last edition in 2011 that to not explore these new fundamentals would be to sell the reader short. The most important change I'm referring to is dealt with directly in the first "secret" and it is the move from retailers holding all the power to a new reality in which it is now customers who have full control.

I used to think that calling the consistencies I'd observed in the best retail businesses "secrets" was somehow disingenuous. They aren't secret – they're pretty damn obvious if you look at enough successes. But what I've also discovered is that whether you are the CEO of a plc or a scary year into your first shop, what looks obvious to a third-party observer probably isn't always obvious to the poor sod at the coalface.

I've called the most important consistencies of modern retailers "secrets" for this edition because I suspect that it flags them in a way that is more helpful to a retailer who is looking for answers. I've always wanted this book to be one that real retailers can take into battle with them – be that the battle to create a credible strategy, or the battle to make enough money this weekend to keep the lights on.

Who needs to know about this stuff if it digs deeper into the theoretical? Of course you must if you are considered a retail leader and, if you are, these seven secrets will be golden for you. But if you're running a single store, leading a department, shaping e-commerce, or just keen to understand better the new workings of the retail machine, then you absolutely must have access to these secrets. Nobody else is talking about them in the way that I do and you have the possibility to work with me in shaping our understanding of these new realities. With big change comes real excitement and fun – it's a great time to be doing what we do.

Modern retail – modern realities

This part of the book comprises seven chapters, each of which reveals a fundamental secret of retailing in the modern age. Some of these secrets are fundamentals that have held true in some form for at least the last 30 years, Big Idea and respectful management of people especially, but others have been rocketed up to the top of the list of essential retail needs by the violent change in power that has seen the relationship between retailer and customer transform as it has.

Much of that change in power has been precipitated by the staggering scope of technology-led change and Secret Six deals with not only the opportunities and necessities of technology but also looks forward beyond the idea of "omni-channel retailing" to a very close reality where retailing becomes entirely "location-agnostic".

The one caveat to the importance of this section is one that I've always given: should you find yourself trading in an under-shopped marketplace where demand outstrips sellers and vendors or square footage (think UK home improvement in the 1980s or video games in the UK and USA in the 2000s), then nothing matters much beyond loading the shelves. I don't see any market like that right now or for the foreseeable future though.

So, like the rest of us, you're probably operating in an intensively competitive market, full of savvy competitors and demanding customers. For you, these seven secrets are absolutely essential to your creation, growth, survival and chances to flourish.

Big times, big words

Okay, I admit it, you've rumbled me. Secrets is a bit of hyperbole, a tricksy artifice that our brains happily and powerfully aid and abet by imbuing with valuable meaning. Bear with me, this isn't a tangent. The reason I've used words such as "secrets" and "fundamentals" is the same reason we retailers must pay closer attention to the way in which we wrap experiences and products with words and frames (among a host of other elements) that help customers feel a particular way about those experiences and products. The third, fourth and fifth secrets deal directly with this idea but it runs through pretty much the whole of this book.

So the secrets themselves are definitely not unknowables that I've pulled out of thin air – but they are definitely insights that are much thinner on the retail ground than they should be. A few truly great retail businesses are doing all of them instinctively, while others clearly have a powerful understanding of most of them, but many are fumbling right now to get to the bottom of the seismic tremors that are rocking our worlds.

What you can be sure of is that almost all currently upward trending retailers have most of these secrets sitting at the heart of their way of doing business.

Retail secret one: low friction and high reward

How customer control means we must reduce shopping friction and balance this with a better understanding of how shopping experiences deliver reward.

Retail secret two: what's the Big Idea?

Why you need to understand what you, as a retail business, are for.

Retail secret three: want? Got. Need!

How to understand and meet customer need states.

Retail secret four: "I'm just looking"

Why discovery is vital in modern retailing.

Retail secret five: I choose stories

How curation and narrative make it easier to decide to buy.

Retail secret six: the everywhere store

What location now means and how online and offline are irrelevant labels.

Retail secret seven: "we love working here"

How great employment experiences are vital to great customer ones.

Guaranteed success

I really should have put a question mark at the end of that heading. If you've bought the book because you flicked through the pages and just read "Guaranteed success", I sort of apologise. But not really – I'm a retailer, we love a hook and you know what we're like – you're one of us. So this is a question, not an absolute.

Does following the seven secrets of retail guarantee you success? No, it doesn't.

Three of them are fundamentals that are always there in retail successes but are also occasionally present in retail failures too. That's another one of the thrilling, pit-of-the-stomach things about what we do. Our success still depends on whether or not other people buy into what we're selling. Very occasionally, they just don't, despite our best efforts. Often, experiments we try, ones that look like real crackers on paper, don't work. That is the nature of trying and learning. Mistakes, dead ends and false starts are also the stuff of success because every single one of those is a chance to learn something and do it better next time. I've often talked about Ray Kroc and his string of failures until, at 52, he recognised something special in the way two brothers named McDonald were operating their burger joint. Kroc wasn't a failure because he never gave up trying.

But if your retail strategy or business don't have at least the spirit or the beginnings of the seven secrets within their DNA, then a failure is strongly indicated. I've seen few successes that don't have the first three sorted. There are also very few retail market leaders that don't incorporate three out of the remaining four in their way of doing things.

The great retailers today, but to a large extent through post-war retailing history across the Western world, all understand what they are for. They trade with a simplicity and clarity of purpose, they put *nothing* in the way of the customer handing over their money. They inspire customers by going beyond the product and instead sell how it feels to unlock the benefits delivered by consuming those products. Also, they understand increasingly that the store is wherever the customer is, that the same customer can be different people at different times (much more on that shortly) and that great employment experiences lead to great customer experiences.

So the seven secrets might not be a guarantee of success, but following them, building them into the absolute DNA of the business is going to take you a significant distance further down the road to it.

I believe that following the secrets is absolutely essential for start-up retailers and there are almost no existing retailers that would fail to benefit from reshaping their strategy around them.

Proof through exception

This is a fun game if you enjoy these things. Take any struggling big retailer and measure them against the seven secrets. I guarantee you'll find at least one of the secrets is missing. Most often Big Idea but failure to inspire will usually be there. How about testing yourself too?

Chapter

The unwritten primary law of retailing, a kind
of customer covenant, is that we must make it easy
for people to spend money with us. So simple,
so often ignored.

Retail secret one: low friction and high reward

In this chapter we explore

- purchase friction
- customer reward in the widest context
- friction/reward indexing.

Maths to describe life

In recent years, I have come to believe that it is completely possible to apply mathematics to every single retail format, shopping visit, contact point, needs state and interaction. To every product, in every context.

If you've read my work before, this revelation is probably a startling one. I talk a lot about instinct, common sense and practical awareness, and that's all still true. But to make sense of the biggest retail change of all time, the shift of power from retailer to customer, to understand purchase friction, shopping reward and the minute levers that can be pulled to influence both sides of that equation, we need maths.

I'm working on refining specific equations to calculate friction/reward indexes in partnership with the University of Oxford and an extremely clever mathematician there. Follow me on Twitter or subscribe to my deliberately infrequent mailing list and you'll get the first updates on what that partnership is producing. It will be practical but it'll be surprisingly scientific too.

But don't wait for the fruits of that refining. I've laid out the base theory here and explored practical ways in which you can begin to apply it. Before you do anything else in your business, I strongly recommend following the structure here to carry out a friction/reward audit.

No other tool I've seen can give you a clearer picture of where gaps and opportunities lie and the best places to allocate time, money and people.

Why friction and reward and why now?

Friction and reward have moved front and centre because of the transfer of power from retailers to customers. Where once we retailers could dictate – this is a store, this is what you can buy, this is how much it will cost, this is the service we will condescend to give you – now we are in an age where customers can get whatever they want, compare a range of prices and circumvent our nonsense at will. The change this precipitates is staggering and few seem to understand it right now. You, though, must or your career in retail will get bumpy very soon.

All successful retail innovation now is happening when retailers do one, or both, of two things:

- Reduce purchase friction and/or
- Increase shopping reward

Customers are going where it's either easy or brilliant and the choice of which is entirely theirs.

A web of wants, frictions, needs and reward

But what considerations, what variables, are influencing customers in that choice?

A selection of friction variables might include:

- travel distance
- time needed to complete a shopping task
- page, app and store layouts
- clarity of communications
- trust
- discovery
- delivery
- product knowledge

- payment
- processes specific to the scenario, such as putting a coin in a supermarket trolley or having to measure a room.

A selection of reward variables might include:

- price advantage
- service quality
- promotional impact on the customer
- brand halo
- additional services
- meeting of needs beyond consumption
- tribal identification
- experiential elements
- fun (yes, really)
- thrill of specialism
- rewards specific to the scenario, such as Amazon Prime membership or early contract redemption on a mobile phone.

Motivating action

Friction and reward. Understanding the interplay between these two lists of variables is what marks out the new successes from the old failures. The new reality is that today nobody has to go to a supermarket, park up, put a massive box of washing powder in their trolley, push it around, lug it to the car and carry it into their house – and huff and puff as they do so.

Nobody *has* to. But they *will* if the reward for doing so outweighs the friction involved. So they will buy that washing powder from Aldi or Lidl and do those physical things if the reward makes it worthwhile. Or they will click an Amazon "dash" button that is fixed to their washing machine where that click will instigate an automatic same-day delivery of their favourite brand of powder.

Lag?

Classical economic models are closed and to work properly require unreasonable assumptions such as "all other things being equal", all while attempting to model a world that doesn't actually exist. Behavioural economics instead attempts to describe a world of biases, nudges, human irrationality and imperfections.

Friction/reward for retailers lives in this real world and will be affected by exactly these conditions. When we run indexing for clients, we attempt to control for these imperfections by incorporating them in the maths. There is, however, one that cannot be incorporated in this way and it is the lag that results from our natural risk-averse decision-making position. You might feel like a risk-taker but the human tribe really doesn't work like that. We need significant nudging to abandon a known state to even try a potentially more beneficial but untried state.

Essentially, what this means is that decreasing friction and increasing reward is just part of the challenge – you then have to find ways to bring risk-averse customers into sampling your improvements. And that's always been how it is as a commercial organisation – you have to be better and be recognisably so. There will be a lag between improving and customers coming to those improvements, but when they do the flow becomes exponential. One person tells three, three people tell three more, those nine tell twenty-seven and so on until you are Amazon.

Walking the trend, not the snapshot

So why is it that millions of people still go to a big supermarket and buy their heavy box of washing powder? I know we have small tabs now, but stick with me. What we are experiencing is exactly the inertia of change I've just talked about. The change has already happened, but habits are yet to universally reflect that, though the signs are already there. How we shop for FMCG as a society has changed dramatically, especially in Europe. The weekly big shop is dying. Top-up, value and convenience are growing because customers are in charge and are able to make choices based on friction and reward.

The difference is snapshot versus trend. Your choice as a retailer is to operate to the snapshot or bravely risk interpreting the trend.

A snapshot of the buying of washing powder taken today will tell you that most washing powder is bought in big supermarkets and taken home by customers in cars.

But the trend shows that the amount of washing powder bought in the big supermarkets is falling while the amount bought in value retailers is rising and the amount that is home-delivered is rising too. The trend shows that building a format or location strategy around people buying washing powder from big supermarkets and driving it home themselves has a limited long-term viability.

But how long? The million-dollar question. Take a look at the previous ten years of retailing and you'll see that the timescale for any fundamental and foundation-shaking change in this industry is shorter than you think. Even better, run a friction/reward indexing audit and you should see opportunities to give customers more of what they want instead of what they currently tolerate.

Let's get these clothes washed

Let's look at washing powder purchase on the basis of friction and reward. What effect might doing so have on our format development, location strategy, interface design, range, service and so on?

The status quo is that large boxes of washing powder are sold mostly in big supermarkets that we drive to. The friction side of the equation is high:

> Drive to the supermarket + find a coin for the damn trolley + push trolley around through screaming kids, gaggles of awkward students incapable of considering that you might be wanting to come past (might be an Oxford thing), avoiding the Bluetooth-headset-wearing gits abandoning their trollies in the middle of the aisle to go and fetch a wheel of camembert + find and lift a large pack of heavy washing powder + queue for a till + unpack and then repack your trolley while under pressure from an angry looking pensioner next in the queue + take your trolley out to the car + load the car + return your trolley + drive home + unload the car + put away the washing powder.

Reward: you now have washing powder.

In the context of a large weekly shop, the washing powder shares a fraction of each of those elements in the fiction equation. But you get the point: this is a high friction purchase.

The new supermarket landscape is that large boxes of washing powder are also sold in smaller value supermarkets offering big savings.

Friction remains high in that the customer still has to jump over some frustrating hurdles. You do all those things listed in the friction equation above, with possibly a longer wait at the till added in.

Reward: you now have washing powder, but you have paid considerably less for it than you would have done under the old status quo. The reward is high enough for you to feel that battling the friction was worthwhile.

Enter the online options where large boxes of washing powder are sold online by supermarkets but also by online specialists.

Friction is much lower: you open your computer or scan a barcode with a phone + click "buy" + complete your purchase + sit back in your favourite chair, drink tea, wear your dirty clothes and wait for the washing powder to turn up.

Reward: you now have washing powder and you may even have paid less for it than you might have done in the supermarket.

Alternative need states

Now throw in another variable, in this case an alternative need state, and the reward part of the equation can change dramatically.

You need washing powder *quickly* because you need to get a wash on to finish tonight and be dry by the morning.

You drive to a supermarket.

Friction: as we established earlier, friction is high.

Reward: you have the washing powder in time. This is temporarily more valuable to you than washing powder might be in your usual need state.

But there are other options too: you walk to a nearby convenience store.

Friction: walk + squeeze round a small store + probably choose from a limited range of powders + possibly pay a premium + possibly buy a smaller pack size because you're carrying it + walk home.

Reward: you have the washing powder in time but you have paid more for it. Again, it is still the case that "in-time" washing powder has a higher value to you than the things that would normally be considered negatives in other need states.

But it's this next version of the transaction that will come to dominate: you order washing powder online at a great price and pay a small fee for it to be delivered to your home within an hour.

Friction: open browser or phone app + order with one click + wait for delivery.

Reward: you have the washing powder in time. You have paid a great price that may even cancel out the small delivery fee. You haven't even had to put on the clothes that you're so desperate to wash. You have ordered the washing powder in your underwear and the experience has been close to friction-free.

Eventually, because this last scenario offers the lowest friction and highest reward, this is the way almost all washing powder will be bought. And because the customer is in charge, there is nothing you can do about it. Whether it suits your business or not, the customer will decide.

The death of physical commodity retail

A side-effect of the friction/reward equation is that all purchasing of commodity products that have no possible additional reward element will shift completely online. Even the Aldi, Lidl and Netto value retailers eventually will not be able to tip the reward side away from the frictionless purchase of commodity items online. Were I a betting man, I would suggest that Europe will be in this position by 2020.

Finding the numbers

We can start to turn each of the above into equations. Doing so will give each need state and shopping experience a number.

$$\text{Friction} - \text{reward} = \text{FR index}$$

The aim should be to create solutions to need states that result in negative numbers. So an index of F – R = –2 would mean that you have a need state and visit experience where reward trumps friction.

"Create a store or shopping tool where reward overcomes friction, and beats competing alternatives, and customers will go for it"

If you discover that customers are either faced with a positive FR or can meet the same need states elsewhere at a lower FR, you know you have a problem. But more importantly, you know what you need to fix.

The aim is to build a matrix of FR numbers across need states, locations, formats and so on. Then do the same for your competitors. Armed with such a matrix, you will be able to see instantly where your strengths and weaknesses lie. It is a better map to retail transformation.

Applying the theory

I've created a model FR indexing audit structure. Even saying "FR indexing audit structure" makes me feel a bit theoretically queasy but it's too important to attempt to reduce it to something Fisher Price.

The aim of an audit is simple: it's a system to identify key customer scenarios and give each a friction/reward index. Then compare that across the business and across competitors so you know where you're strong and where the problems are.

It expresses numerically the relationship between everything you do and how much customers (the people in charge now, remember) can be bothered to respond to it or not.

The benefits are huge as it allows you to:

- identify gaps
- identify opportunities
- target resources where they will have the greatest impact
- visualise why change is useful.

Example 1: Targeting resources

You might identify a shortfall in product knowledge. Normally you would invest in fixing this shortfall as soon as possible. But friction/reward indexing might reveal that actually in most scenarios and customer need states this issue isn't that important to customers. The added friction is more than cancelled out by something in the reward side of the equation. Because this is an audit that looks across shopping scenarios, need states, customer touch points and competitors, you also discover that what customers are massively influenced by is a more generous refund policy. You are then free to invest in the refund policy first, knowing that doing so will drive sales more significantly than fixing product knowledge.

Example 2: Competitor analysis

Your audit uncovers that a particular competitor's web feature reduces friction so significantly that it now trumps your more competitive pricing. You recognise that realistically you are able to develop something similar without losing the price advantage. You thought your price advantage was attractive but it turns out that the reduced friction offered by a competitor was a more powerful attractor to customers. You make the friction-reducing change and customers migrate towards your better priced, similarly frictioned option.

Example 3: Spreading the excellence

It becomes clear that there are a number of scenarios in which you deliver an extremely attractive FR index. There is, however, one where you don't. Drilling down into the component parts of each side of the FR indexes relative to each other, you realise that it is just one policy in the weaker area that is causing the imbalance. You find a way to change this policy such that it is no longer a source of friction. In doing so, you begin to be recognised as an attractive option for customers with that particular need state. Sales rise.

Friction/reward in the real world

There have been some incredible head-in-the-sand responses to customers now being in charge, and it has cost retailers their businesses, employees their livelihoods and customers their favourite old brands. It was a lack of understanding of this shift that killed Borders, Comet and Woolworths. Meanwhile, the likes of John Lewis in the UK and Williams-Sonoma in the USA, traditional old-school retailers, have quietly reshaped their businesses to take the friction out, especially online, and to increase the reward of physical store visits.

Williams-Sonoma now takes 50% of its sales revenue online but concurrently operates fabulous store formats that customers are drawn to because the reward for visiting is high. John Lewis has become an uber-example of the notion of high-reward, low-friction retailing. It is an everywhere store that customers feel is set up to work for them: shopping online, in-store, price matching, after sales. All of it is built not to John Lewis's needs, but to customer needs. That's incredibly prescient and very powerful. It wasn't a cheap change but a little financial pain has provided both these retailers with powerful and flexible platforms that mean they can ensure reward outweighs friction for any given customer need state. And, of course, both updated retailers are thriving year after year.

Here are some case studies that show how retailers have taken out friction.

Ryanair (Ireland)
Complete change of web sales focus

Ireland's famously customer-baiting budget airline Ryanair completely rebuilt its web booking tools, going from an experience that deliberately and constantly stopped customers in order to sell extras, to one that is now recognised as offering among the very fastest booking experiences. In the first full year of the new site profits are up 43 % to EUR 1.3bn.

Apple (USA)
Redefined payment processes

Apple removed the need to queue at a till, as well as the junk of paperwork. You can be advised, stock can be checked and the transaction completed without ever having to queue. I could have chosen any one of a billion examples from Ron Johnson's brilliant Apple Store, but go and check out his amazing Enjoy.com, a retailer that takes even more friction out of the purchase of tech. It's a brilliant, brilliant retail concept.

The great British pub (UK)

Embraced new technology to make transactions easier and faster

Contactless payment in British pubs is removing the need to visit cash machines, worry about minimum transaction values and cause a queue as the customer drunkenly misremembers their PIN. It's a friction-reducing change that is pushing spend-per-customer up.

Albert Heijn To Go (Netherlands)

Physical fixtures that make it easier to put together a meal

Brilliant Dutch convenience format Albert Heijn To Go has cabinets where the same unit can hold a hot breakfast sandwich range and a shelf of chilled juices at the same time. At lunchtime it can change to hot panini and cold Cokes. This tiny friction reduction boosts average transaction values as more customers take advantage of a multi-item meal deal.

And now here are some case studies that show increased rewards to provide more reasons to visit

Respublica (Russia)

Rethought browsing

Expanding Russian bookshop chain Respublica uses clever adjacencies, artist events, cool cafes and DJs to make the stores social and inspirational. Customers consider browsing there as fun and not a chore. Being a Respublica customer feels like a reward in itself. The reward is discovery and belonging.

Halfords (UK)

Eased the option to visit

Halfords simplified its quick-fitting services for small automotive parts, making it easy to come into a store and have a new part fitted. It has also increased staff training and presence dramatically, prioritising advice and practical assistance over shelf-stacking. It has paid off handsomely, with big increases in footfall and a massive sustained jump in ATV, revenue and profit.

Bonobos (USA)

Supports online with a reimagined physical experience

Constantly innovating US upper mid-market apparel retailer Bonobos augmented its existing very strong online business with a chain of "Guideshops", locations stocking all sizes and all colours of all styles all the time – a fashion retailer's impossible dream! At these Guideshops, customers first book one-to-one try-on sessions. At the end of the session, there is no pressure, but everything tried, everything liked has been scanned and the customer sees a clickable round-up of all the things they liked in all the right sizes and colours. They can then order right there or at any time from an accompanying email.

The reward for visiting the Guideshop is huge. Customers have tried things on, enjoyed a stylist's help and advice and been able to touch and see fabrics and shapes. And for Bonobos, customers are in its ecosystem, now know their offer and have been through a unique Bonobos experience. That's massive. Even better, in 2016 CEO Andy Dunn said that the Guideshops are profitable, "drawing customers who tend to spend a little more and buy more [high-ticket] tailored items like suits, dress shirts and wool pants; than online-only shoppers, who gravitate to casual wear".

GAIL's Bakery (UK)

Makes the purchase of staples something special

GAIL's Bakery, the upmarket chain now busting out of London, has created a replicable format based on artisan breads and good coffee. It lifts the reward for buying a commodity (bread) into something that feels special, more pleasurable than grabbing a loaf while trundling around Sainsbury's or ordering online. But the key is that it does so in a format that appears to the customer to be as easy to shop as a traditional baker.

Net-a-Porter (UK)

Invests in credible curation

Net-a-Porter's runaway luxury fashion success is down, in part, to the rewarding quality of its deep commitment to editorial credibility. Fashionistas trust the team and come for the insight, then click for the clothes.

Interior Define (USA)
Bringing "have it your way" to a surprising sector

Chicago-based sofa manufacturer and retailer Interior Define (ID) has specifically targeted customers wanting to graduate from identikit IKEA furniture but who are not ready for big designer budgets. ID's twist is that customers can personalise every important detail of a sofa that will then be custom-made for them. You want the sofa three inches wider? No problem. You want different legs? No problem. The in-store experience is itself built around that playful process of personalisation. It makes it a rewarding thing to go and visit the Interior Define store. It's fun, as the customer you are in control and you feel that this is genuinely all about you and your needs. It turns out it's a commercially savvy way to do things. The average spend sits at $1,700 and margin is high as ID has so neatly managed its manufacturing process. Cash too, which is always vital.

Crate & Barrel (USA)
Teaches customers how to live an aspirational home life

Crate & Barrel pioneered the technique of "vignette" visual merchandising (VM) in the 1960s that displays products, but does so in ways that show Americans how to use that product to live better. Customers will visit stores for the inspirational experience and often leave having bought adjacent products not on the original shopping list. The physical display becomes a reason to visit because it's inspirational and instructive. There is reward in the visual merchandising.

Selfridges (UK)
Offering a constant show that makes visiting an occasion

The classic department store has always tried to provide lots of reasons to make a visit in person, from Harry Selfridge exhibiting Bleriot's Channel-crossing aeroplane in 1909 to the modern mix of cafés, events, theatrical merchandising and inspirational VM. Only these days, few do it well enough – a sloppy cup of tea and a bit of ordinary cake attracts nobody. Harry would be proud that one of those that does continue to be a rewarding destination experience is Selfridges.

Reward state-of-play

It's early days for the creative reward side of this equation as examples such as Enjoy.com are still rare. We all need to start thinking now about how we are going to make the reward side of our FR indexes better because this is the trend and it's now unstoppable.

However, it is still absolutely the case that the basics of great experiences have reward value. Well-trained staff, happy, approachable and giving great advice; easy-to-navigate systems; obvious checkout processes; all the right online efficiency tools in place; clean stores nicely merchandised; lots and lots of demonstrations and hands-on opportunities; the personal touch; easy parking; great availability; nicely curated choice*; all of these things will bring you closer to an FR index that makes you a more attractive proposition for customers.

How to uncover your FR insights

I want this notion of FR indexing to be a practical thing. There's a way to make that so, but it's a proper bit of work – it's an audit. Now I know that audit is possibly the dullest word in the world but it produces insight you can action and action fast. Were I a new CEO or MD, a friction/reward indexing audit is the first thing I would do. It is such an effective way to build a real picture of the health, competitiveness and opportunities in all things "customer".

So here's a model FR indexing audit for you to enjoy. There are seven steps involved:

1. Map all your typical customer journeys.
2. Identify master shopping scenarios.
3. Subdivide each master scenario by common need states.
4. Create a matrix of contact points.
5. Calculate FR indexes for steps 2 and 3 and across all of step 4.
6. Cross reference each index with competitors' indexes.
7. Identify gaps and opportunities.

---

*We'll talk later, in Secret five, about how customers don't really want choice as most retailers understand it.

Let's add some detail using a floor coverings retailer as an example.

1. Uncover the customer journey variables.

   a. These are all the things customers have to do to get from impulse to post-sale. It will include researching, pricing, the buying process, fitting and everything in between.

   b. Identify all possible customer journeys.

   c. Find all the master scenarios.

   d. Uncover typical need states.

   e. Some of the tools you will use:

      i. Analyse existing or new customer insight and research.

      ii. Run observational audits.

      iii. Gather sector evidence.

      iv. Identify the best practice examples across sectors.

2. Identify master shopping scenarios.

   These are the predictable typical things we know customers might want to do. So we might identify one master scenario as carpeting a single room, while another might be thinking of refurbishing and another could be researching carpet styles.

3. Subdivide by need states.

   a. For each master scenario, what might the customers' different need states be?

   b. Taking the carpeting a single room master scenario, we might have need states for just researching prices, another for redecorating the whole room, one for freshening up with carpet only, one for a tight budget, a couple buying for a child's bedroom, a landlord reacting to a tenant, a design/quality-first customer, a customer who has previously had a bad experience, a customer who wants to buy online but also wants physical interaction, and more.

   c. Some of the above can also be looked at in combination.

4. Create a matrix of contact points.

   Where do customers meet our brand? Online via mobile, on a PC or tablet; in a large out-of-town store, high-street store, concession, store in Scotland or East Anglia; on Twitter, Pinterest,

Instagram, Facebook; word of mouth, via sales support phone team or through fitters.

5. Calculate FR indexes.

   a. For every scenario and need state we arrive at an FR index:

      i. Calculated as the result of adding together all sources of friction relevant to that need state.

      ii. Then subtracting from that result all sources of reward experienced relevant to that need state.

6. Cross reference with competitors.

   a. What are their scores?

   b. Do they offer additional contact points? Different types of stores, services such as in-home visits or mobile sales?

7. Identify gaps and opportunities.

   a. Gaps:

      i. Versus different parts of our own business.

      ii. Versus competitors.

   b. Opportunities:

      i. To easily reduce friction.

      ii. To increase reward.

      iii. To spread examples of excellence to other parts of the business.

      iv. To beat a competitor's offer.

What that looks like visually

In the following table you'll see I've used simplified numbers here for ease of example. You would set your reports up so that hovering over a square will reveal the separate friction and reward scores behind the index number. Then a click through should reveal the full detail of each set of friction items and reward elements.

I am also only showing a small selection of the touch-points. You'll have more, possibly many more.

I would also strongly recommend including competitors and at least one retailer that is not a direct competitor, but offers an example of best practice in a related sector. You might be a fashion business so have something in furniture or design in your matrix. You may find there are more applicable ideas than you at first expect.

A few sample interpretations

Nile is very strong in web and mobile. It has an offer that is low friction and relatively high reward. But you have discovered that in Master Scenario 3 it is consistently weak in web compared to you. You use this knowledge to drive a change in the navigation on your site so that customers are immediately aware of this positive difference.

Your urban stores have an issue across Master Scenario 2. Looking into the calculations behind Ret Co.'s equivalent store you find a number of elements on the reward side that you could easily adopt. But you also discover that there are drivers behind your small store scores for the same scenario that could be quickly transferred into the urban stores.

Innovate's new format store is delivering excellent FR indexes, and, drilling down, you begin to understand the specific reasons why and can direct resources towards adapting your new format to meet those customer-led gaps.

You discover that under the specific customer conditions of need state 1c online, you are experiencing high levels of friction that competitors are able to avoid. The difference is stark and you are able to identify ways to correct this gap, in this case by developing a service that increases customer reward.

Your urban store is delivering engaging FR index results across master scenario 3. Drilling down you discover that the combination of friction reduction and reward delivery can be extended across two other scenarios and taken into other store formats. Doing so will strengthen your customer offer versus competitors considerably.

Customers have significantly better options than your small store under master scenario 3. You discover that both Ret Co. and Shop Ltd have found a neat way to reduce friction across the supporting need states so you develop a plan to study and then copy this method.

	Stores									Web							App			Social				
	Urban			Small			New format			Main site							Mobile			Instagram			Skype Bot	
	Us	Ret Co.	Shop Ltd	Us	Ret Co.	Shop Ltd	Us	Ret Co.	Innovate	Us	Shoponline	Web Ltd	Ret Co.	Nile	Innovate	Shop Ltd	Us	Nile	Innovate	Us	Web Ltd	Innovate	Us	Nile
Master scenario 1	-1	0	1	2	2	1	0	-1	-6	2	-4	-3	1	-9	-2	-1	0	-8	-2	6	2	0	-4	-6
Need state 1a	0	0	1	2	-2	1	-4	-4	-4	1	-2	-3	3	-9	-2	0	3	-8	-2	6	-4	0	-4	-7
Need state 1b	1	-4	0	2	-5	-1	2	-8	-8	1	-2	0	1	-9	-2	-1	2	-8	0	7	1	-1	-4	-5
Need state 1c	-3	-1	2	1	6	0	-2	1	-7	8	-3	-2	-4	7	-2	-1	-2	3	-1	8	1	5	-3	-1
Master scenario 2	2	0	1	-1	0	3	-5	-2	-5	3	-3	-3	1	-9	0	3	0	-6	-1	5	2	2	0	-1
Need state 2a	2	-1	1	0	0	1	-4	-1	-5	1	-1	-2	0	-9	-1	2	1	-6	0	4	2	2	0	-1
Need state 2b	3	-1	1	-1	-1	2	-4	0	-5	2	-1	-3	0	-3	-1	2	-1	-5	0	4	-1	1	0	0
Need state 2c	4	2	3	-1	-1	2	-5	0	-2	3	-2	-3	0	-7	1	1	-1	-7	0	5	0	2	2	-1
Need state 2d	6	2	2	-2	1	1	-2	-3	-1	-2	-4	-3	1	-9	1	4	-1	-4	-1	3	1	0	1	-1
Master scenario 3	-4	-2	0	2	-3	-3	2	2	-1	-4	-2	-2	0	3	0	1	0	0	1	-2	-3	-2	-1	-1
Need state 3a	-6	-3	-1	2	-4	-3	2	1	-1	-3	0	-2	1	2	1	-1	1	-1	1	-2	-3	-3	3	2
Need state 3b	-5	-1	-1	2	-3	-2	1	1	1	-4	-1	-3	0	3	-3	2	1	-1	1	-1	-3	0	0	1

Despite big investments in mobile, your app simply isn't competing with Nile's. Nile is both poacher and gamekeeper in that it white-labels IT and systems. Your FR index is so far behind you decide to switch to an app based on its IT instead. You have calculated that doing so will bring your customers' app-experience closer to Nile's.

In web you discover that your performance across master scenario 3 is strong and much stronger than your web performance for scenarios 1 and 2. You discover that there are a number of elements of the reward side of your service that suit scenario 3 that could be adapted to improve your performance across 1 and 2.

An analysis of your FR index for new format under need state 1b versus Ret Co.'s shows that it is reducing friction in an innovative way that you are not. The good news is that looks replicable.

A note on friction

Why have I called this "friction" and not "effort"? The reason is simple: friction deals directly with the things that make it harder to spend money. High-friction things are harder to push along, or through – they are stickier. Low-friction things allow an easy movement and get out of the way of a customer who wants to give us their money.

We also debated long and hard about whether the equation should be expressed as

Reward – Friction = Index

This format would make positive numbers lead. A high-reward experience with a low-friction component would leave a positive result. The higher the number achieved, the better. But we settled instead for

Friction – Reward = Index

This produces negative numbers, because instinctively the task required feels like one where friction must be overcome, removed, made absent, brought to a negative state.

This approach also centres our thought process around the value of zero. It's not going to be about an ever-escalating war to hit 100

▶

or 1,000. Get to zero or even a negative number and you know you are ahead of friction. That is the foundation for what you do next.

Modern technology persistently takes friction out of the shopping experience and that trend will only continue, so aiming to build user-experiences and physical formats that achieve minus-friction numbers feels like the right approach. And, certainly, being able to access a store and conclude that it is operating at an average FR index of –2 across its customer need states feels like more of an achievement than an RF of +2 might.

This approach makes it very clear that achieving a negative friction result is a good thing.

John Lewis Partnership

Until the turn of the century, John Lewis Partnership's department store group was the reliable company that sold nicely designed and tasteful homewares to a contented middle class; a retailer that bought well and maintained excellent ranges and merchandised them strongly. Its clothing offer was high quality but catered, perhaps, to the taste of ladies clutching newly minted pension books. The store was famous for its free extended warranties, its never knowingly undersold promise and for a level of customer service beyond the usual. It was solid, dependable and, in homewares, very strong.

All good so far. But John Lewis was also among the last to open on Sundays, it didn't like opening late and some stores still closed on Mondays. Credit cards were not taken until September 1999 and it was even among the last to accept debit cards in-store. Long after Amazon had entered the fray in 1994, senior management at John Lewis were still dismissive of the internet as a retail tool.

The BBC in 1999 reported John Lewis Partnership's final cave-in to card payments as "one of the last retail groups to yield to plastic cash". At the time, a senior manager explained the change thus: "With an increasing number of transactions over the telephone and with an eye to the internet, we felt the time was right."

Telephone sales! One eye to the internet! A whole eye? It's easy to be cheeky about these things now but, for most, it was easy to do the same back then, too. Amazon served 14 million customers in 1999, taking $1.64bn in revenue, a figure to which it would add another billion dollars just a year later.

The world was changing fast and poor old John Lewis was struggling to come to terms with it. That same September 1999, the group announced a fall in pre-tax profits of 44% and like-for-likes in the department stores were down 5.8%.

Its stores were exactly the sort of honest and reliable old-fashioned retailer the 2000s utterly shredded, as customers found ways to meet their needs with less friction, more cheaply and more easily.

But this is not a case study tracing another loss of a favourite old dinosaur. John Lewis Partnership (JLP) chose change instead of death. It did so quietly and with dignity, moving step by more confident step to take the entire business from a slightly patronising paternal shop to become one of the most completely customer-focused retailers on the planet.

It is a process that saw JLP break the £10bn revenue barrier at the end of 2014, enjoying more than twice the net profit over 1999's figures.

So what happened? It began with a brave appointment and a willingness to listen to a new appointee. Charlie, now Sir Charles, Mayfield joined as head of business development in 2000. Described in a 2010 *Management Today* interview as "[someone who] likes new things and was an early fan of online", Mayfield brought with him fresh ideas and an urgent understanding of the new realities of retail. With a history that included serving as a teenage army officer in Northern Ireland during the troubles, a Cranfield MBA and solid McKinsey retail consultancy experience, he had a situational awareness that helped him to negotiate one of the finest modernisation opportunities any British retailer ever has. He bought the struggling UK arm of Buy.com for a cut price £2m and with it gained the benefit of a tested and reliable e-commerce infrastructure that Buy.com had built with the help of more than $100m in dotcom boom years investment.

▶

By 2002, Mayfield had also supported the fledgling Ocado.com online grocery home delivery service. At the time, many pundits criticised this investment and support, feeling that it would cannibalise Waitrose (JLP's supermarket business) sales for little additional benefit. Again, Mayfield understood that far from cannibalise, gaining an understanding of online grocery with the benefit of the perspective of Ocado's fresh external team would put JLP in a much stronger position in the longer term.

And he was right, in both cases. The Buy.com acquisition gave JLP an immediately reliable and advanced online platform on which to place the John Lewis reputation, and the Ocado partnership provided JLP with a relatively low-risk insight into online retailing and, later, when JLP's pension fund sold its stake in Ocado, it also provided the fund with a tidy £135m.

While this was happening, a wave of change and modernisation swept through JLP and its businesses. Everywhere you might look, the traditional slightly patronising, but certainly customer-led ethos was invigorated by new ideas that would ensure not only that customers were well served but that they were put at the heart of every choice and investment the business made.

The moral of this tale is simple. Sometimes we resist change because change is scary and sometimes we think we're changing "one eye on the internet!", but the reality is so often that we're only floating on a tide that will snap back at us on the turn. But biting the bullet and seeking out the vectors of change then putting them at the heart of the company can lead even an old dinosaur of a business into a state of modern fitness to trade.

Leaders within John Lewis Partnership did that; they hired a person who knew more than they did about what was actually happening in the world. That takes guts, it's brave and it's brilliant. Mayfield is the vector and the leader of the transformation but the credit must be shared with the clever dinosaurs that avoided their own extinction by hiring him.

In 2007, Charlie Mayfield became, at only 40 years old, John Lewis Partnership's chairman. The transition of stuffy old JLP into a modern, young-minded, inquisitive and customer-powered business was complete.

Your new most important thing

Everything else you read in this book will refer either directly or indirectly to the notion of friction and reward. It is the new reality of retailing. Now that customers are in charge, we must build experiences that are absolutely led by their needs, and we must do so in ways that reduce friction as much as possible. In stores we must scale up reward such that customers want to come and experience our shops. In mobile, virtual, whatever, we must create user-experiences that are as near to frictionless as possible.

Whenever you see a TV advert for an app-based store or service there's always a cautionary note on-screen that reads *"Sequences shortened"*. The nirvana of friction reduction is that we get to places where what we boast *is* what happens. Sequences are not shortened, the buying experience is so free of friction that it just happens.

You sit down at a table on your commuter train ready to travel home after work, placing your phone on the table as people do. The table lights up and Papa John's asks if you'd like your favourite pizza to arrive at your house 15 minutes after you do. It knows the train schedule and has geo-located you via Google Now. It knows you from the NFC connection in your phone. It knows your likes and it knows Tuesday is a night you regularly have a Papa John's pizza. You tap the big glowing "Yes" button, smile and nod off to a restful nap. This is friction-free retailing.

If there is one golden rule in retail, it's that we have a duty to customers to make it easy for them to spend money with us. Understanding your FR indexes is the key first step in doing that better.

Now
Things you can do now

- Begin thinking in friction and reward terms by asking these questions of the business: What have we done in the last six months to reduce friction? What have we done in the same period to increase reward? What have our competitors done in that time?

- Identify the five things that cause the most friction when customers transact with you.
- Uncover the one thing customers love about shopping with your competitors. Copy this now, improve on it next.

Next
Strategic considerations for the longer term

- Run a deep friction/reward audit.
- Use the indexing to direct investment and resources.

Chapter 2

The great Sam Walton, founder of Walmart, told
the mom and pop stores who would fight to stop him
opening in their town to "work out what you can do that I
can't, get really good at it and get even better at telling
people about it". As we find ourselves deep into the
twenty-first century, it turned out Sam was right and
those who followed his sage advice have prospered.
You've gotta know what you are!

Retail secret two: what's the Big Idea?

In this chapter we explore

- the importance of understanding what your business is for
- the vital role of emotional context in understanding what it is you really sell
- how to uncover your own Big Idea.

What we really do

The room of hardened DIY retail veterans is silent, save for one measured and clear voice, a voice that barely hides a rising tide of emotion. George Hutchison, one of their own and as battle scarred as any, is describing how he feels when he comes home late after a day on the front line and goes to his daughter's room where she is cosily tucked up asleep. George has told us of the wave of emotion he feels just being in that room, knowing his little girl is safe, warm and loved. He explains that it is a room he and Daisy worked on together; picking out the colours and the accessories and making it into the space she loves and that George has transported us to.

The audience of embattled and practical retailers is silent. You could hear a pin drop because George has quietly reminded them of the reality of what it is that their industry does. It enables people to improve their living spaces, to make safe, attractive and comfortable places they can truly call home.

These retailers have had a stark and emotional reminder that they don't just sell tins of paint. They sell the sanctuary a father builds for his daughter. It is a heart-stopping moment and it is clear that many of the audience, trapped in a conference room as part of their own retail progression, are thinking about the last time they, too, were back in the homes they have made, watching over their own children.

If you know what you are as a retail business and understand the emotional context in which you exist, then you can transform how you relate to customers. Here's the how and why.

Big Idea

Big Idea is incredibly simple and it is there at the heart of almost every great retailer in modern times. It is the rock that brilliant retail businesses are built upon and it is this very straightforward notion: a retail business must understand what it is for.

If it can do that, then it can also get really good at doing and being that thing, and then get brilliant at showing customers that it is this thing. IKEA knows what it is for, Amazon knows what it is for, Bonobos knows what it is for and Trader Joe's knows what it is for. And that knowledge is one of the great secrets of their success. Towards the end of the 2000s, the big four UK grocers lost sight of what they were for – as supermarkets all over the Western world have, too – and have struggled for identity and customer engagement ever since.

When I listed the questions I ask of every successful retailer, I said that the answers uncovered consistencies – things they all do. Big Idea was the most important of all of those – every great retail business knows what it is for. Everyone working there knows why they come to work and every customer understands, sometimes without even being able to articulate what they understand, but everyone knows what makes those retailers special.

Talking, talking, talking!

I've been talking about Big Idea for nearly 14 years now and where once doing so would gain me little but blank stares, we are getting to a point where the notion that "great retail businesses are predicated on a straightforward understanding of what they're for", is pretty much taken for granted.

For this edition of *Smart Retail* I wanted to get much deeper under the skin of what Big Idea really means, how retailers find it, how it's applied and how to pull a conceptual idea through to a practical reality. Part of what has helped in the move towards a better understanding of Big Idea has been the single-minded focus of great online-only retailers. They often present such crisp and clear notions of what they are for. I suspect that when they are presenting to banks and venture capitalists asking for their dough, having an immediately understandable Big Idea makes it easier to win the investment.

Unmuddy the waters

Big Idea is sometimes confused with "mission" or with "retail purpose", sometimes even with marketing strategy. People ask if the company's tag line and Big Idea should be the same thing. No, they rarely are. Confusingly for us when thinking about this, Big Idea *can* be all of those things but those things can rarely all be Big Idea. Big Idea and retail purpose are probably the closest to being genuine synonyms but, for me, retail purpose has been hijacked by big-ticket consultancies to be formulated into a rigid jargon-plastered concoction that is far from customers and their needs. Big Idea is much more human. Big Idea is what we are. What we're here for.

Big Idea does, however, fuel the creation of those other things. If your Big Idea is as eBay's was: "Auctions of everything by everyone", then your mission might be to "Create rock solid systems that ordinary folk are attracted to use". Your marketing slogan however *could* be "Auctions of everything by everyone". It probably is also your purpose.

Can I suggest rereading the last two paragraphs; it's easy to be confused at this point and for that I am sorry but this distinction is important.

We will look more closely at IKEA's Big Idea later, but let's use it now as an example:

- Its Big Idea is to democratise access to great design.
- Its purpose is to take that access to as many people as possible and show how IKEA can put great design into customers' lives.
- Its mission is to open stores wherever there might be people keen to improve their homes, including stores online.

But that Big Idea, that understanding of what IKEA is for at a fundamental level, that is the source of its tremendous power, even if the purpose and mission change or mutate (which they often will).

The central question

The central question keeps coming back to one thing: What are you for?

If you can't answer that in one sentence, then you are already in trouble. If your answer is significantly different in meaning from the answer given by a handler in customer services, a buying assistant or the person who collects trollies, you're in trouble too.

But if you can, if you and colleagues around you can all give roughly the same one-sentence summary that explains why you all turned up today and what it is that you exist to do, then Big Idea becomes a unifying rallying cry for the business – a simple expression of what the business is for.

Everyone at NASA in the 1960s understood what their Big Idea was. The mission was a technical thing that progressed with each launch, and NASA's purpose was wider, but ask anyone from an astronaut to an aluminium polisher to the office services person ordering paper clips and they could tell you that the Big Idea was "to put an American on the moon". That narrative, non-technical answer would brook no objection – it told of the footprint in the dust to come and not of the technical challenges to be beaten. It told a human story that every member of the team could proudly boast of and know they were part of something incredible.

You are part of something incredible too, by the way. When you allow yourself to look beyond product and to what things mean to people, you'll realise that what you sell makes people feel amazing things. Top Shop doesn't sell clothes but the buzz of a Saturday night and the smile a person cracks when they put on something new and fresh that makes them feel just a bit better about themselves that day. Barnes & Noble don't sell books but escapes through stories and learning, as well as human civility through the sharing of our lives and worlds and adventures together.

That's you, Mr or Ms retailer – you directly contribute to making people *feel* things.

But incidentally, if the Top Shop example sounds too high falutin' then consider that Primark, TK Maxx and even Nordstrom Rack all might sell clothes for well under list price but the emotional context is still not about lumps of cheap cloth. It's the feelgood factor of a bargain, the sense of self-worth that comes from a person being able to afford to have a new thing, or the buzz of beating the system with a bargain. Some of those stores are responsible for the incredible self-actualisation from becoming a normal customer when tight finances have made that difficult elsewhere.

Shortly I will ask you to think more about what it is that you really sell and we will look at some more examples to get to the heart of this vital truth.

Big Idea and reward

It should be obvious already that a rock solid Big Idea is essential to finding answers on the reward side of the friction/reward equation. If you know what you exist for, you can use that to create specific experiences, products and formats that provide rewards that your customers can understand and be engaged by.

So, for example, where giant "please all" supermarkets such as Tesco, Carrefour and Safeway struggle for identity and ways to attract new customers without alienating existing ones, Trader Joe's, Whole Foods and Ocado surge ahead on single-minded Big Ideas brilliantly communicated to customers and delivered consistently throughout their customer interfaces.

Working out your Big Idea

Your current Big Idea, even if it isn't formally defined, may not be fit for competition, may not meet new customers' needs or might be beyond the capabilities of the existing business. As a consultancy, we've had to help define a new Big Idea for a client as often as we've had to help them understand better an existing one.

Look outside retail at IBM for an extreme example. There's a business that was literally synonymous with PCs. "IBM-compatible PCs" companies would say. Or "We operate on IBMs." But it had the bravery to find a radically new Big Idea that saw it completely sell off its PC businesses in favour of IT and consulting services and cloud and server hardware.

The Big Idea that built the company over its golden age was to put a PC on the desk of every businessperson in the USA. A very clear and straightforward notion that everyone in the company could work to support. Now its Big Idea is to deliver cognitive solutions. Which sounds nuts if you're not a tech person but which is incredibly exciting if you are because it means "if you work for IBM, we want you to solve client problems with answers that use computer-generated organic thinking". That still sounds nuts but what it means is the difference between make PCs and make this city run better by giving the traffic lights artificial intelligence.

Suddenly, IBM is innovative again, on the cutting edge and attractive to both forward-thinking customers with big challenges to solve: and it makes IBM stand out in a crowded marketplace. It could have kept on making PCs and diminished with its vanishing market. See Kodak for an example of that strategy.

That's a case study that also helps to understand the journey we need to make to get to find what our own Big Idea should be.

The first question that has to be asked is this: **What are people really buying when they buy what we sell?**

In IBM's example, it recognised that the answer was not a personal computer but was something far deeper and much more meaningful. People were buying computers, not for the case and innards but for the opportunities computers could unlock for them: to work more efficiently (when computers were confined to businesses) and, more recently, to share, learn, shop and be part of a bigger, more connected world.

Emotional context

There are hints that where we really need to start is with customers' emotional contexts – how customers feel about the things that their purchase unlocks for them. It's back to understanding what it is that you really sell. Again and again, retailers fail when they concentrate on the intrinsic value of the nuts and bolts of the thing they are selling, rather than on how that thing fits with a customer's emotional and personal life, needs and expectations.

It is why almost no consumer electronics manufacturer can make money by selling televisions, a product routinely reduced to its constituent parts: "10% pixelier pixels with uber pixel dot technology giving you infinite pixel smoothocity and a maker's badge that lights up." Almost never in recent history did the big manufacturers or retailers talk about TV in terms of what it means to sit and watch a film together as a family, or how great it feels to have easy access to quality content, how all these bells and whistles can make it seem as if the screen has melted away and put the human being who is watching, right into the experience. If we can only understand a feature, or even the benefit derived, in nebulous terms, we cannot process that in any meaningful way and we struggle desperately to put value on it. So how do we buy a TV now? On size and price, possibly through the modifier of a brand we like or trust (that last in itself a wholly emotional judgement).

So, for example, when we "buy" a haircut, we don't buy a hair-reduction service, but the feeling we have when we step out of the salon or barber. That's what we're paying for. Even those people who see a haircut as a purely utilitarian endeavour have an emotional context to that purchase that is about feeling organised and efficient and maybe even some of the deeper stuff about feeling personally tidy, too. These are still emotional things. For the rest of us, when do we go for a haircut? When we have an interview, a date, we're going on holiday, we're a bit down and want cheering up, for a change or to get back to feeling ourselves. These are incredibly powerful emotional contexts for something that is quite an ordinary thing in and of itself.

Majestic Wine doesn't sell bottles of wine but the wine that's in the bottle. How that wine makes a person feel: its emotional context. Is it something warm and comforting to enjoy on a winter's night? Something that will make the Sunday roast feel even more special because the flavours go so well together? Or a crisp kick-off to a summer barbecue? I'll upset its inspirational chief executive, Rowan Gormley, when I say this but the wine itself is less relevant than the context in which we drink it. Actually, that might not upset him, as he knows . . .

So B&Q, Lowes and Leroy Merlin don't sell fence panels and bags of sand. They sell, among other emotions, the feeling of achievement, the buzz we get from improving our living spaces, creating safer and nicer homes to enjoy with our friends and families. It's an emotional context that the DIY retail business in general has been slow to pick up on. The old lost British hardware stores knew it, and in the US indie hardware stores that have weathered the Walmart storm, you'll still find an intrinsic recognition that their stores are for people, not for the display of products. Advice and support to get the project done well figure more highly than visual merchandising, and customers have remembered that they like and value this.

One of the things I'm proudest of in this area is when, after two days of going all over and all around Big Idea, the senior team from Kingfisher's Polish DIY business explained that it now understood it wasn't selling nails, hammers and timber, it was rebuilding Poland. That was the Big Idea. Think about that, how does your retail communication change when you know something so powerful about your true purpose? How does the way you sell, the way you merchandise, the range of products you carry?

Find your emotional context

So, that's step one – you must uncover what it is that you are really selling. This looks easy but it's a trap. We are retailers, trained to focus on product, buying it, moving it around the world, setting a price for it, putting it into a range, visually merchandising it, training staff to understand it, promoting it, and so on . . .

Your first attempts to work out what people are really buying when they shop with you are going to go wrong. You will revert to product, but stick with it.

You'll also have worked out already that some people have a different emotional context than others, and that customer need states can change the emotional context. But are there families of contexts that are closely related? As in the Majestic Wine example: sharing, enjoyment of taste, celebration and so on?

Here are some examples of emotional contexts:

- IKEA doesn't sell furniture, it sells democratic access to design.
- Container Store doesn't sell boxes and shelves, it sells ways to get more out of an organised life.
- Starbucks doesn't sell hot water and coffee beans, it sells a little holiday from the day.

IKEA and Big Idea

Swedish furniture giant IKEA's Big Idea is this: make access to great design easy for all.

It is a democratiser of access to design: to attractive things that go together well and that deliver function over form. IKEA is a much older business having been founded in 1943. But it was through the following words, written more than 30 years later, that the business began to really accelerate towards its incredible annual revenues of €30bn today: "We have decided, once and for all, to side with the many."

I consider these to be the most important words ever written by a retailer. They form part of the opening of IKEA founder Ingvar Kamprad's astonishing 1976 retailing manifesto "The Testament of a Furniture Dealer." (Read the whole thing at http://goo.gl/wj1mdV.)

Doesn't it sound like a rallying cry for a socialist political party? And yet, it has made IKEA one of the world's most powerful companies. Here is the full context and quote:

> *"To create a better everyday life for the many people by offering a wide range of well-designed, functional home furnishing products at prices so low that as many people as possible will be able to afford them.*
>
> *We have decided once and for all to side with the many. What is good for our customers is also, in the long run, good for us. This is an objective that carries obligations.*

▶

All nations and societies in both the East and West spend a disproportionate amount of their resources on satisfying a minority of the population. In our line of business, for example, far too many of the fine designs and new ideas are reserved for a small circle of the affluent. That situation has influenced the formulation of our objectives."

Here's where this gets harder to accept. IKEA, the world's largest furniture retailer, is not a furniture retailer. It is a democratiser of access to great design so that as many people as possible can enjoy the benefits of improved living spaces. That's a different thing.

That is IKEA's Big Idea and everything the business does supports that. It considers self-assembly not to be a cost-cutting chore but the customer's honest contribution to the goal of improving their homes and work spaces. So in-store, assembly is constantly referred to as a happy thing, a collaborative effort that will make you feel good. The cynics among us with long MFI memories may snort at that but it is actually sort of true: wrestle with a flat pack and the end-result does make you smile. The commitment to helping us build our Billy bookcases and Schmoogenburgenboos is sincere and is about helping the many. You do not even have to be literate to successfully follow IKEA's language-free assembly instructions.

There's one extremely strong piece of evidence that proves IKEA is not a furniture retailer but a democratiser. That evidence is the mess IKEA's holding company made of Habitat. Presumably Ikano bought Habitat because it had recognised that some customers get to a point where they want to move on from IKEA. They absolutely don't want democracy and to fish from the pool of the many – these customers now want a bit of individuality and exclusivity. So, strategically, buying an existing retailer that was good at meeting that need state made sense. And yet Ikano failed to make Habitat work and eventually gave up, selling the business rather weakly, taking on a ton of debt with its Swedish tail between its flat-pack interchangeable table legs.

Could the world's biggest furniture retailer not successfully run another furniture retailer? No, because Habitat's Big Idea was so completely and utterly at odds with IKEA's. It was *never* going to work.

IKEA delivers on its Big Idea relentlessly. The stores first show customers how to easily group things together, pricing everything in simple round numbers, filling the journey with fun basics, accessories and extras to personalise spaces and then finishing off with an easy collection and payment process all in massive tertiary locations. It's murder at the weekend but that's because lots of ordinary people like you and me are in there buying cheap things that work well and look nice in a room together.

Contrast the experience of buying a first sofa at IKEA now, to when you bought your first sofa, say 20 years ago, from a traditional British furniture store. Six to eight weeks for delivery, a month's wages that probably needed credit and it wouldn't have looked much different from your mum and dad's sofa. Or your nan's. IKEA means everyone can have nice design that functions brilliantly without costing an arm and a leg. That's retail and social revolution, brothers and sisters.

More Big Ideas

Here are more Big Ideas at real companies that shed some more light on this whole thing.

Walmart and Target (USA)

Every item in the store will be offered at the lowest possible price

Walmart invented the philosophy of "everyday low pricing" and does more than any other retailer on earth to drive cost out of its business and harness the power of bulk purchasing. Indeed, it has been the biggest company on the planet (by revenue) at various times. At one point, it accounted for a staggering 10% of all Chinese exports to the USA, buying power demonstrated on a mind-blowing scale.

Take Walmart's Big Idea and contrast it with rival Target's, which is to offer "cool things at lower cost". Both sell in roughly the same categories in the same types of stores. They're classed as "discount variety retailers". Now, what these two different Big Ideas mean in practice is that Walmart must always opt to sell a 10c glass tumbler because it's the cheapest possible price a glass tumbler can be sold for. Target, on the other hand, are able to say "Hmm, that 10c tumbler is a bit cheap and nasty. We're all about selling at lower cost so we can't stock the really swanky 30c tumbler but we've found one that's 12c and is a nicer shape, more consistent moulding and heavier glass than Walmart's so we're going to sell the 12c option."

What this has meant is that Target has been able to use its Big Idea to drive a space for itself to compete against the world's biggest and most powerful retailer. People are very aware of this sort of subtlety and the result is that Target's customers are younger, wealthier and better educated than Walmart's.

Poshmark (USA)

Make it easy for women to share and sell the contents of their wardrobe

The brilliance of Poshmark's business is the wardrobe paradigm. It's a narrative Big Idea that immediately pushes it above the "please everyone" screaming democracy of eBay, or the currently commerce-light Pinterest. It's a structure that is instantly attractive because everyone, from the teams building the software to the users filling their virtual wardrobes, can understand and get the best from it.

That word "easy" is important too because it directly leads to Poshmark's innovative logistics model where sellers are saved the post office hell of eBay because each sale triggers instead the dispatch of a mailing pack to the *seller* for them to use to send the product to their customer.

Aldi (Germany)

Simple presentation of an edited range at the best possible price without compromise on quality

Aldi might be cheap but it isn't nasty and the middle classes across Europe have recognised that quality bargains are a sensible part of the family spend. The stores are plain and very efficient; it costs far less to manage the much smaller inventory at Aldi than it does to manage the exponentially larger range at Tesco or Safeway. "Edited" is the key word here. Aldi is essentially saying "Trust us, we will stock only the low-cost products that work well, taste nice or last a long time." These aren't cheap and nasty imitations, but carefully chosen and formulated to be good and at a low cost for high volumes.

Lululemon Athletica (Canada)

Better performing kit makes an active life easier

The critical bit here is that the company's founder Chip Wilson was a surf, skate and snowboard dude, not a track athlete. That meant he came to yoga with all the high-performance technical kit of those sports but with a laidback and inclusive attitude. He wanted to help people sweat in high activity yoga but for that honest toil to be wicked, smoothed and dealt with so the workout could be the focus and the kit could be the enabler.

So stores are inclusive and welcoming. The clothes are brilliantly made, from genuinely high-performance fabrics and if anything fails for you, at any point, you're encouraged to take it back, talk about your view on the failure and contribute to the continued development of the product. There's even a name now for the kind of clothing Lululemon has pioneered: athleisure. Exercise clothes that are so well made you can wear them all the time.

Space.NK (UK)

A carefully edited selection of high-quality, original and effective beauty products from innovators and specialists around the world

Nicky Kinnaird is an instinctive, natural retailer. She recognised that customers want advice and recommendations free from single brand evangelism, that they want help to find the products that do the best job and that are absolutely on-trend. You can't get that at the Clinique or Chanel counters in a department store. You have to do all the work yourself to work out which bits from whose ranges offer the most effective combinations for you. So Space.NK is almost a living recreation of the "beauty secrets" part of Cosmopolitan or Vogue. It's an incredibly well-focused Big Idea that customers love.

Net-a-Porter (UK)

Sell luxury fashion online through the principles of a style magazine's editorial presentation

Back when Net-a-Porter launched in 2000, it was the received wisdom that you couldn't sell luxury online. Sounds preposterous now, doesn't it? Back then, non-retailer know-alls were already holding their daft conferences evangelising the rules of a thing that barely knew what it was itself, let alone what it might be capable of. Designers and fashion houses were suitably spooked and it took Net-a-Porter's founders a year to find one brave enough to agree to be listed.

Contrast that with today where some fashion pundits feel a listing with Net-a-Porter is important to a designer's credibility and the site is home to 350 collections. The interesting bit about editorial presentation is the winner here. The site was always one that took the conventions of high fashion, the language, the trend-spotting, the secrets, the high regard for designers and for the "art" of fashion and used these to create a place online that was and is worth visiting for the quality of the coverage as much as for the clothes – though the latter produce hundreds of millions in revenue for the current owners.

It is also worth noting that almost every other fashion retailer's online presence attempts to ape Net-a-Porter in part or even wholesale. First-mover advantage keeps the original ahead of the pack but that's only part of the story. Net-a-Porter is built from it's Big Idea up, its power and magic grew from that moment of inspiration its founder Natalie Massenet had when she envisioned a high-fashion web magazine that enabled readers to both enjoy the editorial and directly purchase the featured fashion.

To copy the structure of deep editorial and rich fashion cues is one thing, but it is only ever a cut and paste if glued to a Big Idea that is out of sync or only superficially supportive.

Crate & Barrel (USA)

Draw the template for modern US aspirational living

Every furniture store tries to reflect modern tastes and to create nicely merchandised spaces in which to browse. Crate & Barrel wrote and then rewrote many of the rules of furniture visual merchandising in such engaging ways that customers have a genuine instinctive understanding of what they go there for.

Its founders created, in the 1960s, a store that imported the simple and stylish European furniture they'd been wowed by when travelling. By the mid-1980s, the store had become an aspirational vendor selling to an older demographic. One constant was the "vignette" style of merchandising pioneered by them and which the stores were filled with.

Pirch (USA)

Let people have fun with and fully experience home fixtures, so they can find the ones that are perfect for how they want to live

Truly a business of the friction/reward era, Pirch has created extremely low FR store environments in which everything is plumbed in, switched on and ready to be properly experienced. If there is a tap on display, then water comes out of it, a chef cooks constantly, but you're welcome to join in cooking a meal and try out a kitchen to see if it works for you. It supports this with a bold promise to match prices. "Inspiration is free" it says, and it offers a slick and professional – in its upfront description "accountable" – installation service.

If you want to go and try out the showers at Pirch by having a shower, you can. It's one of the most powerful reward responses to the idea that for customers to bother visiting a kitchen and bathrooom store, there had better be a good reason for doing so. And at Pirch there is: a customer who cooks in a fabulous Pirch kitchen set-up is either sticking the dollars down now or is working out what they have to change in their lives to be able to do so soon.

Mission versus Big Idea

Pirch says its mission is to "make moments count", but it hasn't built a "make moments count" business. It has built a "come and try everything out, really try it, get the results that suit you" business. And it's the latter that is the incredible and powerful Big Idea. It's brilliant and is going to be huge and its competitors are scratching their heads in paralysed disbelief.

Apple Store (USA)

Show people how Apple can improve their lives

Make no mistake, the Apple store is essentially a single-brand PC World or Best Buy, and yet you'd be loathe to make the comparison. Apple's Big Idea for its store identity came from outside electrical retail, in the shape of Ron Johnson, former VP of Merchandising at Target. That's crucial to the story because Ron was able to throw away the baggage of electrical retail (hide things away to minimise theft, look but don't touch, cram it in and concentrate only on price) and create a format that, instead, reflects Apple's focus on using your technology to do cool stuff. He dovetailed that with the availability of lots of support and advice on just how to do that and delivered a format in which the Big Idea means customers get to play, become enthused and be supported in their enthusiasm.

Subway (USA)

Assemble sandwiches "fresh" to order

This is an incredibly successful perversion of the idea of fresh food as healthy. Subway invests heavily in promoting the healthy options on its menu, it uses images of crisp hunks of lettuce and moist tomatoes to lead customers into believing that a sandwich made from scratch in front of them is somehow magically healthier than one wrapped in plastic at Greggs. Every man, woman and child in the USA recognises Jared, the brand spokesman who lost half his body weight on a mostly Subway diet for a year. They recognise Jared now for much sadder reasons too – Google it if you want to ruin your day. It's so pervasive that people have come to subconsciously see Subway as the healthy fast food option, even though what they actually order is a meatball marina with extra cheese every time. It's a powerful use of Big Idea but a bit sneaky too.

Costco Wholesale (USA)

Offers a limited bulk range in vast depth to trade and employee groups

It's easy to see the Big Idea in action here. A massive warehouse stocking few lines but each in massive quantity, turning over inventory incredibly fast at low prices. You have to be a member to get in and be prepared to buy products in big pack sizes. For the small store trade, offices, hotels and restaurants it's another cash & carry, but the extension to employee groups is the bit of genius – putting pressure on companies to offer employees membership of Costco and giving them what feels like a bit of secret access to a part of retail that beats the system.

Media Markt (Germany)
The customer is not stupid and they live where we do

Europe's largest electrical retailer employs a refreshing approach to advertising itself, openly declaring that customers aren't stupid and so should be looked after by knowledgable staff. To deliver great service, Media Markt recognised long ago that store teams who have real say in their store, who get a chance to make decisions and directly influence outcomes, are more likely to want to commit to giving customers great experiences. So stores here are structured as if they were individual businesses with managers having 10% equity stake and, together with their store team, having a say on assortment, pricing and advertising. People take pride in things they feel ownership of and are able to deliver on Media Markt's Big Idea because of that.

WHSmith
Two sides of a different coin

WHSmith is a fascinating case because the retail company actually consists of two separate businesses: WHSmith High Street and WHSmith Travel. The second isn't a travel bookshop but rather the WHSmith stores you see at airports, motorway services and railway stations all over the world. One of these has a Big Idea and one doesn't. One is trading profitably and one isn't.

WHSmith High Street stocks books, magazines, cards, sweets, stationary, DVDs, music and gifts but leads in just one sector; there are better stationers, better book stores and better music shops so only the magazine section is a leading department.

▶

High Street is a business that, for more than a decade, has had no real idea of what it's actually for. Nobody inside the company knows – I've asked.

But WHSmith Travel is brilliant. It's basically the same departments but in highlight form, so you'll have top books with some eclectic promotions, a great range of magazines, batteries, snacks, memory cards, sweets and drinks and headache tablets. Its Big Idea is to reliably equip every traveller with everything they could want to make their journey a better one. The ranges are perfect, the merchandising spot on and the checkout process efficient and pleasant. The Big Idea guides everyone: you know exactly what to look out for as a buyer, exactly what to range as a marketer and exactly how to present it as a merchandiser. You know because the Big Idea is so clear it drives an obvious and practical mission.

Recently, WHSmith has admitted publicly that High Street is a trading problem, whereas Travel is booming and profitable. High Street is without focus and struggles to produce trading profits, whereas Travel knows exactly what it is for and makes a ton. I am sure this is not coincidence.

Pretentious hipster douchebags might be the winning side

Read this quote from a fantastic longer article dealing with the phenomenon that is BrewDog.

"Everything BrewDog does", [founder James Watt] said with great earnestness, "is about the beer. Everything. We want to make people as passionate about great beer as we are. Change perceptions, challenge conventions, but do it on our terms. We've always said we'll either succeed, or be some massive great crash-and-burn failure. But that's fine, because the space in between is really ******* boring."

This sort of overheated rhetoric is just the thing that gets Dickie and Watt called pretentious hipster douchebags on the internet. But BrewDog's astonishing growth may raise the uncomfortable possibility that in an age of media-savvy and brand-sceptical digital natives, ostentatious displays of "authenticity" – known to some as acting like pretentious hipster douchebags – may have become a necessary condition for success. Is it possible that James Watt and Martin Dickie, who make something great but sell it with infuriating stunts and obsessive passion, might represent the future of business?

Jon Henley, *The Guardian*, 2016

That is a company that knows what it is for. Speak to anyone at BrewDog from bar person to the founders and you'll hear an incredibly consistent line that is, essentially, the same as Watt's passionate declaration of what BrewDog is for. The writer Henley's musing that, perhaps, such authenticity and passion are vital ingredients in modern business feels so very right, and his conjecture that it is, perhaps, because of the brand-smashing that has taken place from Naomi Klein's incendiary anti-brand treatise "No Logo" onwards also fits the emerging picture in our industry. This is an opportunity. Become so authentic, passionate and consistent that everyone in the business isn't parroting lines but is speaking from the heart. Then you have something spectacular on your hands. Big Idea is the key to making that happen.

Now
Things you can do now

- Find your emotional context by exploring what it is that you really sell.
- List all the ways your product can improve people's lives and make them happier.
- Consider the Big Idea in play at your competitors. How distinct is it? Does it differentiate them from you? How does it engage customers?
- Repeat for your business.

Next
Strategic considerations for the longer term

- Create a team to sense-check and then redefine (if necessary) the Big Idea
- Roll out a programme to align the business behind this Big Idea

Chapter

3

The military jargon of missions and the business
jargon of channels have no place in working out why on
earth a person, a living and breathing human being,
might decide to spend money with you. The sooner
we start to think of customers as people,
actual people, the better.

Retail secret three: want? Got. Need!

In this chapter we explore

- how customers think in terms of needs, not missions
- the role framing has in setting expectations versus needs
- the reality of customer loyalty (it doesn't exist if you're a retailer).

Regimental thinking

Customers don't shop at your business according to a planogram, or with a map and a five-point strategy. They come to you with a bunch of needs, some explicit, some vague. Some upon which the sale absolutely hangs and some that are the difference between a perfectly acceptable experience and a great one. In some sectors, the customer is so beaten by experience that the meeting of those bonus needs lifts retailers that meet them into the hero category. Think John Lewis electricals department versus 1990s Currys, or Trader Joe's versus Acme.

What sort of needs? The following three categories are a useful way to analyse needs:

- **Practical** – I need to buy a jumper because I'm cold.
- **Emotional** – I need to cheer myself up.
- **Mechanical** – I need to buy a size 14 dress because that's my size.

Needs versus wants

Incidentally, I use "needs" and "wants" interchangeably in this area. It might be incorrect but it's a useful simplification that has no material impact on the actions you can take with the insight.

No sale, buddy!

Need states may not always include actually buying anything. Early sales journeys will often feature the need to research or to compare only because the emotional and practical needs exist right from the start. A customer might *want* to research sizes, styles, pricing and options of a new sofa before buying one, but will bring with them emotional needs too – to demonstrate their design ideas, to make their living space more comfortable for the family, to experience the nice feeling of settling into deep comfort after a busy day. Because these things are there even at the research stage, retailers must always be alive to the opportunity to at least ask if the customer would like to buy now.

It is remarkable how many consultants in this age of the "omni-channel" misunderstanding (see Secret six) will advise retailers to facilitate research and pre-sales activity without any sales element at all. That's just daft. I'm not advocating aggressive selling of the old school type, but a modern customer-led process of assistance that includes gentle attempts to close, assisted by genuinely attractive calls to action, is an opportunity that is foolish to ignore.

If online, then data must be captured unobtrusively and used to make it clear there is benefit to that specific customer in completing the transaction today. In a store, a selling process, both passive and via assistants, must be built around passing on knowledge and tailored, curated recommendations with opportunities to close a sale liberally sprinkled throughout.

Crazy mixed-up people

The need states customers bring to a given retail interaction are rarely singular, but are usually a complex conglomeration of needs, though the emotional are always the most powerful (see Secret two for more on that).

Take one example: a customer wants to buy a new outfit for a job interview.

Practical needs are driven by the occasion:

- Need a new outfit suitable for a job interview.

Emotional needs might go beyond the occasion:

- Need to boost my confidence.
- Need to be taken seriously.
- Need to project an image that fits the job and my personality.
- Need a stress-free shopping experience.

Mechanical needs are likely to be from a stable set:

- Need to be assured that the quality is up to standard.
- Need a 34 trouser and a 40 jacket.
- Need to feel comfortable.

And for every different person, there might be another 20 related needs. Our job as retailers is to look at defeating friction by meeting the practical and mechanical needs and then meeting the emotional by boosting the reward side in some of the ways below.

Just because I want to be happy

We were working on a project for a massive client, part of which was to define a new Big Idea. I love doing them because you get to look in so many interesting places for inspiration, evidence and ideas. This particular client is a great business but operates in a sector that customers and media alike sort of hate. After three months of working, including finding incredible inspiration back in the history of the sector, a time before people despised it, we had a Big Idea.

The Big Idea included the word "happy" in it. And, almost universally, the leadership in that business hated the idea, the MD even said: "We can't make people happy." We argued our case, especially as the Big Idea we'd created was predicated on a series of transformation programmes that would take this business from a dictatorial one to a culture where customers would be in the driving seat.

But no, some felt "happy" was unobtainable, and others, I thought, hated it because it didn't sound businessy enough. Happy isn't a jargon word, they believed it would look strange in an annual report. But customers aren't cattle, and in this particular case, making them happy was not only vital, it was completely possible because we were considering them as people, not as numbers on a spreadsheet.

We do this too much in retailing. We forget that our success depends on Keith, Alejandra, Mary, Derek, Umesh, Priti, Medhi, Sue, Ginal, Rob, Arthur, Rosy, Isabella, Ebele and Indira and thousands like them, deciding to *choose* us.

Sometimes the emotional needs leading to a desire to shop are very simple: to be happy, to be cheered up, to enjoy wandering around websites and stores shopping.

Don't forget that when you consider how need states drive the way your offer and formats work.

There's more than one of us in here

You are psychologically in a different place, your motivations, your patience, even your physical senses are working differently when you dive into South Mimms service area on the M1/M25 to grab a pitstop burger, versus sitting down for a 30-day dry-aged artisanal hamburger with your partner in your local gastropub. Same meal but completely different you. You'll make your choices in each at different speeds, you'll want different things from the food itself, you'll accept quite different standards of service, you'll react differently to sights and smells and your pace of eating will be very different – and you'll pay wildly different prices for the two meals and possibly judge the far more expensive one as the better value.

The customer insight team will describe these as two different customer missions. I hate that kind of labelling because the word "mission" feels so military relative to the reality of wandering into a shop, or lazily loading up an app. A mission is something we consciously plan for. I don't believe the vast majority of what we do as shoppers is conscious at all beyond the initial impulse. Even then, that initial impulse can and will be directed autonomously by the many influences and biases we've built over the years and by other influences we've been exposed to subconsciously seconds earlier.

I prefer the description of those two burger scenarios as being different need states. It's a much simpler idea – we need x from transaction y. We need a pitstop burger for fuel. We need a nice place for a date night so we can spend quality time together.

Thinking in need states is easy too. It's a simple game of getting to what possible needs might people might have when they shop with us.

Once armed with an exhaustive list, it is possible to look at which groups of needs:

a. might be most common

b. we might best be able to satisfy

c. from (b) are likely to be the most commercially useful need states to build our capabilities and customer experiences around.

Some groups that sit in (b) might require an experience that is cheap and fast, some might need significantly more sales support, some might welcome guided experiences, some might react best to clear menu-driven product selections. Some might work only in conjunction with the lowest possible price, while others might react better to a combination of services that unlock the opportunity to improve margin.

There is also a further point, d) need states related to the things we sell that we could or should also meet but that we currently don't. Do our customers satisfy those needs better with competitors? Or by spending money in a different sector instead?

Or the Big Daddy of marketing, e) a set of need states that nobody currently meets because people don't know they even exist.

"They don't even know they want the thing they want" is staggeringly powerful and the people who find those are retiring to private islands in the Caribbean.

"We think you need to take your music out of the house with you – here, enjoy our Walkman."

"We think you'll need to access the internet sitting on a bus – this is for you, try our Handspring Treo smartphone."

"We think you'll need to buy books while sitting on the toilet – here you go, we call this Amazon."

I don't actually know if Jeff Bezos ever mentioned toilets during investment pitches, but I know I'd have had a PowerPoint slide showing someone doing just that, which is probably why he's sending rockets into space now and I still consider a McDonalds milkshake a massive treat. So here's another example.

"We think you'll need your burger and shake within seconds of ordering it – come to our restaurant where we've set up everything in the kitchen to enable that speed of turnaround. We're the McDonald brothers."

Once we know and understand need states

What next? The first job is to make sure you are meeting the needs of the most relevant customer groups identified earlier. This sounds straightforward but I guarantee there are two things you do at the moment that make this harder:

- You will be doing some things that your customers really appreciate but that you take for granted as just part of the deal. If you undervalue these things, so will customers.

- There will be parts of your set-up that make life difficult for customers, that force them to do too much of the work, or that otherwise get in the way. These will be things that you have convinced yourself you can't do much about, but that is a lie you tell yourself instead of facing up to change. See Secret one on friction/reward: change! Change now!

The frame

Framing deals with the physical, emotional and virtual stuff we surround any given product or customer need state with. So the frame around a visit to Aldi is one that is suggestive of efficiency, no frills, crisply getting the job done. But the frame around Aldi-owned Trader Joe's is one that makes us think of fun, new tastes, curated choices and tribal inclusiveness: "I am the sort of person who shops at Trader Joe's."

There are two books you absolutely must read (after you finish this one) that will give you tons more evidence in and around framing: *Thinking, Fast and Slow* by Danny Kahneman and Phil Barden's *Decoded*. The second one takes some of the first's ideas and shows how they work in a marketing context. I agree with a large chunk of what Phil has to say and am very happy to recommend it. One example Phil gives perfectly explains what we mean by "framing" and it is the classic story of two cups of nearly identical coffee.

Starbucks and the Wild Bean Café found in BP garages will both sell you a cup of fresh coffee.

In 2014, Starbucks was able to charge £3.05 for a cup because it was framed as a little holiday from your day. It's relaxing and unhurried. Comfortable. Reassuring. It meets the needs for relaxation, an exhale and a break from the rush.

Wild Bean Café was only able to charge £1.75 because its frame was that of a pitstop: good hot coffee, bought in the queue from a garish red and yellow fast food-themed counter and thrown down in the car, back on the road. Needs such as the mechanical want for caffeine, to warm up and to pay less.

What Phil might not have known is that the two coffees in his example are much closer in taste and quality than you'd imagine. They are both made with semi-automatic coffee machines. Starbucks beans are always excellent but so are those at Wild Bean Cafe where they use a high Arabica blend from Douwe Egberts. In both cases, the milk is fresh and the machine cleaning regimes just as thorough.

And yet, one coffee is £3.05 and the other only a shrug above half the price. We worked with BP on changing the Wild Bean Café frame and made a number of recommendations – leaving the product quality alone, but getting better at showing customers the great Italian coffee machines they use. We suggested replacing outdated red and yellow display tones with natural finishes in wood, exposed brick and soothing blue accents. Fonts went, too, from fast food 1980s to a modern indie coffee house feel. The result? Where BP has made those changes it has been able to raise prices by at least 12% and sales volumes have also increased. Happier customers, feeling the frame was worth more to them, now meeting needs that include such things as to identify with a particular type of coffee experience, to enjoy a good coffee, to find a place on the road where ordering and drinking a coffee was a little less hurried and a bit more quality.

If we were to do the follow-up research by talking to customers of updated Wild Bean Café stores and those of older stores, customers in the new stores, paying higher prices, would tell you the coffee tastes better. We will talk in the next section about just how crazily suggestible we are in this regard.

Selling tea as if it were jewellery

Australian tea retailer T2 sells tea the same way Pandora sells jewellery and customers are drinking it down. Now expanded to the UK, New Zealand and the USA, and having been bought by the world's biggest FMCG company Unilever, the more than 70 store strong chain sells tea from within a modern, glamorous and product-passionate frame.

The stores are sharply designed and packaging looks closer to the sort of boxes in which you might find a high-end watch, rather than looking like an old tea packet. In one of my all-time favourite little bits of retail theatre, every member of staff carries a mug of tea in their hands all day long. It is a lovely bit of old-style theatrical smoke and mirrors – the equivalent of the music hall silvered glass trick. It says to customers on the most automatic level that these people must really love tea so I will trust them when it comes to tea. Staff aren't really getting through gallons and gallons of tea all day, it just looks convincingly as if they really love tea.

Why would Unilever buy a retailer of a product in which they dominate certain categories as manufacturer? Because Unilever is looking to the future, it's trying to understand why customers love a premium positioning such as T2's. It's the frame Unilever wants to understand. It's very sensible and is part of a continuing blurring of lines between notions of what retailers and manufacturers are to each other.

Frames and need states

Sometimes the frame is writ large and as a structural part of the way a business has presented itself, while other times the frame is a more subtle collection of elements. Ask yourself how you are framing product, experiences, stores, sites and apps in the business. Are we pitstop businesses but where customer need states suggest they might respond to a different frame? Can we win "First Visit Advantage" (explained soon) with our current framing or are we their second, third or even fallback choice each time?

Framing, Big Idea and winning FR indexes

There's a gigantic fat link between your business's Big Idea and how you might frame the retail experience. In the example of Aldi and Trader Joe's, it is immediately obvious: the former a no-nonsense and efficient presentation, the latter a fun tiki lounge. More subtle is how McDonalds has been working hard to move its own frame from fast-burger-and-hang-the-taste to one that plays on food quality and European coffee shop cues. One of the ways in which it has done this is through the highly successful McCafé stores, initially operated in Europe. Gone are the red and yellow primary colours of the archetype fast food business and in came euro-style earthy tones, mustard yellow, browns and natural finishes. As the Big Idea moves away from the falling trend of fast food, the frame too moves towards the explosive success of a coffee shop Big Idea.

Net-a-Porter's Big Idea, to sell luxury fashion online through an editorial style-magazine look and feel, incorporates the frame in the Big Idea itself. IKEA's Big Idea to democratise access to great design led to a framing of that idea in spaces that had to show people how things could go together and that had to lead them through the whole narrative, telling the story of how easy it is to achieve high-design results for better living. It's the Big Idea's show and tell.

There is also, and this must be obvious, a huge link between the frame and your opportunities to build richly rewarding experiences that boost the reward side of your FR analysis.

Make me want it . . .

You're a clever person, an experienced retailer and you know marketing. Like me, you never fall for the tricks. You'd especially never be taken in by the adjectives manufacturers now put in front of every single product description. You know that gently sparkling cool mountain spring water is just fizzy water. You know the difference between marketing horseshit and how you feel about a thing.

But you don't. We're wrong. We all are.

The mountain of evidence is now so huge that we have to give in and accept it. Study after study proves that we are cognitive sheep and that our decision making is influenced by the most banal and obvious tricks, more than it is by our experience and biases. Researchers have shown regularly that expertise can narrow the band of our susceptibility but cannot defeat it. For example, in experiments on price anchoring in categories where we are expert, we will still be influenced by external cues but the range of our forced errors will be narrower.

We are experts on retailing, we know marketing and, if even we "insiders" are susceptible, it tells you something incredibly important about framing and description, especially the use of adjectives.

A 'crisp white, cotton summer-weight shirt' sets up lots of very particular thoughts and expectations that "shirt, white" does not. We can no more ignore the runaway freight train of images, biases and expectations the long description conjures than we could ignore a person standing in front of us screaming the words at us.

The language of retailing is incredibly powerful. Brian Wansink of Cornell University's innovating and brilliant Food Lab has shown again and again that the use of adjectives in menu descriptions boosts both sales of the options described that way and that subjects will rate the taste of those items and their satisfaction with the eating higher than those who have eaten the same menu items described plainly.

Wansink's wife Jennifer is a skilled chef, which his friends are aware of, and from time to time they set up an experiment using different groups of friends and an invitation to dinner. One thing the Wansinks also do is to write descriptive, adjective-laden menu cards and put them at each place setting.

The cards and the prior knowledge that Jennifer is an excellent chef set up an expectation that the meal will be great. And so it turns out. Beautifully presented courses are served on beautiful china at a table set with flowers and candles and other lovely things.

After the first two courses, guests are shown that what they've actually just eaten is rather ordinary pre-prepared supermarket food taken out of its packaging, brought to table as if home-cooked and presented wonderfully. There's that moment of "Aha" but what happens next is incredible. Dessert is served, again beautifully and in the context of a flowery description full of powerfully positive adjectives. But this time the guests all know it's a pretty standard dessert from a supermarket that Jennifer has dressed up a bit.

But they still swear that it tastes better than it should do and some will insist that there must be another level of experiment. Maybe the food actually is home-cooked and the test is to see if being told it isn't has an effect. Astonishing that, even given the facts of the framing and descriptions, sensible people like us do not accept the truth.

If descriptions and adjectives can influence us so completely that even when we are in on the joke we still retain the effects of that influence, is it a stretch to suggest that frames and language in retail environments must be at least as important?

A critical insight is that Wansink's hypothesis is that the ways in which description, context and use of positive adjectives set up *expectations* are the source of their power. That we are placed in a state of positive expectation by those things and that natural human tendency to loss aversion acts as a confirmation bias and tells us we were right to expect things to be great, even if they are revealed later to be ordinary.

Northern Quilted's April Fool

American toilet paper brand Northern Quilted released a fantastic April Fool video that purported to be the launch of its new artisanal hand-crafted toilet papers including a single-roll pack

▶

size described brilliantly as "small batch". This advert is a thorough ragging of the hipster maker culture that has risen so giddily in recent years. It's very funny but a weird thing happens when people watch it. It will happen to you too and it is that the wonderfully adjective-laden flowery descriptions of the lovingly crafted product slightly makes us want it to be real. We like things that have love and craft in them, we crave authentic experiences even when it's a patently ridiculous parody. The advert even includes an extra virgin birch option that is a roll of bark tied with string. Watch it here: https://goo.gl/OFyKO1.

This stuff gets to us, there is a movement supported by trend research from source after source and it suggests that authenticity and craft light us up as people because they relate to a desire for meaningful experiences, for connection with more than just things and consumption.

It's incredible that a parody advert for something that is clearly nonsense can still momentarily prod at those same needs.

Starbucks experiments with the coffee frame

You might wonder why I've used a lot of food and drink examples and I suspect it's because the sector changes so quickly as food trends change. So they are great at frames.

Starbucks was among the very first to package the coffee house "small holiday from the day" frame into a repeatable chain format. Rapid expansion, near global domination in a handful of hyperactive years and an incredibly impressive consistency of delivery were all part of the remarkable story.

But that packaged frame is starting to show weaknesses and vulnerabilities around its edges. Coffee trends are changing, customers are beginning to explore new ways to enjoy coffee and the artisanal and maker elements of the hipster movement are beginning to cross over into mainstream. At the same time, there is evidence of more people making better coffee at home.

So Starbucks has developed a handful of alternative framings and placed these in interesting locations around the world. Two of these alternatives are the Starbucks Roastery in Seattle, where the frame has a kind of "world of coffee" credibility, and the fascinating Starbucks Reserve on Upper St Martin's Lane in London. Starbucks Reserve is an attempt to bring artisanal values and maker theatre to coffee. So you'll find the Reserve counter where customers can choose from four different small-batch coffee beans and have those beans prepared in one of four different methods, from Airopress to Clover or pour-over. As the coffee is brewed, baristas engage customers in the story of the beans and the farms from which they are sourced and will talk about the science and pseudoscience of the various brewing options. You'll hear adjectives galore as your tastebuds begin to tingle.

They will charge you £6 for the privilege of enjoying a coffee that may have taken as long as five minutes of manual preparation to brew, and what is incredible is that you will gladly pay and describe it later as a brilliant cup of coffee and worth every penny. Here is where smells, sights, tastes, sounds and textures mingle together to create an incredible coffee experience that feels very special indeed.

The Upper St Martin's Lane store has some mechanical problems, as it is also trialling tablet ordering, ordering by app and table service and is struggling to find the right methodologies to manage those processes as part of the customer journey. The concept accidentally introduces additional friction that in some areas trumps the perceived reward, but battle your way through to the Reserve counter and you will find something really rather special.

These aren't ideas Starbucks has had in isolation. There are indie coffee houses around the world doing incredibly involved things for their customers. We visited a "third wave" coffee place by the name of Bonanza in Berlin's trendy Prenzlauer Berg and found exactly the same principles as the Starbucks Reserve Counter in play, perhaps with a little less theatre but certainly with all the authenticity and artisanal respect for the coffee and for the drinking experience.

This is a great example of the chain business being open to learning from the indie. I should add that I'm the champion of the indie here. Independents can always trump the chains by being faster to change, faster to trial and faster to adapt to new and developing customer needs. Starbucks copying is a compliment that indie coffee businesses should celebrate at the same time as moving themselves ever further forward.

Also placed high up in Starbucks' experimental formats is retail: selling the store experience to customers to take home with them and make part of their home coffee rituals – all the machines used on the Reserve counter are for sale, the beans are for sale, the process of making is for sale.

Starbucks may not roll out a new estate of either Roastery or Reserve stores but the process of experimentation with the frame will find its way into the main estate. This process of iteration through wild experimentation is very powerful, provides far more insight than passive research and is exhilarating for team and customer alike.

I can offer you nothing but my loyalty

With our great engaging frames in place and with all this lovely meeting of needs that we're doing, you might expect customers to begin to show you some loyalty. Which is a shame because loyalty to retailers simply does not exist beyond easily disruptible habit. Loyalty is a consultant's pipe dream, it's a nonsense. Trying to win it or, worse, trying to buy it is costly and pointless. A customer is no more loyal to American Eagle than they are to Gap. They will happily shop at both, they will flow like water towards whichever is meeting their needs better and doing so at the lowest FR level.

When it comes to loyalty to brands, there's a good argument to be made, certainly, but a customer will have far more loyalty to their favourite brand of toothpaste than to the store where they buy it.

You may say: "But it *looks* like my customers are loyal"

Groups of customers might well exhibit behaviours that *look* like loyalty, such as spending loads of money in your stores regularly and giving you a high net-promoter score, but this only lasts for as long as you are consistently meeting their needs and while a competitor meeting the same needs is doing so at a worse FR index. A person who is fiercely loyal to Patagonia, who may even be something of an advocate for a form of responsible consumption that revolves around buying clothes at Patagonia, will eventually jump ship, should another retailer begin to meet those same emotional and practical needs in a convincing and authentic way but at a lower FR number. Fabulously ethical clothes but with an additional re-use dynamic at a lower price brought to their door might do it, for example.

Scheming schemes

Programmes such as Sainsbury's Nectar, Tesco's Clubcard and Macy's Star Rewards are called "loyalty programmes", but they aren't really. They're customer data-for-cookies exchanges: if you nice customers allow us to dig into and learn about how you shop, then we will give you a few tokens as a thank you. Customers are not stupid, they understand full well that there is no something-for-nothing in these schemes, and they are also increasingly aware of the value of their data and that's fine.

Tesco, in particular, has been able to do amazing things with that data. It's a worthwhile exchange and customers enjoy taking part when the rewards are pitched right. But be aware that it can be a gigantic cost of sale and that you cannot claim customer loyalty as one of the elements of your ROI.

So if loyalty doesn't exist for retailers, is there an alternative? Luckily, yes and here it is.

First Visit Advantage

Traditional customer loyalty rather sweetly but naively holds that, given additional incentive, customers will shop with a store so long as it continues to satisfy their needs, and will do so to the exclusion of others. It's clearly a nonsense, even if you read incentive as "reward" and plug it into a friction/reward calculation. A resulting win still isn't loyalty, it's temporary and depends on the maintenance of that new bribe-led improved reward element.

But what if we can build formats so compelling, so focused and *full* of reward, where friction is minimised at every point? What if we can do that so well that customers *like* shopping with us and are prepared to give us the first opportunity to sell to them or advise them on any given set of needs? What if our Big Idea is so clear and engaging that customers will come to us before moving through the remainder of their acceptable store roster?

That would be First Visit Advantage. The retailer whose store or site is the first to be visited as a potential solution to whatever need state the customer is in holds a massive advantage over all others for that customer.

It is the idea that your business can be the place a customer looks to first for any given need or set of needs. Your site or app is the one they open first on any given search, they get off the tram at your end of town first, they choose a retail park because you are on it, they type your name directly into a browser: they give you the first bite of the cherry.

All seven of *Smart Retail*'s "secrets" are packed with content that can help you win First Visit Advantage (FVA), but key are friction/reward, clarity of offer (from Big Idea), format, discovery and promotion and the human experience. For many customers, that human experience of being looked after by nice, helpful people is the most powerful, and it is currently physical retail's unique weapon.

I say "currently" because virtual formats are getting better and better at bringing a human dimension into electronic interactions, from easy two-way messaging of customer service teams to sparky use of social media. Take a look at enjoy.com, an ostensibly online business that centres on an in-home person-to-person component. Take nothing for granted!

Just because we might live our lives through beautiful hand-held slabs of tech, doesn't mean that there is any less value in the power of connecting real people to other real people. We do that all the time as retailers and, while your virtual formats continue to benefit from introducing more and more human elements, the culture of your business becomes ever more critical to great customer outcomes. A culture – be it in-store, in call centres, from delivery drivers to after-sales specialists – that is honest, fun, comfortable, reassuringly knowledgeable (and easily shares its knowledge) is one that provides the best possible foundation for great customer experiences. When it comes to First Visit Advantage, people are a gigantically powerful attractor. Never underestimate the power of eye contact and a warm smile.

ASOS charges customers for First Visit Advantage

Pay ASOS £9.95 and you get yourself premium delivery, a service that buys a year of free next-day delivery, saving either the usual £5.95 next-day charge or a wait of three to five days for standard free delivery. It's sort of counterintuitive to charge customers to shop here but really it's based on internal insight that understood that customers loved ASOS for the fashion but also for the convenience and reliability of delivery and return. ASOS had become an everyday shop for many of its customers and that opened up an opportunity to strengthen the relationship at the same time as delivering an easy premium.

The customer psychology goes along an obvious path: need something fashionable in a hurry?

"ASOS will *definitely* have something, though I could shop around a bit, I suppose. I've got their premium delivery service, so I might as well go there first and order something. It'll be here tomorrow and I can easily return it if it's not right."

ASOS gets the first bite of the cherry, the first chance to make a sale and does so by charging customers to reduce the friction of their shopping experience. You can do these things if you've built a sufficiently valuable proposition and become reliably consistent in delivering it to people who trust you.

Now
Things you can do now

- Run the "Needs states" exercise described above, address the opportunities and identify the gaps.
- Write up a definition of your current retail framing.
- Ask how the frame looks when viewed from a friction/reward perspective.

- Consider your favourite frames used by competitors.
- List everything that you feel might win you First Visit Advantage.

Next
Strategic considerations for the longer term

- Realign all customer interaction with identified need states.
- Commission a project to consider a future framing for the business. An effective way to explore this is by briefing out a "future format" type of exercise: create and operate test format, then consider pop-up testing of aspects of the frame.

Chapter 4

Every time anyone browses a store, they're wandering around the pages or aisles, shouting at the top of their lungs "COME ON RETAILER! INSPIRE ME, MAKE ME WANT SOMETHING!"

Retail secret four: "I'm just looking"

In this chapter we explore

- the role of discovery in customer engagement
- merchandising for inspiration
- why customers crave this inspiration.

Even a pencil can surprise

New York store owner Caroline Weaver's left forearm features a life-size tattoo of a pencil. This might give you a clue to the nature of her store's stock. Caroline likes pencils and has made selling pencils and pencil ephemera her business. Don't tease me but so do I. I do a lot of this writing malarkey and there's something about scratching notes with a favourite pencil that is more satisfying than writing with pen or straight into the computer. But though I'm a weirdo who likes to buy the odd dozen box of Tombow Mono 100s, plenty of ordinary customers have stumbled upon and fallen instantly in love with Caroline's crazy but certifiably brilliant shop, and online business CW Pencil Enterprise (cwpencils.com). In her first year, Caroline has sold 109,896 pencils at an average per customer spend in-store of $20 and $50 online.

What Caroline has done is a template for brilliant customer inspiration. She has instinctively landed on a coherent Big Idea. Her incredible knowledge of the product, way beyond that pencils are generally made of California incense cedar and have a marking core, means every customer can rely on great suggestions for odd little unique pencils that perfectly meet that particular customer's need state. But it is in the discovery, curation and storytelling that CW Pencil Enterprise so excels. These humble little analogue pencils are lifted to become something special, personal and meaningful. How Caroline has done this in-store is especially brilliant: the tiny shop's precise but incredibly accessible visual merchandising screams discovery. You want to pick pencils up and explore their stories.

I know your instinct as a reader is to tease us mercilessly, but I challenge you as a retailer to visit CW Pencil Enterprise and not come away full of ideas and admiration. Each pencil is celebrated and collections precisely curated. There are the Portuguese scented pencils that make great gifts, there are the semi-synthetic vintage IBM test marking pencils loved by crossword puzzlers, there's a poster from a great writer explaining how a dozen soft-tip pencils pre-sharpened in the morning help his ideas flow through the day. There's a lovely physical illustration of the process of making a batch of pencils from wooden blocks to finished article. All of it enriches the discovery experience through curation and narrative.

Because pencils have a credible use, this single-minded store is able to transcend its novelty status. It's more like a guitar shop than, say, a place devoted solely to popcorn or ice cream sandwiches (both of which are actual stores that exist within a five-block radius of this one).

New York Times

Even the problem of the very low average price of the product is addressed by stocking high-margin pencil sharpening machines, premium options and offering a bespoke service to imprint pencil barrels that will become more popular only as the service becomes better known. You need to visit Caroline's store to work out what of its brilliant construction you can transfer to your own formats. And trust me, there is a lot.

But it's still just a pencil

And then there's the cult Blackwing pencil. If you want an example of pencil-related madness, it is the near legendary

Blackwing 602, first made in 1934 by the US arm of Eberhard Faber. But this is also a story of how a humble product can be positioned such that it transcends inherent value and becomes something around which a retailer can build discovery, curation and narrative.

The 602 was distinctive for two reasons: at the blunt end, it featured a flat and wide ferrule (metal bit) with an innovative clip mechanism that held a proper removable eraser, but it was the graphite that was special, a unique formula gave the pencil exceptional writing properties that produced a dark line even without the writer pressing hard. The pencil's barrel carried the slogan "half the pressure, twice the speed". Sold for a few cents each, over time the 602 became a staple favourite with writers and artists including John Steinbeck, Chuck Jones and Stephen Sondheim – until we all went mad for computers in the late 1980s and early 1990s when the pencil, in general, began its sales decline. The end for the Blackwing 602, late in the 1990s, was especially ignominious. The machine used to stamp and form the clips holding the removable eraser broke and nobody in the factory could see any point in fixing it. Once the stock of clips ran out, the 602 was dead.

Then, in 2010, US pencil maker Cal Cedar Products bought the trademark and set out to recreate the lost Blackwing under the Palomino brand. The resurrected legendary pencil is selling by the truckload, at $22 for a box of a dozen, incredibly expensive in pencil terms. Do a Google search for Palomino Blackwing and marvel at the cult status a pencil can achieve. There's even a club for people who modify their Blackings. What do you stock or what sits within your specialism that you could build such appreciation around with a little authentic history and a design twist or two?

And if you want an original 1950s Eberhard Faber Blackwing 602, Caroline Weaver will sell you one. For $75. And she says they do sell. That's customer psychology in a nutshell. We value, and will pay a premium for, the emotional payload of the thing that most satisfyingly meets our need states, but as customers we need the inspiration of discovery, curation and narrative to get us there.

Pencils made more – a selection of Palomino Blackwing models

Source: Koworld

Inspire me and you've got me

Let's take stock. We've begun to think of our customer interactions in terms of friction and reward, we've worked out what our retail business is for and we now understand what needs customers bring to us – and, hopefully, you're looking at ways to meet those needs.

We've got customers reliably browsing us, they're on our websites, they're noticing our social media, they're coming into stores and opening apps. Now we need to inspire those customers to buy our things.

"Inspire" is a very deliberate word. Unless you operate in one of the extremely rare retail sectors in which demand outstrips available points of supply, you must actively work to inspire customers to click on a product, request a test, choose from the menu, handle a product and look at it.

Do that, and you increase the potential for a sale dramatically. In the physical world, Paco Underhill's observation business Envirosell discovered that up to 80% of customer journeys are fulfilled by the customer either buying (or coming back to) the very first thing they interact with. It's a form of bounded rationality where we make decisions based on the immediately available information rather than considering all possible alternatives and outcomes. In this case, where an alternative solution to need states might be distant and nebulous, because we haven't found or seen that alternative yet, so the one in our hand takes on a greater significance. After which, loss aversion kicks in. We've found a solution we like and we then measure all other alternative solutions against it, all the while becoming slightly nostalgic and fond of the original solution. Everything the customer considers after interacting with that first solution has to work much harder to fit need states and *beat* that first solution.

Think back to the last time you bought an item of clothing and you'll recognise this. You find something that fits your need states but you know there are other options out there so you might leave the first and explore the alternatives. Sometimes, one of those alternatives is the one you end up buying but think about how much internal persuading you had to go through before deciding that it definitely was a better option. Loss aversion forces you to measure the new alternatives against the original one that was unaffected by comparison.

"Long story short – get a customer to interact with something and you've kick-started a complex tangle of behavioural economic theory. You've made them put that first thing on a nice little psychological pedestal. Which is good for you as a retailer."

Online, the hard and fast numbers are less well-established in terms of how many purchases are satisfied eventually by the first thing a customer interacts with. It feels instinctively right, though, to assume that the same psychologies that bias towards the first item of engagement in physical interactions are in play in virtual environments. Though perhaps it is in a weaker form, given that it lacks the tactile triggers. Mind you, we're not far away from devices that will enable us to have multi-sensory interactions with virtual items.

Three things that inspire engagement

In the past we could open a store and line shelves with product. If the product was right and the shopfit appealing enough to the right customer segments, then people would come and buy. Online, retailers tended at first to replicate this format: a shop front in the form of a logo header, and then grids of product. It is online that the cracks in this approach are most obvious in that nothing stands out, scrolling pages of product fast becomes a chore. For many retailers, especially those without first mover advantage, despite relevant product and keen pricing, people didn't come.

It is no longer effective to follow this basic model. It has all the sophistication of a toddler playing shop and no retailer can thrive under it. The task now is to inspire interaction through discovery and I have a structure for that, based on my observations, research and conversations with the world's best retailers. Often, those retailers will see their own circumstances differently, might even give their "system" a proprietary name, but what I've done here is package all those successful ideas and systems into a set of universal tools. It works and running your own business through these processes will pay dividends.

So, there are three things that are consistently in place within those winning retailers:

- **Discovery:** they build formats that force discovery by incorporating it strategically and structurally.
- **Curation:** they creatively limit choice using curation and editing of ranges to prompt interaction.
- **Narrative:** they tell stories in which customers can easily recognise a benefit that relates directly to themselves.

We will deal with curation and narrative in the next chapter. For now I want to look at discovery and explore its powerful role in making it natural for customers to want to engage with you and your product.

> Inspiration to interact happens when retailers build discovery-rich formats, populate those formats with curated ranges of products and services, and then use strong narratives to show customers how easily they can put themselves into those stories.

In practice

Here are two examples of modern retailers that are doing all three brilliantly. In the first, I've chosen to concentrate on Williams-Sonoma's physical mastery of discovery, curation and retail narrative but it is a retailer that also does the three of them extremely well online. In the second example, I've looked at Everlane, currently only online, but, as you'll see in Secret six, that is a label that is fast becoming meaningless.

Williams-Sonoma
Prodding the senses and the imagination

The smell of pumpkin-spice cider, a warming deep autumnal scent, transports me away to a New England autumn with the golden leaves starting to cascade from the trees . . . Williams-Sonoma has got me. Outside it's a grotty urban mid-western afternoon, cold and mean but inside I've taken just a few steps yet travelled a thousand miles.

This high-end cookery and housewares retailer gives the absolute masterclass on sense-based retailing: smells of food being cooked all around the store, the sight of seasonal cues everywhere, taste of the samples dotted about. It's that pumpkin-spice cider. Pumpkin bread there. Mash and sweet gravy in another section. Even sound gets a look in as, on a proper full gas hob, there's a big pot of something nice bubbling away in a satisfying chatter. What does that leave? Touch? Well there's plenty of stuff to for that.

Client after client tells me this sort of thing is impossible in their stores. Nonsense. You want to create a taste of what your product leads to? You can do it. This particular Williams-Sonoma, packed with the emotional context of its market sector, is selling the pleasurable and satisfying feeling of cooking good food for friends and family. It isn't even that big at around 300 square metres, yet packs demonstration and discovery into every corner.

Everything in the range feels curated, as if to say, "If we stock it, you can trust it." One fantastic example of this is positioned with considerable narrative skill. An extremely expensive collection

---

▶

of pans is promoted with, "This is the last cookware you'll ever buy" and the display then goes on to explain that this is heirloom cookware, pans you will pass on. It's such a simple, yet powerful, story. It lifts a bunch of saucepans into something laden with wonderful images of longevity and family.

Williams-Sonoma is built around discovery of things that will make you not only a better cook but will improve your experiences of cooking for the people you care about. It's warm and cozy and very shoppable.

Everlane.com
Transparency and rewarding virtue

64% of millennials, Everlane.com's target customers, would rather wear a socially conscious brand than a luxury one. That truth, one that is reflective of a trend that means if you're reading this two years after I've written it, that 64% will be higher still, is the narrative, where an amazing level of price and manufacturing transparency provides the discovery. In this case, customers discover that they can make both a socially conscious purchase and do so at a lower price than they would expect. Powerfully, Everlane's price transparency – every item has its materials, labour, import duty and transport costs shown together with Everlane's mark-up – makes customers feel that they are part of a fair trade.

Everlane's format is founded on a Big Idea that is to be a radically transparent retailer of classic wardrobe staples. So a T-shirt isn't a sweatshop-produced basic but a classic imbued with the story of the factory in which it was made, the people who made it, the narrative of socially conscious production and the discovery that these things can be bought at a reasonable price.

Research business Forrester says there are 8,000 places where you can buy a white T-shirt online; for Everlane to have discovered a way to make theirs attractive is a big achievement. The business sells "tens of thousands" of them every month.

The company does something that, on the surface, might appear to be anti-discovery. Rather than offer seasonal collections, it adds products one at a time. Some items have been in the collection for all of the five years Everlane has existed. Founder Michael Preysman says the clothing has "a current point of view", but suggests that items "can also be worn in ten years" and encourages customers to wear items for as long as possible, as part of a sustainability message.

Each new item has a story of its manufacture and pricing built around it, again imbuing everything with an authenticity and character that is very effective. The whole range covers just 200 pieces, all of which fit a recognisable Everlane look. It is a curation that customers love – they like being part of the Everlane story and trust the company as a source of socially conscious fair-priced classics.

The three keys to inspiration

So let's break down each of these three essential tools of customer inspiration. We will start by looking at the ways retailers can build discovery-led formats. In the next chapter we will move on to the power of curation and narrative.

Discovery

All three of these ideas are roughly talking about the same thing: the moment a customer interacts with your product or service because they've found something that fits their need state. The benefit of prompting discovery, of inspiring customers to pick something up or click on it for more detail is gigantic. Here's how to make that happen.

Discovery features at some point every time anyone shops, online or off. Even the customer who is certain they just want Heinz tomato ketchup week in and week out is disruptible by a good promotion or interesting new alternative – and they delight in it. The point at which discovery is made may shift but no shopping trip is ever made without it. As retailers, we can benefit if we can manage discovery to our advantage, and the good news is that there are some usefully formal ways to do that.

Sometimes the discovery will be made before leaving the house or opening the page, research having been done online, via media and among friends. That type of discovery certainly applies to a more significant degree to big-ticket items but even then the decision reached is observably disruptible, especially by promotions but also through knowledgeable intervention and definitely by stock availability.

Many customers who leave home knowing what they want, having extensively researched it and used all the tools online to help with that, are still open to persuasion once they arrive at a store and begin to actively shop. We see the same thing online where customer journeys that have come direct to a specific product page are stymied by an out-of-stock item or by a recommended alternative.

Discovery makes people interact with things. Make a customer say "Wow" and, more often than not, you've got a sale. Discovery is not just about showing customers surprising things, it is the complete process of helping to guide them to the highlights of your range, to the great promotions, to using great service and support to lead customers to the right choices.

A reputation as a store that can meet customers' sub-conscious desire for discovery will drive your clicks and footfall. So long as you're consistently meeting needs and you've got the framing right, creating formats where discovery is at the heart, will also actively contribute to your business gaining First Visit Advantage.

There are broadly four approaches to integrating discovery: promotion-led, service-led, product-led and total-format. Some retailers can combine more than one of these. When you get to the Stew Leonard's case study, you'll find a great retailer that combines all of them.

1. Traditional promotion-led discovery

Traditional promotion-led discovery is still the most common way retailers incorporate discovery and, if you're able to offer great deals, it's very powerful. The availability of those deals is only half the story, though. Promotions must be supported with great visual merchandising that brings them right to the surface.

The key elements are:

- creative promotions
- a variety of promotions
- a near-guarantee that there will be a deal for every customer, every time
- consistent low prices on core products
- a retail-type that encourages regular revisits
- a celebration of the offers by putting them in good locations and regular inclusion of the "good stuff"
- store layout that includes plenty of hot-spots
- a planned customer journey that leads visitors between those hot-spots.

Tesco (UK)

Tesco is the international blueprint for promotion-led discovery. Go as an observer and learn how to select, place and promote offers brilliantly. The business might have gone through troubles in the early 2010s but its singular ability to offer killer promotions remains intact.

Aldi (Germany)

The powerful trick Aldi has pulled off is to persuade customers that the entire store is one big price promotion. Aldi isn't just about being cheap, though. Efficiencies in logistics, ranging and buying, as well as reduced location, store-fitting and staff costs are all positive, but the product itself is good and sometimes extremely good. Watch middle-class couples ransacking the incredibly cheap, but very high-quality, steak section for evidence. On top of this, Aldi specifically operates a discovery element by introducing revolving special buys: one week it's very good value cycling gear, the next it's gardening, and so on. Every visit to Aldi over a period offers the chance to discover something unexpected that is incredibly good value. Ever since I bought a £5 snow shovel in 2013, we've seen not a single flake of snow in Oxford. Thanks for that, Aldi.

Lowes (USA)

Lowes has always been good at promotional deals but what puts Lowes into the premier division of promotion-led discovery is its approach to pricing core project items. Let's take decking. The deck planks themselves are priced almost to give away, a few dollars only for each 3m length. A wandering customer will do their initial value calculation, the one done in your head when you've actually come in for something else, based on the cost of the decking planks alone. That makes the cost of the project appear to be very low. It is only then, when adding the cost of frame timbers, posts, screws, joints and finishes, that the true project cost emerges. By this point, it's a bit academic because you've already pictured yourself out on the deck enjoying a summer barbecue.

2. Service-led discovery

The humans in your business are amazing – all of them. They offer you the very best opportunity to tell the best stories about your business and your products. They are also one of the best ways to deliver on discovery through honest advice, thoughtful recommendation and after-sales service. Keys to achieving this are written up in the team section of this book (see Chapter 8). Go do it and your customers will love you for it. Love you with their wallets.

The key elements are:

- Make clear to everyone in the business how directly their effort affects customers.
- Make it clear that you trust your team with your customers and that your number one priority is the satisfaction of both.
- Create and evangelise your Big Idea and make it easy to understand and act upon.
- Treat your people with respect.
- Offer them great training and lots of it.
- Allow and enable your people to experience the products you sell, give them free stuff and generous staff discounts, and operate loan programmes for big-ticket items.
- Get all your people exposed to the supply chain, show them how things are sourced and made, as doing so will help them

to enthuse about your products and, more importantly, identify what makes your stuff great.

- Structure your reward programme such that it is biased towards customer satisfaction and away from sales volumes.

- Put in place a recognition programme and use it to say thank you each and every time you see your people go the extra mile for customers.

- Value knowledge highly but also encourage your team to be open-minded and make sure they understand that every customer has their own set of needs.

- Stress the value of listening to what customers tell us they need and show how this is more important than telling customers what we assume they should have.

The Container Store (USA)

Brilliant at discovery, The Container Store provides phenomenal levels of training, wonderful employment experiences and works incredibly hard to build stable customer-focused teams. The result is a business that punches well above its weight and that enjoys a near fanatical level of customer advocacy. One of my favourite retailers anywhere in the world, it provides an average of 210 hours per year of staff training, great staff discounts and has featured in *Fortune*'s 100 Best Places to Work in the USA list for more than a straight decade.

Enjoy.com (USA)

This is what Ron Johnson (creator of the Apple Store) did next. Well, not next, so ignore the horrible bit at JC Penney and fast forward here. Enjoy.com is the first new thing to happen to electrical retail in decades. Start with a price-promise backed web store, supported by a sprinkling of physical area "houses", but throw in home delivery and set-up by its experts, who will take the product to customers at home and then sit patiently with them to find out what that customer wants to get from the product and then show them how to do it. The discovery here comes post-sale (or partially pre-sale from press and word of mouth) that buying a phone, a router or a camera can turn out to be such a reassuring and deeply satisfying experience. This isn't deliverymen in overalls with sack barrows stomping muddy boots through your home. Enjoy's people are exactly the sort of boys and girls you'd meet in an Apple store or at a benign cult: service-trained, friendly, knowledgeable and empowered to make customers happy.

John Lewis Partnership (UK)

A byword for honesty, quality and great customer care, customers are drawn to John Lewis because they trust it and are confident that the experience will be one that is complemented by staff worth talking to. Elsewhere in retailing, extremely poor employment practices have meant the reputation of the in-store retail assistant has been damaged, but John Lewis has been able to prove to customers that it doesn't have to be this way. It has been especially good at doing this in high-ticket electricals and computing, areas perhaps not traditionally associated with the store but that, nonetheless, customers let John Lewis guide them through both online and in-store.

3. Product-led discovery

This is where the product is the star. Innovation, fashion, trends, great iconic design are the critical factors in stores where the product leads discovery. So we're talking about the kinds of stores that are great at buying and merchandising and at refreshing the ranges. But it's more than that – it's critical that the top team in this sort of store has an innate understanding of the principles and power of design and that they have a sense for the zeitgeist among their target customer groups. A lot of expensive single-store businesses start up in this category and an awful lot of them fail. They fail because the owners mistake knowing what I like with knowing what customers need. When done right, though, the approach can be incredibly successful. The very best fashion and furnishings stores are great examples of product-led discovery businesses.

The key elements are:

- Curate ranges, do not offer choice for choice's sake.
- It's all about your buying team, spotting exceptional products at the right price points.
- Hang on, maybe it's all about your visual merchandising team – showing off those products in inspirational settings?

- Study all the sources of information on trends that you can lay your hands on.
- Watch very closely what goes on in competitors' stores for clues on trends.
- Talk to customers, formally if you want, but on absolutely every single store visit you must talk to customers and get feedback all the time.
- Ask customers what's hot, encourage them to make recommendations on new finds and new directions.
- Ensure key products are given room to breathe and are displayed to their absolute best.
- Be prepared to drop poor performing lines early (or at least to change emphasis, if you can).
- Refresh ranges often but show respect for important classic lines too.
- Do not presume to dictate taste but do try hard to influence it.

Objects of Use (UK)

This tiny one-store miracle is typical of a new wave of specialists with young artisanal sensibilities grafted to commercial instinct that makes product discovery the foundation of its Big Idea (see also Caroline Weaver's brilliant CW Pencil Enterprise, Chicago's quirky art and music store Transistor, described by *Time Out* as "your coolest friend's apartment", and the icy cool, but brilliant, Labour and Wait in London's East End).

Objects of Use's Big Idea is to be "a source of enduring household tools and functional items". Those two words "enduring" and "functional" are important: they carefully curate a range that is full of thoughtfully made long-lasting items that are entirely focused on the function for which they exist. The store is thus filled with lovingly displayed and described items that transcend ordinary by virtue of their timeless craft and quality. They are items that, by their inherent nature, are both lovely things to own and great for gifts, and around which that process of discovery is fuelled.

The store is always packed and the tills always busy. All of the businesses I mention above are also supported by robust and attractive online stores in which product is fetishised and celebrated and sold by people who clearly love what they stock, and for whom an online component is not a separate thing but a natural part of the business. It's what they've grown up with and is second nature to them. It is also entirely no surprise that Objects of Use stocks the magical Palomino Blackwing pencils.

ASOS (UK)

Back in 2000, when ASOS launched under its long-form name "As Seen On Screen", the Big Idea was to sell clothes seen on celebs and actors on telly and in the movies. The business quickly outgrew that space as they discovered that it was good at tracking screen-seen fashion but even better at understanding and stocking bang-up-to-date fashions in general. That awesome instinct for fashion, and a focused concentration on the 16 to 34 age range, has driven product-led discovery and created a store that customers love to regularly check out.

Zara (Spain)

Zara is built on an incredibly efficient supply chain that enables it to bring new items into stores twice a week, every week. That's an astonishing commitment to product-led discovery and it leads the fashion retail industry on logistics and is able to take an idea from initial design to retail rail faster than anybody else. It's obvious to see why customers might react positively to such fast change and ever-shifting variety.

Warby Parker (USA)

Though Warby Parker's Big Idea leads on making glasses cheaper, the team never compromise on quality or design. It almost fetishises style and form; its visual merchandising in the physical store chain is of an extremely high quality and produces the sort of interiors you'd expect to find on Bond Street or Fifth Avenue. For those of us who remember our first super-nerd NHS glasses (for US readers, imagine glasses given out on welfare), the idea of own-brand specs conjures horrible memories of teasing at school and worse, but Warby Parker's cheap specs are beautiful and bang on trend. It's a terrific twisting of the expected norm and generates exceptional volume at respectable margins.

Here is Warby Parker's description of its Milton frames: "Each pair is crafted from lightweight Japanese titanium and wrapped in premium cellulose acetate coils (handmade in Italy!)"

Crafted. Wrapped. Handmade. Sounds like a description from a menu item at a top restaurant. Ingredients are raised by being Japanese titanium and premium cellulose acetate. Titanium is titanium, wherever in the world it's mined and worked. Cellulose acetate is essentially plastic, albeit a natural one.

And this for a pair of glasses retailing for less than half the price of an equivalent designer-branded pair. This is product-led discovery in powerful form.

Total-format discovery

There are a number of retailers that have based their entire Big Idea and format around discovery and paths to discovery. These are the stores you find full of handwritten notices recommending products. They are the ones in which you see little notes to you, the customer, all over the place that connect you with the products. Everything in the store is about making sure that you are made aware of how brilliant a product will be for you, how you will feel, what a difference it will make to your health, well-being or lifestyle. That sounds a bit "ad-man" written down. It's worth saying that, in order to properly convince, the format must be honest, credible and authentic, too. It's important, too, that format-led discovery works only if there is service-led discovery in place too.

The tools include:

- Create an authentic voice for the brand.
- Use your values to ensure that the voice properly represents your Big Idea and mission.
- Create a compelling conversation throughout the customer journey, make use of space on product, bags, shelf edge, in changing rooms, on product cartons, walls, editorial, at the till, and so on.
- Provide honest advice everywhere.
- Celebrate the great products, be enthusiastic and explain to customers why you think an item is so great.
- Constantly refresh displays.

- Get customers involved with recommendations.
- Make good use of customer advocacy, so make it easy for customers to tell others about your store and range.
- Remember that it's the conversation that's important.
- Make good use of seasonal and "occasion" events.

Story (USA)

The ultimate expression of total-format discovery is the Story store in the heart of Manhattan's cool Chelsea neighbourhood. It is a retail space that changes every three to eight weeks as a new story is told. One period this might be a story themed around wellbeing (http://goo.gl/VrZZaH) and next it could be a Lexus-sponsored store of discovery wrapped around creativity. The result is a 200 square metre space that customers are drawn to because they might discover something new, that features constant time-limited calls to action, as in the wellbeing "last weekend" campaign, plus unique new product collaborations fitting the current theme. Story is a place where brands can experiment and play with concepts and products. An article at CNBC puts the cost of those brand sponsorships at a minimum of $400,000, with no shortage of brands wanting a slice of the Story pie.

In five years, Story has run 28 unique "stories" and held 400 events, featuring 3,000 brands. This is ever-changing discovery and curation as the format itself. It has made for an exciting and energising physical space that ramps sky high the reward side of the friction/reward equation.

Apple Store (USA)

The iconic retail bases for Apple's products are entirely about discovery. They are built ground-up around the notion of non-Apple people discovering that Apple meets their needs better, and of dedicated Apple-users discovering they belong to a tribe that cares about them. So you have every single part of the Apple range, in quantity, out on the shop floor, set up so customers can touch them, play with them, have fun with them and discover new things with them. Then the Apple team, extremely well-trained customer advisors, make themselves easily available to give advice, recommendations and solutions. In the early days,

I wondered if the Apple Stores would turn out to be a heavily sub-sidised brand promotion rather than profitable stores, but the opposite is true, as the stores are very profitable as well as being stunningly successful discovery zones for loyal and new Apple customers alike.

Pret a Manger (UK)

These sandwich shops do authentic conversation better than any other retailer in the world. Should you find yourself reading this book while sitting at one of Pret's stainless steel counters, you would find that the coffee cup you're drinking from has a note on it that explains how Pret's coffee has come to taste as good as it does. That cup would explain too how Pret supports the grower of the beans your coffee was made from. You might then dab the corners of your mouth with a Pret napkin that tells you it's made from unbleached, recycled fibres that explains why that's a good thing.

This conversation Pret a Manger has with its customers is power-ful and is about helping customers to discover a lunchtime option that meets a perceived deeper set of needs. There's a lot of research evidence that proves that our sense of taste is effected by contextual information – telling somebody that they should expect to enjoy their sandwich more because it's fresh increases the likelihood that they will enjoy it more. You can use that in lots of ways in retail. We're generally really bad at communicating emotional or sensual information so directly to our customers.

Urban Outfitters (USA)

You'll notice that I categorise most fashion stores in the product-led discovery category. Urban Outfitters makes the jump because of the innovative way it has constructed its display sys-tems, the credible addition of non-clothes ranges and the con-sidered inclusion of branded ranges. All displays at Urban Outfitters are mix and match – tables, shelves and rails can be easily combined, moved and re-merchandised. This makes it easy for the team to constantly refresh the store and use a form of convection to bring different items to the surface before allowing these to settle back into main stock as new items get pulled to the surface.

> ## Stew Leonards
> ## Being authentically great fun
>
> This case study is essentially the same one I included for the first time in the 2007 edition of *Smart Retail*. All I've had to change is to put another hundred million dollars on the revenue total. Stew Leonard's keeps on ramping up and up. It's an amazing business and more retailers should go out of their way to visit. I first had that pleasure on a mammoth drive from Lake Winnipesaukee up in New Hampshire down to the bottom end of Manhattan Island via Danbury in New York State. We arrived at the Danbury store in the dark and through driving rain feeling exhausted and miserable after hours on the road. I'd long wanted to see a Stew Leonard's but my partner and I were grumpy and hungry and this visit felt a lot like work. An hour and a half later we were back in the hire car buzzing, having been boosted by one of the most vibrant and fun store experiences we'd ever had.
>
> Stew Leonard's is barking. Often literally. And it's baa'ing, moo'ing and clucking too, much of the time. Stew Leonard's is a chain of just four stores (with a fifth planned), all in the north east of the USA that together take $400,000,000 a year. They turn more than $5,000 per square foot of sales space and achieve revenue-per-employee that is around $180,000. Staggering, stunning, mind-blowing numbers.
>
> And what is Stew Leonard's? A family-owned dairy store that sells a limited selection of 2,200 dairy and dairy-related products, 80% of which are fresh, serving 130,000 customers each week.
>
> And, although I suspect current boss Stew Leonard Junior wouldn't call it by this name, discovery is what sits at the heart of the amazing performance of this business. The entire format is built around discovery and theatre: loads to see and do and a massive single aisle that snakes customers past every last part of the big store. Promotion-led discovery is there in spades and in massive volume. Product-led discovery, too, is important with, in particular, what they claim to be the freshest milk in North America, which comes from their own herd of cows, cows you can see milked on the live webcam feeds shown in

the milk area. Service-led promotion is incredibly important, too. The employment experience at Stew Leonard's is of a very high standard (and regularly recognised as such in *Fortune Magazine*'s 100 Best Companies to Work For annual list).

The customer is king, but only because the staff are allowed to make it so. "You can't have a great place to shop without first making it a great place to work." That's a slogan you'll see written up in the store but it's more than words as the management team deliver on that too.

Stew Leonard's gives every employee a real say in how to best service customer needs. If an employee thinks that doing x is good for an individual customer, they will get on and do that thing. If they think y is good for their customers in general, and they really do mean "their", then they will suggest the business gets on and does that too. There is a great story Stew Junior tells that illustrates this in action. He calls it the tuna fish story: "I unwrap one of our tuna fish sandwiches, and this package of mayonnaise rolls out. I figure the sandwich has enough mayo already. So I call Bill Hollis, my deli manager, and tell him '. . . get rid of the extra mayo, it's expensive'. So next week, I open a sandwich, the mayo rolls out again. I call Bill, and he says '. . . you gotta talk to Mary Ekstrand, she makes the sandwiches'. I call Mary, who says 'Sorry, Stew, the customers want the extra mayo, so I'm packing it again.' You know my reaction? Bravo, Mary!"

Stew Junior has a cheesy, but perfect, acronym that illustrates his management style nicely: STEW. Satisfy the customer, work together as a Team, strive for Excellence at everything you do, and get the customer to say Wow.

That "wow" thing is a foundation principle of all forms of discovery. It means customers have found stuff that meets their need states. The team has created what the *New York Times* calls "The Disneyland of dairy stores", and it is banjo-playing robot dogs singing Dixie, and animatronic milk cartons (The Farm Fresh Five) dancing near a model cow that tells jokes when kids pull its bell. Staff dress as cows, ducks, chickens and bananas while patrolling the aisles, giving out free ice cream and helium balloons. They put on these daft costumes, not because they are told to, but because they decide for themselves what to promote and how to

▶

celebrate it. They use their own budgets to go out and buy these costumes. Free food samples are everywhere and staff offer them accompanied by warm, genuine smiles. There are petting zoos, outdoor BBQs, beach grills, cafes and singing broccoli and carrots. Shoppers don't just come here to buy a quart of milk, but for the experience. An experience built on discovery.

This store might feel like it's lots of things all just thrown together, but that's not really true. This is a place built by its people. Those 130,000 customers come along each week because they like the products, but they come for the atmosphere and, mostly, I suspect, they come because the human experience at Stew Leonard's makes them feel good. That is down to the dedication, imagination and vision not of just one man but of a whole motivated, passionate team. A retail family.

Now
Things you can do now

- Find five ways in which your current formats inspire customers to interact with product. Consider what it is about these five things that connects them. Are they random? Is there a pattern that might suggest this inspiration to engage happens *because* of you?
- Work out what sort of discovery business you are now – product, promotion, service or format?
- Take an honest look at the answer above and decide if it is compatible with your Big Idea
- Look at how you measure up with the "key elements" list for the type of discovery retailer you are.
- Identify three of these key elements to work on strengthening.

Next
Strategic considerations for the longer term

- Is your current discovery positioning compatible with the current strategic vision of the business?
- What structural change might be required to better deliver discovery to customers?

Chapter

5

We think in terms of stories – it's how humans make sense of the world around us. Retailers need to be storytellers and we need to build those stories around carefully curated benefits and the solving of problems. We need to do this because stories go deeper than facts or even ideas.

Retail secret five: I choose stories

In this chapter we explore

- the use of curation to prompt spending

- the fallacy of choice

- narrative selling – how we think in stories and why that's important.

Curious about curation?

Curation is the process of being active in recommendation either from products available within your sector or from within your own range. It can be either a targeted limitation of choice in general (everything you stock fits a theme or your own defined tight criteria), or products surfaced from within your own ranges, so you might stock 20 variations of an item across the store but bring just 3 into focus under a family heading.

It's worth admitting, though, that the word "curation" has come in for a bit of stick recently, having been identified as a symptom of a me-too maker-culture sickness. Claims to have curated bank accounts or curated socks stretch credibility. Some wags will shout "CURATING? NO, YOU MEAN CHOOSING." But stick with it as those are different things. Curation is the process of narrowing down wild choice into easier to shop logical and related small families of things, where "choosing" is about looking at all the options available.

Choice versus curation

On the surface, curation appears to be the last thing customers want you to do, especially if you only look at the headlines in customer insight:

- If you ask customers if they want choice, they will say "yes" because choice has become a synonym for freedom.
- If you analyse common retail complaints, wanting a bigger product range comes near or at the top all the time.

So retail CEOs and chairmen stick "expand choice" down in their strategies as a KPI. And then they do, indeed, write in their annual reports things like: "We increased customer choice and range by 10%. We now offer the greatest range of choice in our history."

But look closely at the second point above and you find that, actually, what people are complaining about is that it's hard to find the thing that's right for their particular need state. They say "give us more options" when they mean "I couldn't find the one that was right". There's stuff around loss aversion in that, too. Choosing between a million similar options is less satisfying than choosing between a limited number of very different ones.

When you have all day and a cup full of tokens, choice is a good thing but these circumstances are rare in retail

Source: Koworld

Why? Because many of the similar ones could have satisfied the need state in play and, after purchase, we are subject to a nagging doubt that one of the other options could have done the same job better.

Very few retailers curate choice properly, which is where the solution lies. Offer a wide theoretical selection (go into the Amazon store in Seattle and you can order any book, but you're much more likely to buy one of the carefully curated options in front of you), but constantly pick out and display what amount to decision trees as curated selections.

You give me no choice

I'm going to argue here that less choice is better than more choice and that presentation of product, no matter through what medium, must be in curated and related forms. At it's most basic, that means putting sandwich, drink and crisps together and calling it, with powerfully narrative effect, "lunch". At it's most creative, it's Story, the store I mentioned in the total-format discovery section (see Secret four), where new product might be specially commissioned to fit curated story themes.

For decades, the received wisdom in retailing has been that large ranges are the ideal, that customers want to be able to choose from the widest possible selection. There's some easy cod logic in that more choice means more opportunities to sell stuff and more opportunities than our competitors mean more customers for us. It's a logic that is especially nagging when you've been commercially brought up to put product first (product is the most important thing, therefore more product means more better), but those retailers who truly put customers first have discovered that what customers really want is to be exposed to those choices that are most relevant to their particular needs in a given situation.

More technically, there is a big issue in choice that is linked to our natural tendency toward loss aversion. Curated choices that give the widest range of distinctions between the perceived benefits of each option are the most shoppable. So, five shades of grey T-shirt are harder to choose between than five distinct combinations of patterns and colour. Worse, the perceived benefits of the slightly lighter or darker grey persist *after* purchase as near and therefore possibly better options. Choosing a red T-shirt that says 'Happy' on it, when the ones either side were different colours and slogans, is provably more satisfying than the choice between those five grey T-shirts. There is more about choice later but establishing the focusing of choice as the root of curation is essential.

In a right old jam

A greater understanding of the value of curation versus inhibited choice began with an experiment on jam nearly 20 years ago. Psychologists Sheena Iyengar and Mark Lepper, over two Saturdays, set up a display table outside a posh supermarket in Menlo Park, California. On one of these days, the table was laid with 24 different flavours of jam from Wilkin & Sons (described gloriously in the subsequent research paper as "a British jelly purveyor"). On the other day, just six flavours were displayed.

Every customer who stopped and sampled the flavours was given a coupon for $1 off any subsequent Wilkin & Sons jam purchase in the store. The coupons were tracked, as was overall footfall versus customers stopping to sample.

On the day featuring 24 flavours, a huge 60% of people stopped to try a bit of tasty British jam, whereas on the day of a curated six flavour table, just 40% of people stopped for a taste. But subsequent purchase behaviour uncovered something remarkable:

- Of the 24 flavours group 3% of coupons were redeemed.
- Of the six flavours group a gigantic 30% of coupons were redeemed.

Work that across a sample size of 100 people:

- 24 jams: 60 people sample the flavours but only 2 (1.8 rounded up) go on to buy a jar of jam.
- 6 jams: 40 people sample the flavours and 12 go on to buy a jar of jam.

The large display attracted more interest, generated more pre-sales buzz, but the curated choice table generated significantly more sales. Why? The difference is straightforward: most of those testing from a wide choice of 24 jams leave the table with *some* impression of the general quality of Wilkin & Sons jams. Most of those testing from six jams leave the table with a distinct perspective on Wilkin & Sons strawberry jam versus Wilkin & Sons blueberry jam or any of the other easily remembered four choices.

Those customers are forming opinions and buying intentions around specific jars of jam because 6 flavours can be kept in memory much more easily than can 24, and they have formed preferential views within those 6, such as, "I like the strawberry more than the blueberry". If their need states include jam, then they take along with them a specific set of ideas around an easily relatable specific product. The result is that those customers go from a vague appreciation of one brand's jams in general to a focused confirmation bias towards a specific jar of jam they then see on a shelf.

In a similar commercially driven test, Swedish supermarket giant ICA cut down chewing gum choices at the till from more than 30 options to 5, and experienced an absolute increase in sales. Their view was that this increase arose from customers seeing the five distinct choices and experiencing a switch in their internal need state from "Do I need chewing gum?" to "Which chewing gum do I prefer?"

Sweet sugary snack and soda spot

When it comes to general choice, there is a sweet spot. US research has shown convincingly that increasing choices of snacks and soft drinks at convenience stores often leads to decreasing overall sales volumes and decreasing customer satisfaction. And, certainly, the delightful novelty of the first time a Brit walks into what looks like a small gas station retail section to be confronted by 200 choices of soft drink and a billion possible snack choices wears off when you're in a hurry and can't find root beer and those insane bags of crisps that have M&Ms mixed in.

But it's absolutely not a linear curve. If snack and soft drink selections are critically narrow, then the attractiveness of the offer is damaged. Too large and poorly delineated a selection and customers experience a paralysis and frustration of choice. For some, they don't have the time to make a choice, while for others their habitual choices in those two areas are swamped, and other customers experience selection blindness. They simply cannot see a choice that is right for their immediate set of snack and drink needs. For them, increased choice just means increased friction for the same reward level.

Finding that sweet spot relies on instinct and test, change and re-test. It's also important to improve the quality of your visual merchandising, to help the process of choosing. Take, for example, those customers frustrated that you've given everything equal weighting. You *know* your dependable high volume favourites so don't just put those at eye level, consider multiple locations for those: entranceway, range section, queue line, lunch section. But also be creative in each. So flow secondary choices out as adjacencies from the favourites, use promotions to tell a story, use compression to create blocks of instantly recognisable colours and brand assets, and so on.

Sephora
Actively curating choice

Great examples of creative visual merchandising for curation can be found throughout Sephora stores. In particular, they feature large "Sephora Favorites" displays in hot zones that carry a small curated selection of bestsellers, hot product and customer favourites on them. These favourites stands are large but might only carry four choices in each of a small selection of categories.

One recent example showcasing primers (it's some part of the make-up routine but I'm lost, to be honest) featured headings across the four stages of priming. Under each of those were four favourite products in a column. Each product had an accessible sample and a big display card explaining why it was selected. Behind these cards are packaged products looking exclusive but easy to grab. It's a display you can linger at and take your time, while the layout makes selection and interaction a very natural process. It's easy to see customers taking a product from each column. This is Sephora cutting through its deep ranges and making choice an easier, more rewarding and much lower friction process.

Sephora also sells pre-packaged favourites in various categories, both multiple examples of one item such as lipstick, or selections for a specific task, such as hydration on the go. These cut-across brands appear to be properly curated to provide Sephora's best recommendations and examples across each pack.

This frankly terrifying beauty-blogger video illustrates how Sephora packages and promotes curated favourites: https://goo.gl/qvrvhl and here's Sephora's own page on the selection boxes: http://goo.gl/2wBTKF.

Online, Sephora's curation tools are varied and excellent, including "Editor's Picks" prominently on most customers' view of the front page, and "editor" is a terrifically evocative word, immediately prompting thoughts on curation, independence and advice. To a tightly curated "Choose 5 from 12 samples selector", and on to the brilliant Beauty Board on which customers can post their own make-up looks, then browsers can click on pictures that interest them, and then all the required products are listed just a teasing "Buy now" button away.

With curation, Sephora is playing an active role in advising customers and then getting those customers to buy. Sephora customers can be confident that a visit to the store or website will result in them easily finding inspiration and product that meets their need states.

Sephora has done the work for the customer by making it easier for them to spend money.

"I still reckon customers want choice"

The Daily Telegraph published a story in 2015 on the future of retailing with the following headline: "After 20 years of online shopping, why the future could be about less choice for consumers, not more."

The article was well researched and offered some useful retail insight, the summary being that online retailing will continue to grow and will, at the same time, become more and more focused on individuals and their personal needs and shopping trips.

What's curious is that headline, as it hints that the Telegraph feels that massive choice is good and limited choice is bad and that customers want choice, so any restriction in choice is a bad thing. Perhaps restricted choice is okay online, the writer suggests, because there's a useful trade-off: the smaller range of choices are likely to be better targeted. But still the headline makes one thing clear: less choice = customer sad face.

But the real truth is that customers have *never* wanted huge choice. Choice is paralysing, it demands effort in the sorting and sifting. Making customers do the legwork in finding something is utterly upside-down. You have one primary job as a retailer: to make it easy for people to buy things from you. Call it a retail covenant, if you will. If you're a retailer, your commitment to the customer is to make it easy for them to spend money.

But the customer insight managers and market research drones yell: "Whenever we ask customers, they tell us that they do want choice."

Of course, customers tell researchers that they want more choice. Put a box on a form with the word "Choice" next to it in a list of things people value and they will always tick it. Why wouldn't we? Nobody votes to restrict choice because we're so inured to the idea that choice and freedom are synonymous. Leaving "choice" out of a list of things we like would be madness.

Barry Schwartz's book The Paradox of Choice is still, more than ten years later, the bible on understanding the negative connection between choice and happiness. You must read it. Here is Barry bringing the book to life in a TED talk: http://goo.gl/P6Tf14.

Do we know we don't like choice

You shouldn't ask customers about choice at all because, however you ask, we will give a dumb answer that is entirely biased to what we mistakenly think choice represents and to the way in which you ask the question.

Customers rarely vote for a restriction of choice, but, in practice, they crave just exactly that restriction. IKEA, Aldi and ASOS are all examples where choice is curated (in order, by function and design, for price and effectiveness, and for style).

Amazon, too, is a business that *looks* like it offers the ultimate in unlimited choice, but that's a mirage. Many customers find it highly frustrating when attempting to browse for inspiration along its myriad paths, but it doesn't matter. Amazon's curation, inspiration and discovery is done for it by media and customer reviews, by brands' own marketing and by word of mouth. Amazon as a business is staunchly and philosophically anti-curation, yet depends on it for sales.

Another brilliantly curating retailer, one that some may not even recognise as a retailer, is Netflix, whose vast library of films and TV isn't easily visible in one standard customer-facing database. Subscribers find their inspiration, and experience discovery, largely through curated recommendation. So, instead of lists of all movies beginning with the letter A, as would have been the case at Borders, or 500 films listed under World Cinema as at HMV, subscribers might get 30 films in a section entitled "Quirky Comedies" or 30 in a chunk under the title "Because you watched *It's Always Sunny in Philadelphia*".

So vital is recommendation to Netflix's success that the company has awarded more than a million dollars to independent researchers able to beat Netflix's internal recommendation algorithm. The Netflix Prize shows how highly valued recommendation and, by turn, curation are. And, of course, part of the Netflix Prize is that the winners' processes are then used to improve the Netflix recommendation algorithm still further.

Like illustrated spreadsheets

Switch back to an example of the tradition of choice in retailing. If you were to visit Clarks' UK website now (May 2016) and select mens/smart shoes, a not unreasonable search, then the result is a list of 74 pairs, all identically photographed and sized, and presented in the form of a rigid visual grid. Or, more accurately, you see an illustrated spreadsheet, with all the lack of retail engagement that suggests. Clarks, as do many other retailers, expects customers to do the legwork; this is choice as chore.

Let's try again. Select mens/casual shoes. 188 pairs! All identically represented.

To be fair to Clarks, it does include some good curation accessible from the home page and the company works very hard to seed online blogs and social media. In the case of the home page tools, though, I have to actively choose to find them. I have to click around a bit first, which is still asking me to do too much. The basic stock-in-trade of the site is still the grid listing: 188 shoes with absolutely no sense of differentiation.

Complaining about choice might really be about lack of discovery

Qubit.com runs a very credible big data system to survey complaints customers have about online retailers and, in 2015, published the latest of its reports, in this case covering 1.2m data points.

Number one complaint was about product range, which, on the surface, seemed to suggest that customers want to see greater range and more choice. Drill down into the types of complaints and it starts to become clear that making sense of choice is what's really being complained about. The logic goes, "If I can't find what I want, then surely the answer is for you to offer me more things?"

Qubit offers three representative examples: "More sandals and pumps please", "View all items in a category or be able to select more items to a page" and "Show more brands".

All are absolutely not about there being limited choice, but about not having been able to find something that meets the customers' need states. The second, especially, is a desperate plea for the retailer to put loads more on the page so that they might actually find something.

There is one area where choice and availability *could* be a problem and that's when a customer is determined, especially online, to find a specific brand or a specific product. In many cases, there will definitely be brands and lines you must stock because they are predictable and regular purchases. Your ability to then vend those successfully depends on how customers perceive you as a retailer, your price competitiveness, your logistics efficiency, and so on. So there is a dual strategy here. You must cover the predictable range bases but then also use the tools of curation to drive the most common customer, the browser desperate for inspiration, to solutions to specific need states.

"Unfiltered" isn't a positive hipster food choice

It's not just online, such as in the earlier Clarks example, that we find smothering examples of unfiltered choice. Before their respective administrations, British retailers HMV and GAME merchandised their bricks and mortar stores as if they were clumsy physical databases. As digital media and social sharing made it easier to find that perfect new song, game or film, flicking through racks in those stores lost its appeal.

Contrast that with music retailer Rough Trade, whose inspiration, discovery and curation-led approach is so successful that this British team are now the proud owners of New York's largest record shop. Theirs is a seemingly trend-bucking success story that is down to creating stores that customers want to visit because, and I quote a random customer: "Going to Rough Trade East [a 500-square-metre store hidden off the street down Brick Lane in London] is a risk because it's so dangerously easy to spend money."

"Dangerously easy to spend." That's the retail covenant fulfilled, right there.

Rough Trade isn't afraid to tell customers what to like, to be active in that recommendation, and its popular subscription service fully dictates a regular selection sent to customers but chosen by Rough Trade.

In book retailing, another sector seemingly doomed, the stunningly lovely Respublica (Moscow) is surging ahead. In part, by matching books to music, film, gifts and memorabilia with such skillful use of adjacencies that items appear to spring up and beg to be bought. Each book is treated as something special and racks of titles are minimal. Instead, modestly merchandised tables dominate. Everything has space to breathe, to be seen and picked up, taken in and enjoyed. There's a café and a DJ during evenings and weekends, but it's matched so absolutely to the offer that it all seems integral.

Even Respublica's terrific website (www.respublica.ru) is built on the principles of curation and adjacencies. Rough Trade and Respublica are like retail in the old days – places you'd go just to be in, safe in the knowledge that you'd definitely discover something great to bring home.

Contrast, too, Marks & Spencer's failing "throw everything at it" approach to clothing with ASOS's incredibly successful curated magpie merchandising and skillful use of social media; Tesco's stuttering cover-all-bases philosophy with Aldi's singular curation on the basis of cost and effectiveness. Never make the mistake that customers love Aldi on cost alone, by the way. It's the German efficiency of curated quality at a brilliant price that we've grown to so love.

Risk and reward

There's an issue of bravery here. A CEO or marketing director who chooses to limit choice is worried they are taking a risk. And they are to an extent. Curation is harder than unfettered assortment, merchandising for discovery is tougher than standard VM, inspiration requires active communication and creative adjacencies. The response to that fear is, so often, to not only make sure "all the bases are covered" with massive ranges offering lots of choice, but they'll even turn it into a positive for the annual report: "This year our ranging and logistics management have resulted in the largest ever choice for our customers."

Nobody ever got fired for providing 'the widest and deepest choice', but maybe they should because unfettered choice is confusing and disabling. It's not effective retailing.

Trusting your choice

The ultimate case studies on curation can be found in the exploding subscription retail sector where customers are sent regular packages of one type of product or another. Sometimes these boxes are tailored to information customers have already supplied, while some are user-driven selections through a preferences or selection tool, and some send the same selection to everybody.

In each of those three variants, curation plays a critical role. Whether the customer has further narrowed down their selection or not, that narrowing is done from a carefully edited and chosen range that closely matches the brand's values and positioning.

Some great subscription retail examples to take a closer look at include:

- Pact Coffee (UK) – artisanal coffee: www.pactcoffee.com
- Stitch Fix (USA) – fashion: www.stitchfix.com
- Dollar Shave Club (USA) – blades and razors: www.dollarshaveclub.com
- Birchbox (USA) – cosmetics: www.birchbox.com
- Field Notes Colors (USA) – retro notebooks: fieldnotesbrand.com/limited-editions
- Simply Cook (UK) – meal-by-meal ingredients to add to fresh produce: www.simplycook.com
- Graze (UK) – healthier snacking: www.graze.com
- Nerdblock (USA) – collectables: www.nerdblock.com
- Blackwing Volumes (USA) – Blackwing pencils. Even they have a subscription option: each quarter Palomino creates a special edition Blackwing. Subscribers get a dozen, plus a specially boxed and sealed extra pencil to "archive". So far we've had Blackwings lacquered to look like a sunburst guitar, a pencil tribute to the founding of Yosemite National Park, one that relates to John Steinbeck's writing process (he'd sharpen 24 pencils at a

time, place them in a box and then transfer them one by one to a second box as each dulled its point), and one that is printed with every single frame of Georges Méliès' 13-minute 1902 sci-fi film, *A Trip to the Moon*: http://goo.gl/h2OHKJ.

Stitch Fix
Awesome confidence in curation

Stitch Fix is a fabulous retail concept, one of those you wish you'd thought of yourself because it's so simple. Fill in a questionnaire and click a few preferences and then Stitch Fix will send you a personalised selection of five items of clothing every month. Keep the ones you love, send back the ones you don't.

As a retailer, the accompanying offer of a 25% discount if you keep all of them makes me incredibly happy. It's proper old-school, market-stall selling and it's brilliant. In the midst of new technology, new customer relationships, there's still the instinct at Stitch Fix to drive ATV and stock turn. Further proof that hardcore retail skills are still an essential component of successful modern retailing.

The pitch from Stitch Fix is this: "For busy women on the go, Stitch Fix is the personal styling service tailored to your taste, budget and lifestyle that helps you look and feel your best every day." So it's not just a bucket of random clothes each month, but positioned as something special, a bit of expert help to get you looking your best. "Hand-picked, personal-stylist, personal shopper" are expressions you see a lot in their communications as part of setting an exclusive scene, a narrative for the discovery and curation that tells a story of you, the customer, being given special treatment.

Stitch Fix charges $20 for the initial "styling" that comprises the questionnaire and related preferences. This, too, is very clever as it puts a value on the process of styling and says: "This isn't a throwaway process, this is worth real money." That last is something to remember more generally as people tend not to value things given away free. There's always a nagging doubt that the thing must in some way be without worth. Brilliantly, customers are told upfront that they can have the $20 back as a discount on the last thing they buy, should they ever wish to cancel the service. So they've attached a real value but removed almost all the risk.

There is also a gigantic hidden benefit to Stitch Fix in the method. For every delivery, the company asks customers to give their feedback, and most do, as it's neatly integrated with the buy/return process. Customers explain which things they loved and why they're keeping them, they give notes on sizing and fit and they say why things are being sent back. This generates fabulously rich data that Stitch Fix uses not just to improve individual customer recommendations through an incredibly clever adaptive algorithm but also to improve their buying and erchandising.

Other fashion retailers are in awe of the power of that individualised data. Business Insider quoted founder, and genius, Katrina Lake on this: "Buyers love working with us. In traditional retail stores know that some things sell and some things don't, but they don't know why. In our model we actually know why. If we have a sweater that doesn't work, for example, we can isolate whether [the problem] was the color, fit, or fabric."

Stitch Fix is roaring along, and was estimated to have done $200m in sales over 2015.

Subscribe now

No matter what your business, there is almost certainly an opportunity for you to find a curated subscription angle. From a few thousand customers to a few million, it's well worth the opportunity to take up to a year's worth of pre-sales cash, or nice regular monthly payments, from each of them. Creative and curated subscriptions, put together with a bit of inventiveness and love are attractive, a lot of fun and an opportunity to lock customers into happy relationships.

If you're scratching your head for ideas, think laterally: a box of your stuff every month might be okay but take a look at the Field Notes Colors and Blackwing Volumes to see how inventive it is possible to be. We even managed to find an angle for BP's Wild Bean Café, but I can't tell you about it yet beyond there being a physical item mailed out each quarter, linked to in-store redemptions of extras. I really hope they do it because it's a cool subscription but also another solid opportunity to move the Wild Bean frame to an even more valuable position.

I should add, too, that you might want to move quickly on this. Don't let your retail business be bypassed by a nimble start-up offering a low-friction, high-reward subscription in your product sector. I lecture fashion students on University of Westminster's fabulously commercial merchandise management course, assignment in and assignment out, those talented final year students are constantly coming up with subscription ideas that will make certain existing retailers irrelevant.

Curation's egg?

So curation is a tool to focus customers' attention and to move their need states to a position that is more likely to generate an immediate sale. Curation can create strong emotional bonds between customers and retailers too because it appears that you, the retailer, are on the customer's side. You're helping them by honestly and creatively curating collections that more immediately meet their need states. You're an advisor making things easier, cutting through the noise and confusion of unlimited choice and pointing customers to the best and most appropriate things.

Narrative selling

In retailing, narrative is about finding ways to present product as a part of stories that people can relate to and want to be part of. There is enormous power in making it easy for customers to put themselves into the simple stories you tell through communications and visual merchandising and more.

Once upon a sold

Retail experiences that work to put the customer into the story are hugely engaging. So much so that I strongly believe that the best modern retailers are those who instinctively understand narrative.

Most of us, when we see a picture like this one, will find our brains immediately start to attempt to explain it in narrative questions: Who are the people? What is their relationship? Where are they? Why are they there? What's in the box? What is the man saying and to whom is he saying it? The handrail on the far right and the patch of light set off a chain of thought about what is out there. The door on the right: we will construct the idea of a room existing beyond that door, whether there is really one there or not. We are humans, we use stories to make sense of the world. And in case it's bugging you: that's my dad and my eldest son Arthur. They're in the saloon of a boat and I think dad is probably telling me that he needs a beer! What's in Arthur's box? I'll take the secret to the grave with me . . .

Source: Koworld

Great chunks of human interaction depend on storytelling and narrative. We use stories to describe what we have done, what we are going to do, our aspirations, our relationships, our state of mind. Narrative, the basic description of things linked together in a logical and cognitively sensible way, is at the heart of how we make sense of the world and our context within it. It is why we see meaning in coincidence and why we create faces out of chaotic shadows.

We think in ordered narrative. It is inherent to human development and human survival. Psychologically, order and connective meaning help to reassure the primitive bits of our brain so that the world around us can be explained and therefore mastered. It is one of the direct sources of comfort in what some of us eventually discover is a random and cruel place. A bit heavy for a book on retailing, but it goes a long part of the way to understanding why stories are so compelling and engaging. It is that they are one of the things that stop us going mad, they are the foundations of morals and civilisation. They are the foundations of learning and culture, they are how we think.

Why wouldn't you use stories in a retail context, where a substantive part of the task is to help people to imagine themselves enjoying the benefits of whatever it is we are selling?

Random un-randomness

Here's a simple experiment you can do that shows how desperate our brains are to give everything meaning, relative to everything else.

1. Find a novel.
2. Flick through the pages and randomly put your finger down on a noun, verb or adjective.
3. Write down that word.
4. Flick through again and randomly select a second noun, verb or adjective.
5. Write it next to the first one.
6. I just did this here (using J.G. Ballard's *High Rise*) and got:

Jacket building

Now look at your two words. What you're feeling as you look at yours is your brain suddenly sparked into a frustrating wrestling match with those two words. Whether you like it or not, you have imbued each with the power and the mystery of the other and what your mind is desperately thrashing through is an attempt to find a narrative that removes the random element and gives these two words a useful relationship. A reason to appear together. It's how we attempt to make sense of the world and why humans are so uncomfortable with coincidence and lack of context.

In my case, a ferocious fight went on. Is this about jackets being made? Are we at the Jacket Building? Is jacket building something people do? What is the jacket like? What sort of building? Who is doing the building? Do they own the jacket?

Put two adjectives, nouns or verbs together and it must mean something, we reason. The need to create a meaning, in the form of a story, begins with just two words coincidentally grouped together.

Looking for the stories you didn't know you were telling

Take a look at any place you present your business and its products and services. Look very closely at the adjacencies, look too at the sum of the narrative elements within any given field of cognisance. Are you placing gold leaf next to corrugated card? Is the dissonance between those two useful or confusing? Is the symbol you use to represent a shopping basket at odds with the type of products you are asking customers to click to place in it? Are you displaying a very expensive bottle of wine next to a sign for a toilet? What story is that telling?

Here's a great example of a positive selling adjacency from, USA grocery. You will almost never see a banana without there being next to it a packet of mix to make a banoffee pie. The narrative is that this banana isn't just a nutritious and delicious meal in itself but that that tonight you and your family can enjoy time together eating a great dessert, all warm and comforted at home. Pick up the packet of mix and you'll notice that on a rack below it are cookies for the base, condensed milk for the filling and cans of instant whip for the topping. Before you know it, a hand of bananas is in the basket and so are four additional products. That example is also symptomatic of a certain type of supermarket's reflection of its customer's fear of fruit but it's powerful example all the same.

So go through everything you present to customers:

- The random stories two things next to each other tell.
- Where things fall together on a page or screen.

▶

- Colour and font associations.
- The words in headlines and product descriptions.
- Symbols and materials.

Before you know it, you'll be armed with a hundred opportunities to tell better-selling stories to your customers.

Talk to me

Stories are fundamental; we communicate "Buy me" messages better if we use stories to contextualise the engagement and benefits of our products. The first stage in doing that is telling stories about the stuff we sell. Let's start with an obvious and simple example from the world of home improvement:

"New kitchens improve life at home."

The narrative is still simple: it's not a statement or a demand to buy a new kitchen, but a simple story that describes what happens when people buy new kitchens – they tend to then find that life is a little bit nicer for a while.

The second stage, the killer stage, is putting the customer into the story, so now we get:

"A bright, modern new kitchen will make your life easier, bring everyone together and make your cooking more fun."

So, now, the customer is directly addressed and told a story that starts with buying a new kitchen and ends with a nice picture of them being happier and enjoying a better life.

I'm not suggesting so much that we use these stories in written form but that the idea behind the story, and the inclusion of the customer in the story, should absolutely drive the way we visually merchandise stores, and the way in which we stimulate and engage customers in our offer.

Easy ways to get narrative into the store

I've found six simple ways to bring narrative into the store and there are probably more.

A tractor in the fresh produce section at Rewe Richrath tells an instant story: it cues a cascade of related ideas around traditional farming and the popular notion that produce tasted better when it was farmed "honestly". A red tractor is an icon; putting it in that island of food makes customers feel differently about that food and that store.

Source: Reprinted courtesy of Wanzl (https://www.wanzl.com/en_DE/company/success-stories/rewe-richrath-d/)

1. Service

Service that involves asking customers questions about themselves is a fine foundation for authoritative narrative-selling.

Container Store (USA)

The selling process is completely story-driven. It's the customers' stories that are gently probed in order to uncover ways in which Container Store's products could contribute to improving the customer's life. More on Container Store soon.

2. Visual merchandising (VM)

Static product on shelves tell no stories but creative VM can be used to tell instantly recognisable and irresistible ones.

CB2 (USA)

Crate and Barrel's "younger" format uses arrangements of product to tell instructive lifestyle stories. A great example might be the fixture that tells customers "How to make an entrance", that is visually presented as the entrance way to an apartment and that includes full instructions on how to recreate the utility and look. Each item is placed within a context of getting that part of the house right and with a card on it explaining its role in setting the scene for a comfortable and stylish home.

3. Demonstration

Demonstrating function is boring, but put benefits in the context of real people's lives and you create stories that are powerfully engaging

Williams-Sonoma (USA)

Walk into any Williams-Sonoma and you'll see, hear, smell and taste seasonal good things being made and cooked in-store. As soon as you smell pumpkin spice around Halloween you are in the thick of a narrative about the perfect celebration at home.

4. Product

Simple product can be transformed from utility into a key element of a story.

Sainsbury's (UK)

There are competing claims for this one, but I'm crediting Sainsbury's with having invented it on account of that's where I first saw it done. So, the ubiquitous chicken tikka masala ready meal is not a story but a utility, an easy solution to practical and mechanical needs, possibly with a bit of comfort thrown in for good measure. The Sainsbury's Curry-House-Style Meal Kit in a box is a story – that's a special night in with all the trimmings. You'd get in the car to go and fetch one of those, probably not for the lonely ready meal on its own. Utility versus narrative. Doing the work for customers in putting together packages can have hugely uplifting results.

5. Deal

It's possible to use what looks like a simple price promotion to create narrative occasions

Marks & Spencer (UK)

The classic Marks & Spencer "Dine in for £10" deal is a supreme example of creating a story out of price and product. Suddenly choosing a main course, side, bottle of wine and a dessert isn't feeding, it's a "night in together". The customer considering that deal isn't just thinking of the individual components, they are heavy with the expectation of the context in which they will eat them. It's a very engaging and simple idea.

6. Calendar

Throughout the year there are simple stories happening that everyone recognises and that you can align with, such as Easter, summer holidays, Valentine's Day, back to school and Christmas.

Ann Summers (UK)

It's easy to snigger at Ann Summers, but there is loads of proper craft in the retail format. Especially around Valentine's Day when the windows tell a very broad story of how to perk up your relationship. My partner Emily would probably punch me in the spleen if I got her a pair of fluffy handcuffs on 14 February, but what they're doing with occasions is making them into stories laden with expectation that customers need to do very little to place themselves into.

Container Store
Placing narrative at the heart of the business

As a consultant, you get asked which is your favourite retailer a lot. There are a few that would be easy to give in answer: Amazon has to be in with a shout, IKEA is incredibly good, I've huge respect for Trader Joe's and Warby Parker, I love Selfridges and I've probably spent more of my own money with Wiggle over the last decade than I should have, but that's because I'm a middle-class, middle-aged, fat-bellied man who thinks lycra is a sporting necessity.

▶

Then there are the exciting esoteric independents: Stew Leonard's and Oxford's Robert Moy – Tuscan Pots is awesome, a bit lunatic, which I like really and only opens for two hours a week like some sort of mysterious retail religious cult. The same happy feeling goes for a store that looks like an Iowan kid's bedroom in a late 1970s Spielberg film, American Science & Surplus. I adore Foyles, I love visiting markets and have a big soft spot for Chaos City Comics in St Albans.

But my favourite? On measures such as retailing skill, sustained success, authenticity, profitability and likeability, there's one retailer head and shoulders above all the rest and it's The Container Store. The staggering audacity of founder Kip Tindell's vision to sell what amounts to shelves and boxes with a creative life-changing flair is amazing. Even his incredulous dad asked him how he was going to make money selling empty boxes.

What Tindell has achieved, and please do read the story in his own words, as found in the entertaining and insightful "Uncontainable", is stunning. It's a success that almost beggars belief. Container Store doesn't think in product; everything the business does is linked to thinking exclusively about customers' needs, problems and lives. You see that in the levels of pay that are way above retail averages and that include very high basic wages, because Tindell believes that people should be able to count on their income and that bonuses should be exactly that. You see it in the huge investment in training. Its employees see 210 hours of training a year and don't even get on the shop floor for the first few weeks. Our industry average training hours per employee a year is a measly six.

Then there's the training itself: Tindell calls the service method "man in the desert selling", and it is a 100% narrative-driven process. Trainers ask staff to imagine they're running a general store at an oasis in a desert and a man walks in from the desert asking to buy a bottle of water. In the traditional retail model in Tindell's view, you sell that man a bottle of water and mark the transaction as a conversion of a motivated customer. Big tick.

In Container Store's model, you don't sell him the water immediately, but ask the man what brought him to you. You give him some water for free because that's the right thing to do, but you keep asking questions and you keep uncovering needs. Perhaps he's been lost and been walking for a long time; water is his immediate practical need, but his shoes are broken from the walking, he has sunburn, his family are worried about him, he's tired and a little scared.

Uncover the customer's story and instead of selling one bottle of water, you sell him a shady spot under an umbrella by the oasis, new comfy shoes, lotion for his skin and a hat to protect him in future, you sell him a phone call back to his family and you sell him a cocktail to celebrate his survival. Along with respite, rest, recuperation, safety and relief. You uncover his story and then weave what you sell into it.

And that's exactly what Container Store's well-paid, friendly and motivated staff do. Pick up a letter tray in-store and soon an assistant will ask you some variation of "What's got you looking at organising your mail today?" Before you know it, you and the assistant have established that you don't have a problem with letters, it's the way you organise your desk and together you create a package of storage and organisational tools that promise to transform the efficiency of your home office.

Ask a question about picnic bags and hampers and your question will be met with an authoritative stream of questions in response. Where do you like to go for your picnics? How many people typically come with you? What sort of food and drink do you all like? What does your perfect picnic have in it? How did your last picnic go? You buy the picnic bag you came in for but add half a dozen other items that you are now convinced will make the fantastic family picnic you now have firmly visualised in your internal narrative a wonderful day out.

It's no surprise, therefore, to learn that while the average unattended customer buys 1.2 items per visit, customers who have contact with an assistant buy an *average* of 8. The impact of story at Container Store is truly astonishing. What is more, customer satisfaction is through the roof, and that's no surprise because people, in general, love to come away from a shopping visit with the full kit. It's enabling and fun.

Container Store is brilliant. Tindell took the business public a few years ago in order to fund further expansion. Wall Street

▶

hasn't always been an easy ride for him, as many there don't get it. They question the high wages and challenge the need for so much training. Container Store delivers very healthy profits, but the bean counters look to the spreadsheets and wonder aloud if there aren't some pips that could be squeezed. They don't understand that if Kip Tindell gave in and reduced the business to a seller of empty boxes, rather than continue to run it as a creator of great personal stories that transform the lives of customers, then his dad would have been right all along. There is no money in empty boxes, but there is in helping people to save time, enjoy life and solve problems.

Some narratives are easier to visualise than others

Look at a glorious picture of a garden furniture set shown on a sunny day and with the table not only dressed but shown in use, as if a person has just got up to get themselves another cold beer to enjoy outside. We can instantly put ourselves right into the heart of this particular narrative.

A set of garden furniture and a barbecue displayed on a shop floor or leading an online section instantly tells an almost trivially recognisable story – that being outside in the summer is nice.

A customer is immediately able to put themselves into that narrative because the visual arrangement closely replicates the stories they already know: "Sitting outside in the sun is lovely. We love having barbecues and, if I buy these things in front of me, then we will immediately have fun."

But put that same customer in front of a pile of decking planks on a shelf, or show them the components of building a garden deck on a standard grid layout on a website and the story breaks down. A narrative still exists: that building a deck gains the customer a lovely place to sit in the summer, increases the living area of the house and delivers a fulfilling sense of pride and satisfaction at a job well done.

But the customer has a significantly harder time putting *themselves* into that narrative. The building of the deck itself becomes a prequel story. One characterised by questions and doubts, such as, "Am I able to do this correctly? Do I have the tools? What size will I need? How do I price that? What extra items will I have to buy? How long will it take?" If the customer can't easily visualise the solutions to all of those complex elements, then they can't put themselves in the second more powerful narrative of enjoying sitting out in the sun on a nice new deck.

Contrast that with the garden furniture and barbecue example, the only questions customers need to ask there to put themselves in the story are: "Can we afford it? Have we space? Can I take it home now or can it be delivered fast enough?"

There is no spoon

Professor Charles Spence is an experimental psychologist at Oxford University who specialises in "cross-modal research", which broadly means how cuing one sense can create a response in the others and how such cues lead people to describe their experience of the world around them. Prof. Spence consults with big companies on all sorts of sensory subjects, but we retailers could also learn a lot from his insights.

This is a quote from his 2016 appearance on BBC Radio 4's show *The Digital Human*: "If I show you a picture of food and I have a spoon approaching that food, and if it's approaching say from the right-hand side, the side that most right-handers would use, then you will like that food more, even though it's just a picture of food, because you can simulate the act of eating it more easily because that's like *your* hand. If I put the same spoon on the left side of the plate, suddenly you don't like it as much. Why not? It's the same food but your brain has a harder time simulating what it would be like to eat it."

Charles Spence, incidentally, was the first man to prove that food could taste different, depending on the sort of crunch the eater hears when consuming it.

As retailers, we are using cues, visual ones especially, all the time to generate responses that will help customers to better imagine themselves enjoying the benefits of the things we want them to buy. What are your equivalents to Professor Spence's spoon? How are you managing sensory cues to create narrative?

The narrative store

So what do we, as retailers, do with that pile of decking planks that are not yet a deck, the cakeless food mixer, a context-less television set or a camera that has yet to take a photo? We must create retail experiences that put the customer into the narrative. This is especially true in physical stores where we have access to so many of a customer's senses, but it also holds true online where we must join the dots more easily for browsers to show them the story of ownership beyond the screen. We must prod and poke at those senses and draw the customer into the story.

So, back in a store, let's get those deck planks off a shelf and merchandised in a space that is itself a deck with the smell of oiled planks and sawn timber. Samples of deck stains that turn the question, "Will I have to stain a deck" into, "What colour will my deck be?" A touchscreen that makes it easy for a customer to size and price the job for their garden that will even put a 3D model of the deck into a photo they've brought in on their phone, together with a top-down image of their garden pulled from Google Earth. Co-merchandised in the space would be comfy sample furniture and all under a warm heat lamp operating at the same colour temperature as the summer sun. With all the tools they need, available to hire as part of a total easy package.

Online, embed those things above into garden blogs where the stories are already written and use customers describing their own stories to bring this one to life. Create planning tools and incorporate little teasers to lock customers into the "once upon a time" part of the story by, say, asking a question, "Which of these would be your favourite way to use a new deck?" All the way through, link materials with the advice and support exclusive to your customers and package things in novel ways that make them harder to side-by-side compare with other suppliers' offerings. I'm writing this while sitting in a garden office from an online business called Dunster House that is a superb asker of questions and packagers of unremarkable components in novel ways.

Dead stories

The television set merchandised against a warehouse wall on a black metal shelf playing the same picture as 99 others in the same space should, instead, be on a digital wall that allows customers to put domestic living room finishes behind the TV. Show shelves filled with books, patterned wallpaper, modern, classic, and so on. Provide a simple scanner that a customer can either scan their own colour into or share a picture of their own wall scalable on to the digital wall. Give them loads of choices of the things they like to watch on it and a sofa from which to experience this. Train the sales team to ask questions about the customers' own narrative, rather than parrot the dull mechanical story of the manufacturer's specifications, "So you and the family like to watch animated movies together? Here are the two buttons to press to get Pixar on demand. Have you ever seen *Toy Story* look so lovely? What about the sound? It's like Woody and Buzz are in the room."

The food processor, not plonked on a shelf or blandly listed in a web-shop database but, instead, cooking happening all around, customers and staff baking and selling at the same time, customers asked about what they like to make, the flavours and tastes they enjoy. A room-set full of equipment that says that your life at home can be better if we can help you to bake a bit better, easier and more often. The narrative is of a happier and more fulfilled life, with contentment through cake, and where the means to join in that story is simply to buy this enabling product.

Are these last two examples extremes? Perhaps, but at the very least, in the basic fundamentals of visual merchandising and communication with customers, using stories and putting customers into the narrative creates more compelling, inspirational and shoppable experiences.

Now
Things you can do now

- Identify five examples of curation in your business.
- Create five new ones.
- Ask yourself if your web store is curated or is an illustrated spreadsheet.
- Identify ten areas where the choice you offer is confusing. Create a plan for each to make choices easier to make.

- Identify the stories told throughout your business. Do this your-self physically in-store, not theoretically in the office. Walk the stores or shop the website in minute detail, taking a screenshot every part of the online or app journey. Ask customers and staff.
- Of the six "easy ways to get narrative into the store", which do you have current examples of? Identify one new one from each of the six categories to test.
- List your equivalents of Professor Spence's spoon

Next
Strategic considerations for the longer term

- Consider trials to AB test fixtures that introduce elements of curation offline and online.
- How would you need to fundamentally change the business to tell more engaging stories?

Chapter 6

Now that it is possible to exist everywhere
and anywhere, should you?

Retail secret six: the everywhere store

In this chapter we explore

- location agnosticism versus omni-channel
- the irrelevance of distinctions between online and offline
- the new meaning of location.

The benefits of reach

You don't need me to tell you that the digital age has made it possible for you to reach more customers in more places than ever before. As a result, I'm sure we've all seen those strategy documents or business plans where, under the section on "target audience", you find something along the lines of:

- Target audience: *everyone*.
- Age range: *10 to 100*.
- Location: *everywhere*.

You could argue this is a bold and uninhibited plan, the sort of blue-sky thinking that we need around here. If you're not drunk, then you'll recognise it as a scarily unfocused plan that makes it hard to work out any of the proposition, branding, offer or merchandising.

But, even the omnipresent, ubiquitous Amazon started out with a plan that went something like:

- Target audience: internet-aware book buyers.
- Age range: those old enough to have credit cards and young enough to be comfortable with the notion of using the internet to buy items, so probably around 18 to 30.

- Location: USA but with the infrastructure in place to ship to wherever the US Postal Service can manage.

Within two months, Amazon had sent books to customers in 45 different countries, such was the pace at which news of the great idea of discounted books spread. But those deliveries were facilitated in English, through the Seattle offices and via an existing third-party logistics network. Only when the time was right did Amazon extend its strategic and structural ambition to sites specifically for other countries in local languages, with warehousing closer to the final delivery location and the formation of local management and customer-service teams.

There was sensible caution and careful consideration before each move to expand presence. The product range was only expanded as Amazon became confident enough in its ability to do so at a reliably great level. In terms of target audience, Amazon worked really very hard to make a wider range of people feel comfortable buying over the internet.

Be focused but think big

Thinking in defined audiences and around specific customer need states doesn't mean limiting the scope of your long-term thinking or saddling yourself with underpowered systems that cannot grow easily. Martha Lane-Fox, co-founder of Lastminute.com, suggests businesses should build for scale right from the off. Imagine a large customer base and make your online business accessible and relevant from the start. That means building systems that are robust and straightforward to scale into locations, virtual and physical, as you grow opportunity. But it doesn't mean dilute everything you do from the off by initially trying to hit every target with every activity all the time.

The end of rigid online and offline definitions

And now Amazon has opened stores. Stores that function really well, partly because Amazon built everything, right from the start, with an eye to scale and efficient function across multiple-use cases and locations. Just three stores are open at the time of writing and each is very different from the other. More pertinently, sage grand oracles of the retail industry, together with over-confident CEOs have written off these stores as, "Amazon clumsily meeting specialist needs in unique cases, though without ambition to *really* do physical retailing".

When the first opened, those same clever observers said that was a unique case. And then there were three. If you're reading this book a year from now, I bet there are a dozen stores; 2 years after and it'll be 50 to 100. Still not a devastating march of the Amazon retail reaper, but the continuation of a sensible programme of putting stores, virtual, physical or whatever, into wherever customers are willing to spend in them.

Omni-channel thinking

This is where we get to the problem with one of retailing's hottest buzz strategies: omni-channel. Omni-channel is tool-centric thinking, where I believe the thinking must, instead, be location-centred.

Omni-channel is defined as providing the customer with a seamless shopping experience, whether that customer is shopping online, researching through the website, in-store, on the phone or reaching the retailer through some other channel. Immediately, that word "channel" is challenging because it suggests that customers and retailers are separated by some third thing. That's dangerous thinking because it really isn't true. If I'm on the website, I'm not separated by the computer. If I'm having a moan with a service bot on Twitter, I'm not kept at arm's length by Twitter, I'm right in there, point for point with the retailer. If I'm in the app, I'm not kept remote by my phone, and so on. Website, app, in-store, on a call, in a chat window, on Twitter or inside Pinterest, in each case I might have been kept initially remote by having to find the app on the App Store, search for the website on Google, search for the store location in Google, get the Twitter address, but, when I am face to face with the representative of the retailer, I am there. I am in the relationship and there is no channel.

In each case, I should be able to experience the same pricing, the same tone of voice, the same availability and I should feel like I am dealing with the same organisation.

We used to call that, in bricks and mortar retail, the left hand knowing what the right hand is doing. It is common sense and it is no surprise that one of the richest sources of customer dis-satisfaction is when pricing is different, or when you are passed around bits of the same company (try cancelling your mobile phone contract for a taste of this particular sport), or the person, app or website cannot give you an answer without a long delay in getting it from elsewhere. If you want to call *this* omni-channel, then knock yourself out, but be aware of the effect that word "channel" has on your thinking. More about that later.

This is a shop now. A location not a channel. When that customer gets back to the beach, what might we sell and how?

Source: Koworld

Becoming location-agnostic

There is a second part of omni-channel, which is where the big-gest mistakes are currently being made. It is in the idea that an omni-channel strategy is about customers being able to reach your store across all platforms and sites. "But that sounds great", you cry, and it sort of is, but omni-channel forces retailers to think of each of those platforms and collections of sites as distinct channels. It introduces a tunnel vision that makes building the app more important than understanding how, when and, crucially, *where* the customer will use it.

But there is a way retailers used to think about how to reach customers. It was called location strategy. Retailers thought about every place in which they could serve, advise and sell to customers as a "location". What has changed? Nothing! Every place that you do that, regardless of whether it is through an app, in-store or via an interactive customer-aware tabletop on a train, all of these things are locations.

I strongly believe it is time to move the thinking on to become location-agnostic. To use the power of digital to be wherever our customers are, but to think of each of those places as a location, with all the fundamental retail disciplines in place in each.

Location-agnostic retailers think not of channels and ways to bridge a notional space between the retailer and the customer but, rather, do a much more powerful and elegant thing: they put stores wherever the customers are. Stores that are relevant to the need state in that place and at that time, with all the additional retailing impulses fully in place. So the app can be a research companion, but it's full of compelling yet unobtrusive calls to buy. The physical store is structured to provide an experience that is rewarding and that welcomes browsing as well as buying.

Oasis
Seamlessly blending platforms

The left hand knowing what the right hand is doing – essential retail basics. So integration of systems and consistency across all your locations, be they real or virtual, is absolutely essential. That part of the circus around omni-channel is right. UK fashion retailer

▶

Oasis is typical of those retailers that have understood and implemented this properly. Walk into store and the staff all have transactional tablets and access to both product information and to stock availability. See a piece you love but the last one in your size went this morning? Staff can check stock elsewhere, take your order immediately and process your card purchase without having to go near a till. It's seamless and low friction.

But here's why this is such a good example of where omni-channel is a blocking jargon. You'll find what you've just read, written up as a case study in various omni-channel example articles. Most will start by pointing out that Oasis has fused its online, mobile and store experiences into one seamless continuum.

But what does that actually mean? At it's most basic, it means that the Oasis companywide plumbing has been made to talk to all parts of the business properly. Stock can be found and transferred, whether it's in a different store or allocated to the online business. Product descriptions and information, such as sizing, consistently percolates its way to all places that customers and staff can access it and, if one location is up to date, all locations are automatically up to date. So far, so good.

I would argue that in an age of digital opportunity, far from being a stand-out achievement, that's actually a minimum requirement to operate and compete because it provides a foundation for all the cool stuff you might want to do with digital tools. I know the hell that such integration can be, as many of my friends are IT experts involved in doing exactly these things and they wear the thousand-yard stares of conflict veterans when you ask them how things are going.

As a modern retailer, you must make these brave choices just to stay in the game. I know one huge manufacturer/retailer that makes millions of its product, but cannot tell you reliably where any of it actually is at any one time. That's unsustainable.

The plumbing, though, is the vehicle's sub-frame. It isn't the shiny exterior that attracts customers, and not the brilliant driving experience that keeps them delighted. The location is where you meet customers, it is the body and experience and, as such, is the critical thing. Your systems must be up to scratch, they must work seamlessly and they should be unnoticeable to the customer. In the Oasis example, it doesn't matter to the customer how these things have been enabled. What matters is how the digital tools either reduce friction or add to the reward of a visit to that location, real or virtual. It is the location that leads, not the tools.

Under pressure

If you're a CEO of a listed company, though, your chairman will have sent you, at some point, an email asking what your omni-channel strategy is. If you're in the business of arse-covering middle management at any large retailer, you too have been banging on about omni-channel since at least 2011.

My problem with this is really straightforward. That the alternative to omni-channel is so much more compelling and instinctively right. What location agnosticism proposes is that every way in which a customer can be reached should be considered as a store in a specific location. So the store on the high street is a location. The store in an app on a mobile device is a location. The store on a web page viewed on a tablet is a location. The store that exists only on the wall of a train station is a location. The interactive window on the out-of-hours shop is a distinct location. The transactional insertion in a blog is a location. The QR code on a poster is a location.

The question should not be, "Which channels should we operate in?" but should be, "Where do we want to be located?"

Thinking of this question in terms of location has the huge benefit of taking the question away from systems and IT and putting it back into location strategy. Excellence in location strategy has always been one of the skills that separates a great retailer from a good one. It is somehow fundamental to the question of making it easy for customers to spend money with us.

At its heart is this. Location agnosticism means putting the store anywhere and everywhere that it is relevant to a customer. Just as in physical locations, different virtual locations are likely to require different formats with alternative ranges and services. This is not a one-size-fits-all kind of thing.

Once you start to think of all the different ways in which you can reach customers as locations, it instils the discipline that goes with any other form of location-planning. How many people will, practically, be able to access this location, what are the competitive alternatives in the same location, how do we attract customers to it, how is the space, be it real or virtual, merchandised, and how will we sell within this space?

Far too often, omni-channel box-ticking strategies deliver expensive apps nobody uses, websites that ignore all the basic rules of retailing such that they are unshoppable. Or fantastic websites that nobody knows about. It is no coincidence, by the way, that the list of global top 50 online retailers is dominated by old-school bricks and mortar businesses. They know how to create shops and sell in them.

Omni-channel means a brute insertion into all and every route to market. Location agnosticism means being sophisticated in choice of location, be that location physical, virtual or both.

The opening in Seattle of Amazon's first physical store means it has become the first retailer to be truly location-agnostic rather than merely omni-channel: to exist wherever the customer is ready to spend.

There is no offline/online retail. It is *all* location. Amazon's move provides the clearest evidence yet that omni-channel is a dangerous misidentification of the job retailers have to do in order to maximise their opportunities to sell to customers.

Manufacturers can, legitimately, claim to reach customers via channels. They must balance a mix of retail partners, resellers, wholesalers, possibly even direct sales channels – these are distinct routes to market and the channels are the guided navigation paths. For a manufacturer, a channel is a point-to-point canal but one where they must hand over their product to an independent narrowboat owner at a lock who may even hand it over again, eventually delivering that product to the final sales destination, which is also the place the end-customer is active. That end-destination is a location: it is where the retailer retails. But read the following Warby Parker case study when a manufacturer becomes the retailer and the channel disappears.

Warby Parker
Pureplay? Nonsense!

Originally an online-only business, Warby Parker now boasts a 27-strong, and rapidly growing, store chain. Warby Parker's Big Idea is to "make glasses more affordable and more accessible without compromising style or quality". It has delivered on this brilliantly: instead of cheapening the product, it has simplified the supply chain and distributed its in-house designed products direct to customers.

In cutting out the middleman (us retailers), it has become a retailer, but it's not that simple. The team at Warby Parker always had the instinct and spirit of retailers. They have brought a retailer's perspective to the design and manufacturing part of the chain. Everything about the company is customer-facing and transparent; what could be considered to be own-brand manufacturing and the intent to cut prices are not hidden, they are celebrated. The founders even tell a great story to illustrate where they approached the problem from: "Every idea starts with a problem. Ours was simple. Glasses are too expensive. We were students when one of us lost his glasses on a backpacking trip. The cost of replacing them was so high that he spent the first semester of grad. school without them, squinting and complaining." This story humanises a rational, but massively attractive, proposition.

The accessible part of the Big Idea is fascinating, too. It's come to mean two things:

- Be wherever customers need Warby Parker to be, be that online or with a Warby Parker person physically fitting glasses to customers' faces.

- For every pair of glasses sold at retail, give away a pair to charities, serving to get desperately needed specs to people in parts of the world, or in economic circumstances, that make buying glasses extremely difficult.

They do this second thing one-for-one. Buy a relatively cheap pair of glasses and you will be directly responsible for putting a second pair on to the eyes of another human being

▶

who also really needs them. Retailers being a force for good in the world . . . there's a thing!

The first part of accessible, though, that's the one that has certain retailers and "experts" scratching their heads and gibbering, "But Warby Parker is an online business, that's its model, so how can it work as a bricks and mortar retailer? It doesn't make sense." It only doesn't make sense if you subscribe to the notion that retailing is done via channels and that those channels are all distinctively separate things.

The founders of Warby Parker never said they were an online business. They just set up a glasses business with a sector-challenging Big Idea and then put it wherever customers might be in the right need states to buy glasses.

This is the absolute essence of location agnosticism. You, as a retailer, aren't a hard concept operating in a walled channel and then fitting that into other so-called channels in an attempt to expensively cover every base. You should be location-agnostic just as Warby Parker is. Exist in whatever locations make sense to you and your customer.

Retailing happens in locations

For a retailer there simply aren't channels to customers, there are only locations. Those places where customers can be interacted with and ultimately sold to. Sometimes that location might be a URL or a physical store, it might be embedded in a blog, it might be pinged off a beacon, it might be the surface of the café table in front of you, but each is still just a location. They have to be engaging, easy to shop, safe and low friction. Thinking in channels makes retailers constrict their strategy, narrowing it to the tools and apps, putting the customer down at the distant end of a mythical tube. Retailers thinking omni-channel become blinded by the tools, seduced by the apps.

Chasing an idea labelled "omni-channel" is a retailer's current modus operandi and it so often leads them into big strategic mistakes. Call our strategy "omni-channel" and the mindset concentrates on the route itself, not enough on the location. How many retailers are now stuck with expensive and pointless apps because they never properly considered if customers would be motivated enough to use them?

Instead of asking, "How do we get in front of those customers in group x?" we should be asking one much simpler question: "Where are the people in group x when they might want to buy the stuff we sell?" Are they holding a mobile phone? If they are on that phone at home, is their need state different from when they look at it on a bus or in the office? Are they at an airport? Are they inside Pinterest? Are they keen to touch and feel our product in-store? Are they looking for a physical browsing experience near them? Are they keen to travel for a bigger experience?

. . . and stores exist in locations

A retailer's presence on a mobile phone isn't an app delivered at the end of a channel. It's a location. Even if it's a buy-it button inside a blog, it's still a location. And what do retailers do in locations? We build stores, even a one-product, one-button location still exists as a store. Do customers trust us and that button, and do we support the sale at the lowest possible level of friction?

Being wherever the customer needs you to be

Described perfectly by Gadgette.com as "like a really slow acting self-destruct button", Domino's has launched what could be considered the uber location-agnostic format. It's a single button housed inside a miniature pizza box that, when pressed, requests your favourite Domino's order for ASAP delivery.

Domino's considers the physical part, the button, to be a PR gimmick. Pressing the button just initiates an order via a connection to the standard Domino's app on the customer's phone. I hope it realises that, in fact, it is one of the most incredible retail formats ever created: a working physical Domino's store that sits in a person's home, nagging away at them. It's shaped like a pizza box and you flip the box lid. For the love of thin crust!

▶

If we've learnt just one thing, it is that our dumb animal brains are weak and are susceptible to even the most basic of narrative constructions: see pizza box, think pizza, want pizza, feel hungry, definitely want pizza, press button, pizza arrives, eat pizza, happy. See pizza box a day later . . .

This is the location-agnostic equivalent of putting a man on the moon. It is a fully functioning, though extremely focused, store that can be placed at any strategic point in a customer's house or office. Press button, pizza happens. I'm feeling slightly delirious here, and probably need a pizza, but I prefer Papa John's, to be honest.

Turning the question on its head

The alternative to omni-channel is to do as Amazon has done in the Seattle University Village and think in terms of locations only. What sort of store do we need if our location exists in physically browsable form? How do we engage, inspire and then service customers?

Explicitly, Jennifer Cast, VP of Amazon Books, has said: "We've applied 20 years of online bookselling experience to build a store." That isn't omni-channel thinking, where one thing exists distinct from another, albeit wrapped in a consistency of customer experience, but format development strategy. It's: "What do we already know from our existing locations that can make this new one great?" They haven't come in and said: "So that's how you do things in this channel; we need to do that too."

See, too, James Daunt's ostrich-style mocking (quoted on the BBC's reporting of Amazon's new store) of the decision to merchandise most books face out, like they do on their web store because they've realised that customers like to judge books by their covers. James is thinking in terms of range depth and space productivity because he's bound by traditional channel thinking.

And I am willing to bet my shoes on Amazon also using this opportunity to uncover some ideas it can roll back into other locations, such as the one that lives in your phone, or is embedded into associate websites, or the one on your computer at home.

Fear of a new world

Words lead thinking. I had an email today that used the phrase "traditional omni-channel roadmap". It's only been a handful of years. How can there already be a tradition? Because of the way we allow ourselves to be sidetracked again and again by the desperation to make sense of a fundamentally fractured and explosively changing retail landscape. But here's the thing, we don't get to dictate what happens in this new world, where once customers were limited to what we gave them, in the stores we opened, with a single payment point and whatever staffing level we set.

As we explored in the first secret, the customer is doing the dictating, and we can no more create an app and expect customers to automatically and gratefully shop it than we can expect them to adhere to any of our rules.

Here's an example. In 2015, Samsung launched its fabulous Samsung Galaxy Note 5 phone. I love the Note series and wanted to upgrade my current 4 to a 5. But there's a catch, as, for whatever reason, the 5 isn't being sold in the UK. The big retailers that could sell it to me are playing by Samsung UK's rules and dutifully selling through their Note 4 stock and aren't parallel importing Note 5s.

But I'm the customer. I don't care about Samsung and its channel issues. I only care about finding a location where I can buy a Note 5 now. None of Carphone Warehouse's locations can help me. None of any mainstream UK retailers' locations can help me. Not even the location Samsung trades directly at my computer in my house can help me.

But I don't care, as I'm in charge now because I'm a customer, so I have a Samsung Galaxy Note 5 in my hands bought from a nimble little outfit that chooses to trade at a low-friction location easily accessible to me: eBay.

Maybe Samsung UK will have shown some control of the UK market but, in doing so, they've pissed off the customer and, ultimately, it has only held back a few sloshed bucket-loads of a tide it cannot stop.

Samsung, in this case, is channel-bound, whereas, as a customer, I am location-agnostic.

Kwik Fit
Inconsistency and obfuscation

Here is a great example of a business that resolutely thinks of online and offline as completely different worlds where customers belong to only one or the other. It is an extreme example of old-rules retailing and a cautionary note on the customer's new-rules response.

In 2016, it was still possible to roll your car into a branch of Kwik Fit and be charged a premium for having the temerity to do so without first having bought a tyre online. The walk-in customer pays price x while the internet customer still has their fitting in the same tyre centre but pays the lower price y.

In just one example, a customer told us they arrived, wanting what looked like a puncture to be diagnosed or denied. A screw in the tread confirmed that it was, indeed, a puncture and so this customer was offered a Michelin replacement for £121. The tyre was changed and she was on her way, with her temporary spare wheel tucked away for another day.

Now this customer was well aware that Blackcircles.com could have sold her the same tyre for significantly less money, but she felt that it was worth going straight to Kwik Fit, as they are a friendly expert service that is easy to access in a rush. What she didn't expect is that she could also have bought the same tyre from Kwik Fit online, and had it fitted at the same centre and have paid just under £97 for it. Even more annoying, a Pirelli tyre to the same specification was available for just £86, but that option hadn't even been mentioned at the centre (though it might not have been in stock that day).

The only catch with ordering online from Kwik Fit was that it would mean waiting three more days for fitting. This customer told us she would have happily waited for the sake of either a £24 or £35 saving. But more pertinent is that this is, effectively, a Kwik Fit imposed "offline tax" and it has converted this customer into a person who (a) will never use Kwik Fit again because she feels it attempted to hoodwink her, (b) will tell anyone who will listen to the awful story and (c) will give Black-circles.com a chance in future, even if it means waiting a day to get the job done. Once Blackcircles has got that customer, do you think she's going to want to go back to Kwik Fit any time soon? No, nor do I. Inconsistency is a customer turn-off.

No more Canute

So, instead, lean into the on-rushing tide and ensure that, as retailers, you exercise your power to place yourself at all locations that are relevant to customers, with product you believe they want and you can sell. Don't give in to taking the broken end of a manufacturer's, largely irrelevant, channel to market.

Some readers may say this is mere lexical semantics – and they would be right, in a way. This is an issue of semantic interpretation of the words "channel" and "location", but to write that off as unimportant is plain wrong. We bring our experience and cultural baggage to words in our responses to those words.

$$F**K$$

That popular profanity is merely an arrangement of symbols and shapes but, for all who read the word, even with the missing letters, there is a power and meaning attached to those symbols that can be as deep as shock or disgust. Semantics matter. The word "channel" forces thinking to focus on the method of reaching customers and distracts from the real job of what to do when in front of them.

And it is semantics and the desperation for order that leads to retailers appointing heads of omni-channel, as if channels to market exist for a retailer (which they don't). A retailer exists in only one place: locations. Locations where customers are hot to buy. A channel is a route to somewhere. A location *is* that somewhere.

We have heads of supply chain but, God bless them, we don't let them dictate the form of the stores they deliver to. They facilitate the successful operation of whatever location strategy we have in place.

So why do retailers allow heads of omni-channel to dictate the form of the locations that live at the ends of their so-called channels? Because we're a bit scared by the technology, we're being pressured by the City to up our omni-channel "game" because everyone else is doing it.

Well, here is the news: everyone else isn't doing it. Warby Parker is location-agnostic, Enjoy is location-agnostic, Domino's is location-agnostic, and the bomb that went off under all retailing in 1994 turned out also to be location-agnostic. Amazon has asked the question, "Where are people when they are in the mood to buy the stuff we sell?"

That's why Amazon is opening physical stores because, in this case, it has answered that question with, "Lots of them are wandering around streets going to coffee shops, spending their money on things that aren't bought from us and, if we located ourselves on some of those streets, then we might make enough new sales to justify the cost of doing so."

It's not omni-channel, it's part of a forward-thinking location strategy from a retailer you keep consistently losing out to. Omni-channel is a dead end. Retailers must become location-agnostic and do so fast, as they're already playing catch up on this, so catch up now while that's still possible.

Extending our reach

The fist fight between omni-channel thinking and location-agnosticism may be rumbling, but on one thing both approaches agree: you must use digital technologies to reach as many customers over time as you possibly can. All those great new-wave specialist stores I mentioned in Secret four put a companion store on to customer phones and computers as well as a lovely physical one into a choice neighbourhood. Their virtual stores reflect them and their physical values and the editorial of their advice perfectly. That the new-wave specialists do this is because they have tended to come into retail from other places. They are makers, collectors or artisans first and do not bring retail baggage with them. They naturally include virtual versions of their stores because it makes sense.

Should all offline businesses also trade online? Yes, absolutely, provided they can do so in a way that either reduces friction or that maximises reward. Simply matching prices and product with other online vendors isn't enough.

Should all online businesses also open physical stores? A qualified no. There are, certainly, some online businesses where maximum resources are employed in servicing and growing their online trade, but those are possibly quite rare now. The facts are that customers are keen to have fun with physical experiences and stores that deliver more than dreary old shelves and a till. Most online retailers will find they have some of the magic that could be profitably applied to the creation of great physical stores.

Where to put them? Location strategy right back again. The answer isn't necessarily to put them in expensive primary high-street or mall locations. A strong enough proposition, especially when it is already supported by a big online customer following, might be better located somewhere off-centre, opening up opportunities to locate in bigger and directly accessible spaces.

The reality of everywhere

You can put your retail business anywhere you want to. Your challenge is to construct a location strategy that ensures no big opportunity is missed and that all locations work to the best combination of friction/reward. For some retailers that will mean a business that exists on mobile, as stores, embedded into other online spaces, as a website, as home visits. Each one a distinct location but each playing a role in serving the customers' need states while gently extracting cash from their wallets. Do not consider creating tools unless you've thought about how the store part of that tool behaves as a location.

So your location strategy that once meant placing stores on a map now exists as a customer-led plan to put stores wherever and however customers need them to be. Be location-agnostic, consider every place you serve and trade as part of a modem location strategy and you'll make better choices in your delivery of it.

Now
Things you can do now

- Consider all the locations your customers might be at in a need state you can meet. What is your presence there? How consistent across each are you? Does that presence, whether virtual, physical or pop-up, fulfil enough of the customers' need state such that it can lead to a transaction, either delayed or immediate? If delayed, do you understand enough about where customers go to fulfil the rest of the need state?

Next
Strategic considerations for the longer term

- Brief out requirements for any or all missing formats to meet gaps in current physical and virtual estate.
- Integrate your channel strategy under your location strategy with decision making falling under a single location-led view.

Chapter

7

If you don't treat your people with respect, if you undervalue them, how on earth do you expect them to respect and value your customers? The best customer experiences depend on the best employment experiences and I can prove it.

Retail secret seven: "we love working here"

In this chapter we explore

- the links between what it's like to work for a given retailer versus shopping there
- service profit chain theory
- why people make better choices on your behalf if you trust them
- the fundamentals of great employment experiences in a retail context.

The big joke, Trader Joe's

It's my first night in Chicago and I've wandered out from my apartment to take in what feels like, in London, would be a big slice of hipster nonsense, but that will turn out to be authentic and fun: a night of alternative stand-up in a tiny indie comic-book store, the magical G-Mart on Logan Square. I arrive early and, when the store's owner asks me what comics I like, my English accent, somehow posher than normal, stands out as a novelty and I feel the room's attention on me. We have a nice chat, I buy a book and everything is good. Still, I'm a bit shy and typically English and glad of the six-pack of beer I'll be settling down with soon when the show begins.

The comedians are great, but one stands out and he's the reason I'm mentioning stand-up in a book about retail. Danny Maupin supports his burgeoning comedy career by working days at

Trader Joe's. As coincidence would have it, I'd been to Danny's store earlier that day and been wowed by the energy, fun and pitch of the place. I know Danny works at Trader Joe's because he used a lot of his experiences there in his act. You'd expect comedy about working in a supermarket to lean towards the bitter and cynical, but it was the opposite. Working at Trader Joe's sounded like fun; there were jokes about how laidback the place is, about how nice the managers are and about the ubiquitous Hawaiian shirts staff wear.

The Trader Joe's material was warm and funny, everyone smiled and laughed but, more than that, the audience, as customers of Trader Joe's, instantly recognised Danny's portrayal of the store as an irreverent, enjoyable place to work where people matter and bosses are good fun. They recognised it because that's also how it feels to shop at Trader Joe's. By this time, deep into my fourth can of local brewer Revolution's Anti-Hero IPA, it hit me that here was the best evidence I was ever going to get for the power of the employment experience to directly influence the customer experience.

The yin and yang of looking after your teams

Employment experience drives the direct customer experience, especially in stores. That much can be directly proved, but I am convinced that you see the true spirit, values and employee happiness, or otherwise, in virtual representations or when talking to call centre or services staff too.

An example of how that spirit permeates through every part of the company can be found at BrewDog. *The Guardian's* Jon Henley heard this from barman Dave Bruce, working in the company's Aberdeen location. Bruce said he had spent 18 months trying to get a job there and added: "This is a special company precisely because it gives a shit. Everything it does is about its beers and its people. Okay, it's a bit over the top sometimes. But I'm super proud to work here."

It's more evidence of the power of having a simple and translatable Big Idea. Henley added that BrewDog also rewards, with a pay rise, everyone who passes the beer professionals' exams run by the US firm Cicerone. (The top grade, Master Cicerone, involves

12 hours of essays plus a blind tasting of 100 beers. Nine people in the world have passed it, and two of them work for BrewDog.) What is your equivalent? Do you view training as a part of the job, or do you reward members of the team for making themselves more valuable to the business and more aligned to the Big Idea?

Service profit chain

Some years ago, I was introduced to the basic idea that within retail and service organisations, it's the employees who have the biggest impact on customer experience of the brand. It sounds obvious when you put it like that and it's true. What service profit chain theory does is turn the fluffy bit of that equation into a way to measure the pound note impact of treating your employees with respect, care and integrity. It steps through the linkages from the idea to the impact. Whatever way customers interact with your business, service profit chain holds true.

"Nice" means profit

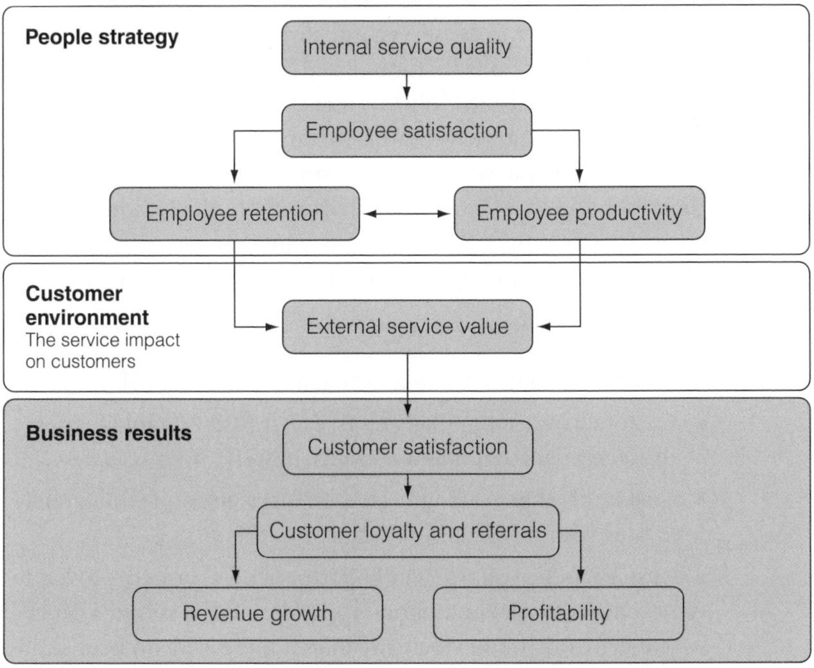

People strategy

Internal service quality

Employee satisfaction

Employee retention ←→ Employee productivity

Customer environment
The service impact on customers

External service value

Business results

Customer satisfaction

Customer loyalty and referrals

Revenue growth

Profitability

Source: Adapted from Smart Circle Limited

Let's step through the boxes.

Internal service quality: treating your people well is good.

Employee satisfaction: because happy, motivated and respected staff are more satisfied.

Employee retention: they stay longer with you.

Employee productivity: they get better at their jobs.

External service value: happy, stable and productive teams tend to deliver the best customer service experiences.

Customer satisfaction: which makes customers jolly happy.

Customer loyalty and referrals: they come back more often, spend more cash with you and they recommend you to their friends.

Revenue growth: which means you take loads more money.

Profitability: goes up and we all start ordering Ferrari brochures.

Improved customer service

Customers prefer to be served and supported by happy, friendly people and every observational and feedback study proves that conclusively. Tied into improvements in employee retention are corresponding improvements in employee effectiveness and knowledge. People who stay with you longer tend to get better at their jobs and that filters through directly to the customer experience. This is especially important when supporting customers remotely. Friendly people making good decisions are vital.

But why is great service so important? Here are some reasons:

- Customers come back more often and they shout about you.
- Customers are more likely to give First Visit Advantage to those retailers that have served them well.
- Customers share their great experiences, most of which relate to how your people have looked after them.
- Customers also share their bad experiences, but are proven to become more positive about a retailer that has solved a problem generously and efficiently than if there were no issue in the first place.

Then there are the cost savings:

- Reduced shrinkage – happy people don't steal from you and they care more about reducing customer theft as well.
- Reduced employee turnover – happy people, and people who feel valued, stay with you longer and that means savings not only on advertising for replacements but also savings on training and your time.
- Mistakes have an inverse relationship to tenure – keep people longer and they waste less through errors.

Walking the talk

We cover values and vision statements later, when I'll explain why these are so important to the success of your business. A great team and store culture makes an excellent starting point for making values and vision statements really work for you. Walking the talk also means that new ideas tend to be adopted more readily and more happily by the team: everybody is up for driving the team forwards.

Support

You *could* create a happy team by letting everyone run riot, throw sickies whenever they want and help themselves to whatever they fancy from the warehouse. That wouldn't do anything for the performance of the business. A great culture still encompasses the unpleasant things, such as sacking people who don't make the grade and reprimanding staff when they let the team down. However, if you have got that great culture and you have a happy team, they will tend to be far more supportive of you in those difficult decisions. That's useful because it helps keep the disruption of such moments down to a minimum and the team gets over it more quickly.

Enjoyment

Happy teams are nicer to work within. Fun is a powerful component in a high-performing team. Shopping is, in itself, fun. In all but a few circumstances, customers *like* visiting stores and websites and buying things with a few taps of their phone screen, so it's reasonable to aim for a fun retail team culture too.

How to build great teams

Happy teams make you more money. You know that anyway, but service profit chain proves it. So does Container Store, Trader Joe's or Dixons Carphone. The best customer service is delivered by happy and motivated people. The best performance improvement strategy I could ever recommend is make your team happy.

A happy team of friendly, motivated people, pulling together, having fun with customers, bristling with ideas and enthusiasm, people with passion for the job, can build huge performance improvements. Like so much in retail, the recommendation to create a happy team is obvious, but is also a massive challenge. The best of us still struggle to get every new recruit right, to always make the best decision in a given situation, to not drop the ball when the going gets tough. Management is hard to do right and that is why business values good managers so highly.

A consistency I've seen through great retail businesses is that they understand their Big Idea, tend to be very clear on what the business is trying to do (vision), allow people to behave like grown-ups (respect) and are very good at recognising positive behaviours (recognition). Let's call these three things cornerstones: vision, respect, recognition. Wherever the three are in evidence, great cultures emerge.

- **Cornerstone 1 vision:** we understand what we want to do for our customers.
- **Cornerstone 2 respect:** we make sure our people know they are empowered to do those things.
- **Cornerstone 3 recognition:** we reinforce those positive things by recognising them when they happen.

The three then exist as a self-reinforcing loop. The clearer we are about what our business is for and the better we enable our people to do those things, and the more we notice and say thank you when they do them, then the better we become.

I'll go into each cornerstone in more detail in the next chapter, but first I want to illustrate the value and importance of leadership.

Leadership

Things get a little bit tricky when we start to think about leadership and teams. I have a heartfelt belief that leadership cannot be taught. Indeed, we once lost out on a large bit of consultancy business because I fundamentally disagreed with the notion that leadership could be taught. A UK retailer with 1,300 stores was looking to improve store cultures and was very proud of the expensive leadership programme it had pushed 1,300 managers through. But, when we peeled back the detail of what had actually happened, it became clear that any gains it had seen as a result of this leadership programme were pretty much down to the fact that those managers had spent two days out of their stores and were hyper-aware that senior people were watching them post-course.

It was also clear that gains would evaporate quite quickly. And here's where we lost the relationship. I'm not sure that the role of human resources is to teach a fundamental in-the-genes skill such as leadership. I believe its job is to find the best existing leaders out there within the total workforce and then to put those natural leaders in the right roles. Pointing that out led to a huge disconnect from that particular client and we've not been back since. When I say disconnect, I mean "hissy fit" and, as expected, its leadership programme didn't work and it has experienced flat or declining performance in the years since, ended up being taken over, then taken over again and is definitely in a pickle right now.

So, do you have to be a good leader to be a great retailer? Do you have to be a good leader to create a strong culture? The painful answer is that, to a large degree, yes you do. You might want to do a bit of soul-searching for a moment on that. It might help if I define leadership. It's really about answering one question: are you able to inspire others to line up behind your chosen course of action? To rally around a Big Idea and a vision?

Now we get to the notion that great leaders can, and sometimes do, still fall on their arses. Being able to lead is essential to the job at hand, but understanding where to lead and how to structure the journey is essential too. And that's where the three cornerstones come in handy. It's like a leadership map: follow those steps and you'll get to where you want to go.

Market Basket
Sharing the spoils and leading kindly

Managing director of the leading retail analysts Conlumino, Neil Saunders tells the story of how an incredible strike by staff and customers proved nice guys can win in the end.

How loyal are you to your supermarket?

Do you have one you prefer to use over others? Probably. Would you make most of your food spend there? Perhaps. Would you drive miles out of your way to shop there? Some-times. Do you consider it an important part of your life? Unlikely. Would you make a sacrifice and join a protest move-ment to protect it? Unimaginable!

This tells us something: namely, that when it comes to food shop-ping, what often counts as loyalty has shallow roots. It is tran-sient, tenuous and turbulent. In fact, it isn't proper loyalty at all.

There is one supermarket, however, that's different. A super-market people drive miles to get to. A supermarket that is a real part of people's lives. A supermarket that people sacrificed and protested to save. A supermarket that has the genuine loyalty of its shoppers. That supermarket is Market Basket.

A once little-known New England grocery chain, Market Basket came to prominence in June 2014 when its CEO, Arthur T. Demoulas, was sacked by the board of directors.

Despite the chain's profitable growth and expansion during Arthur T.'s tenure, other family members who co-owned the company objected to his management. They contended that he was paying staff too much in wages and profit-sharing bonuses and that prices in stores were too low. Without Arthur T. they could, they believed, maximise their profits.

On learning that Arthur T. had been sacked, six Market Basket senior executives resigned. The next day, a rally was held out-side the company's flagship store.

News of Arthur T.'s treatment spread rapidly. Store managers, cashiers, warehouse staff and administrators protested. Some held rallies at their stores, others stuck up posters demanding the return of their former CEO. Local media picked up on the story and reported it.

And then something extraordinary happened: customers walked out. Not just some, but thousands and thousands and thousands of them. They refused to shop at Market Basket until Arthur T. was reinstated. This, they said, was their store. They liked the way it was run, they liked the staff they interacted with, and they didn't want "corporate types" coming in and changing things.

This was not an action they took lightly. Many relied on the low prices of Market Basket to make ends meet and shopping at more expensive alternatives was a sacrifice. As if to underline this, every day, former customers came and taped the receipts they had received from rival stores to the windows of Market Basket's shops.

The protests grew. Store managers closed their shops. People gathered in the parking lots to protest. Some suppliers joined in and terminated their contracts with Market Basket.

The move by the family, designed to extract more profits, was costing the company hundreds of millions. It was fast on its way to bankruptcy.

Late in August, after the governors of both New Hampshire and Massachusetts had intervened, the family members agreed to sell their stakes to Arthur T., giving him control of the company and putting him back at the helm.

After it was announced, staff immediately returned. They worked around the clock to restock stores and get the supply chain moving again. Suppliers helped out. And customers returned too, in greater numbers than ever before. Arthur T was back – and so was Market Basket!

This state of affairs – a demonstration of almost unprecedented loyalty to a store, to its proposition, and to the man who ran it – raises a question: how did Arthur T. do it?

The answer is surprising in its simplicity. Arthur T. treated people well, he treated people fairly, he treated people honestly, he empowered them and made them feel like they owned the business.

The excessive wages and bonuses the family saw as a waste of their profits were no such thing. They were a just reward for a

▶

workforce that was highly productive, a workforce that would go above and beyond to serve the business because they felt it valued them and wanted their ideas and contributions.

The lower prices that the family saw as an erosion of their margins were no such thing. They were an essential point of differentiation based on Arthur T.'s understanding of his customers and what mattered to them.

Most critically, these two things went hand in hand. Arthur T.'s business model wasn't predicated on maximising margins, but on maximising the productivity and efficiency of employees. And his low prices weren't just low prices, they were low prices together with exceptional staff, motivated to give great customer service and to look after their stores and products. Something that added up to fantastic value for money.

He achieved this not through micromanagement, meaningless performance targets or complex hierarchies, but by simply making people feel passionate about the business they work in, by letting them know that they matter, by rewarding them for success and by treating people as people.

Arthur T. may well be nice, but his business is also highly successful. Profits have doubled under his leadership and the firm continues to expand, opening its 76th store in Portsmouth, Massachusetts, recently. More openings will follow.

So, that's ultimately what real loyalty is all about: genuine interactions with people, both staff and customers. And, strangely enough, it's what good business is about too.

As Arthur T. puts it: "If everyone in the workplace is equal and treated with dignity, they work with a little extra passion, a little extra dedication. I think that's a wonderful business message to the world."

Be excellent to each other

The thing is, the logic of this process is inescapable and can be seen at work inside the world's best retailers, yet it's rarer than it should be. Putting mission, respect and recognition at the heart of your management style will deliver this good stuff. Great employment experiences drive great customer experiences and that is a modern retail essential.

Now
Things you can do now

- Open a feedback channel for all employees that encourages them to tell the CEO. Use a secure private messaging tool where feedback can be gathered anonymously, if necessary.
- Consider opening a private space for employees to share ideas on the employment experience, but make this shared space one in which real names are used by the participants. Slack is an ideal tool here.
- Run a survey asking questions relating to the employment experience. Commission a specialist agency to write the questionnaire, but use a low-cost or free tool, such as SurveyMonkey, to conduct the survey itself.
- Walk through the service profit chain and list what you do as a company at each stage, and identify gaps and weaknesses.

Next
Strategic considerations for the longer term

- Use the output of the steps above to rebuild the employment experience.
- Review reward and remuneration to ensure it's both a positive element in the employment experience and that it's structured to encourage behaviours that meet whatever customer expectations you have set up through your Big Idea.

Part

2

A bit of doing it

US Patent no. 1,242,872, granted in 1917, shows Clarence Saunders' revolutionary self-service store; but what's next?

Source: US Patent Office

Retail legend Allan Leighton, the man who made Asda a contender, called the first edition of Smart Retail *"a book about doing it", which, though dry, was a high compliment, if you know Allan. These chapters are the ones Allan would most identify with doing retail!*

Introduction: practical people

The practical core

Part 2 is the practical core of *Smart Retail*. It is a set of ideas, suggestions and tips on doing retail, all taken from observations of the consistencies present among the world's best retailers. I'm going to concentrate on three areas: team, customer and store.

There is no order of importance as each is as important as the other. When it comes to store, I will make some distinctions between types of stores and give specific thoughts on virtual as well as physical stores. Philosophically, I am more convinced than ever that the fundamental principles of customer and store apply to every type of store, whether that's a one-button, one-product Amazon Dash store located in a customer's kitchen in Arkansas, or if it's a retail palace on the North Circular in London.

What gives?

Inevitably, there is more that could be covered than is possible without extending your reading time unreasonably. The two areas I don't cover in detail are buying and the maths of retailing. The first is because buyers are all unknowable lunatics, highly prized but insane and what they do has rarely been adequately captured in print. What I've tried to do is cover principles of product to at least get you to the point where you understand what you ought to be selling as a business, how that should be priced, at least philosophically, and why customers might engage with that product.

I would love to cover retail maths because it is, possibly, even more important than the subjects I do cover, in that without it you are hamstrung. But it would take a whole (possibly quite dry) book to take a person from scratch to comfortable competence and this isn't that book. Instead, I am assuming that you at least understand general sales and stock maths and that you can apply the advice and ideas I go through using existing knowledge.

I also know that many readers are retailers of many years' experience for whom the maths is like a second language. Just in case you do want a crib sheet, *EDI Provider* maintains a useful list of all the core retail equations and calculations: https://goo.gl/KlO10.

Chapter

David Brent, that famously clumsy oaf of a manager in *The Office* said: "You've seen how I react to people, make them feel good, make them think that anything's possible. If I make them laugh along the way, sue me. And I don't do it so they turn round and go 'Thank you David for the opportunity, thank you for the wisdom, thank you for the laughs'." The fictional leader of Wernham Hogg's Slough office generally knew at least half of what made for great teams but would then trip over the other missing half. Yet one thing he's right about here is that a significant element of building great teams is to make all members feel that they can achieve together, that anything is possible.

How to build great teams

In this chapter we explore

- the three cornerstones of team building

- why people make better choices on your behalf if you trust them

- the fundamentals of great employment experiences in a retail context

- how to build and lead high-performance retail teams.

The three cornerstones

This rather handily follows on from the seventh secret. If we're all about great employment experiences driving great customer ones, then this is how to go about putting some of that in place. Team, here, obviously applies to individual store teams quite easily, but I extend the definition and techniques to everyone in the business who has a direct impact on customers. They might be writing web copy, answering phones, managing email communications or setting the tone in social media.

So, going back to the last chapter, I mentioned three cornerstones as essentials of building great employment experience:

- Cornerstone 1 vision: we understand what we want to do for our customers.

- Cornerstone 2 respect: we make sure our people know they are empowered to do those things.

- Cornerstone 3 recognition: we reinforce those positive things by recognising them when they happen.

Vision

For most of us, the very words "vision statement" set our skin crawling. We tend to think of them as marketing waffle, and with good reason because often that's all they are. That's a shame because a good vision statement is an incredibly powerful tool. It becomes a rallying point for the whole team.

Has your company got a vision statement? If it has, does it make sense? Does it make clear what it is that the business wants everyone to aim for and to do? Does it help you make choices and decisions? Above all, does it reflect the Big Idea? If the answer to those questions is no, then you are going to need to rewrite it. Once you have done that, you must make that statement live and breathe, then refer to it in every team meeting and offer up every decision and choice you make against it.

A strong, clear vision statement can be a fantastic tool for improving and securing best performance. Make it simple, obvious, reinforcing and make sure that it addresses practical objectives. If people know what the company exists for (the Big Idea) and they understand what the company wants them to do for customers, then there is a very good chance everyone will work consistently to deliver that.

Halfords
Clear and unified

As the 2000s drew to a close, one of the UK's largest multiple retailers, the 114-year-old Halfords, appeared to be trudging through its own end-phase. Maybe it would have another ten years, maybe the internet would kill it now, but poor results and generally declining performance suggested the business had good cause for pessimism. Then nine profit warnings from 2010 to 2012 intimated the patient was possibly terminal. Enter Matt Davies as new CEO.

Arriving from his first big retail role, successfully transforming Pets at Home from a quiet little specialist to a national profit

---

powerhouse, the affable Mancunian quickly rallied the troops. He convinced the entire team that they had a place in the world and invested in areas constantly cut by previous CEOs. Those areas of investment included at the time unfashionable cost lines such as staff numbers, wages, training and store fabric.

Above all, Davies has a knack for encapsulating his vision, the strategy and the actuality of delivering these things in very simple terms and in really clear objectives. If you work for Davies, in any position from the shop floor through to the board and all points in between, you know what he wants you to do. Even better, you know exactly how he wants you to look after customers.

And, wow, did Matt Davies revive Halfords. Setting out with a clear mission to deliver a £1bn in group revenue by the end of 2016, Davies presented the business with a simple Big Idea as vision and supported it with an elegant purpose. The Big Idea/vision is to help and inspire customers with their life on the move. They would support drivers of every car, inspire cyclists of every age and equip families for their leisure time away from home.

Here's how this fits together:

- Halfords' Big Idea was to "help and inspire customers with their life on the move".
- Its purpose was to support drivers, inspire cyclists and equip families for leisure.
- The mission was to deliver group sales in excess of £1bn by the end of financial year 2016.

Some retail leaders would read all that back and declare it a load of old tosh – meaningless words where retail discipline was what was needed. But they would be so wrong. Look at those words. Just take "support drivers". It means something very real, which is to be ready in-store to help diagnose, to advise, to fit. If a customer, a driver, asks for help with selecting the right battery, the assistant knows that's the most important thing they should be doing at that moment. The manager knows it, their regional manager knows it. Everyone in the business knows it.

Now that is huge. That is the triumph of simplicity of vision over complexity of strategy.

▶

Beyond this Big Idea and purpose, the strategy was further articulated as five programmes that would "get Halfords into gear for 2016". And, again, the whole thing is supported by seven values that anchor this customer-centric, optimistic and human strategy.

Halfords' group sales were £865m in 2012. Davies aimed to hit a billion in four years. It took him and the team only three: Halfords delivered a whopping £1bn by 2015, and did so on massively improved profitability and with significant like-for-like growth, proving that the success was in the changed customer experience rather than estate growth or accountancy weaves.

Tesco poached Davies in May 2015 to operate as CEO for its UK and Ireland stores. By Christmas 2016, the national basket case that was Tesco was already beginning to post encouraging and positive improvements. At a speech for Retail Week Live in June 2016, Davies explained that he had asked his team one key question on joining: "How do we turn Tesco from a company that runs shops to a company that serves people?" Those positive green shoots that began to sprout just six months after he joined suggest Davies has found some answers.

Halfords expressed their strategy in a simple graphic that displayed the following headings and content.

Under the unifying Big Idea 'We help and inspire our customers with their life on the move' followed:

Three strategic pillars

- Supporting drivers of every car
- Inspiring cyclists of every age
- Equipping families for their leisure time

Supported by specific programmes

- Service revolution
- The 'h' factor
- 21st century infrastructure
- Stores fit to shop
- Click with the digital future

And all displaying these values

- Be helpful
- Earn trust
- Aim to win
- Have fun
- Think customer
- Inspire others
- Work as a team

And what of Halfords in the year since Davies moved on? New CEO, new approaches, that's fair enough. Davies' replacement, Jill McDonald, has dismantled the strategy illustrated here, though McDonald might describe it as having "moved it on" or "finessed it". Tellingly, the new strategy is explained on Halfords plc's investor site in page after page of detail with little clear summary.

To be fair to Jill McDonald, it's too early to see her long-term impact and I wish her the very best, but I already miss the clarity of Matt Davies' Halfords vision.

Complexity kills – simplicity liberates.

Values

This is another area where a lot of rubbish has been made up by management gurus. It means that talking about values can feel a little ridiculous. This is a shame because a set of defined values becomes the practical tool that helps you to apply the vision statement to the everyday running of the business.

Where the vision statement tells you what the company does, the values tell you how it wants to go about doing it. They are a reflection of what the company stands for. We're talking about a list of words, such as innovative, fun, honest and inspirational. The trick is to mould these values into a set of practical sentences that tell us how to apply the values to the jobs we do every day.

In 2016, Aditya Chakrabortty wrote a damning piece for *The Guardian* entitled "How Boots [the UK chemist/drug-store] went rogue". In it she describes a culture where values have been skewed: "That fear comes wrapped in the corporate language of empowerment. A chemist advising a customer – 'You know, like I've done my entire career,' as one Boots lifer puts it – is now having a great conversation. If the satisfied customer then compliments the chemist that is now a 'Feel Good Moment' (although in performance plans they are unfortunately referred to as FGMs – so a chemist must notch up, say, five FGMs a week). This is pure Apprentice-speak, an attempt to turn pharmacists into estate agents, career pedants with a duty of care into hustlers in labcoats."

Contrast this with the values founder Jesse Boot wrote about in 1919: "Common hope, common sympathies and common humanity bind us together, and whatever fosters this happy union is valuable." These things are important as they set the context for the customer experience. I worry for Boots and have been vocal in that worry for some years now. I hope the latter values do, once again, come to be seen as more valuable than the fear-inducing former.

For the full article, including attribution of the statements above, see: http://goo.gl/ER97VB.

A great way to think about values is to fix in your mind the perfect customer experience when interacting with your business, then imagine talking to that customer afterwards. What five emotions might they tell you they felt during that experience? Write down that list of emotions and then ask yourself this question: if my customers come away from an interaction with us feeling those five things, are they likely to come back again? If the answer is yes, then you're on to something good.

Walking the talk

Defining a good vision statement and then living the values across locations, both virtual and physical (walking the talk), is good for you because it improves the customer experience and builds stronger teams. This, in turn, increases business performance. A good set of vision and values reads naturally: it uses language that a normal person can easily make sense of. Simple things, strongly stated.

Using values to change staff behaviours for the better

Here is a solid, practical example of the way in which values can make a significant difference to the everyday functioning of a shop. This case study is about a British clothes retailer. One of the very obvious values that applied to this business was that buying or selling clothes was about fun. Customers wanted a happy environment and staff wanted to enjoy their jobs. In fact, that was one of the things people told us had attracted them to the business. Working in fashion retail looked like it might be more fun than stacking shelves. So we included "fun" as a value. It really supported the company vision: "Delight our customers by giving them affordable access to great high street fashion."

See, fun! Nothing more fun than a sad clown failing to get served his pint

Source: Koworld

Fun is a value that many people believe, and I agree, should be part of the working environment for almost any retailer. I don't mean mindless larking about, but the generation of genuine "this is cool" moments for customers and staff alike. Fun helps make shopping enjoyable. We are all in the business of making shopping fun, whether we are selling washing machines or watches.

One of my favourite methods for making values work every day in-store is to rewrite job descriptions. Out goes the dry HR-speak and in comes practical stuff about what to do and why. In the case of this retailer we had identified one particular group of employees who were really hard to engage. There was a set of 16 to 18-year-old girls who all worked one weekday evening and then all day Saturday. They are notoriously hard to engage. You hardly see them all week, then suddenly they are there on your busiest day when you've got little time to give them. It's crucial that you have these girls on board and pulling for the team or they can become a disruptive and negative element in the store. They are also famous for mickey-taking degrees of lateness and for being uncommitted when they do finally arrive. This was especially true on hungover Saturday mornings!

We looked at their job descriptions which I doubt any of the girls themselves had read (and I don't blame them). One of the most important responsibilities, the first task they were supposed to perform on Saturday mornings, read like this: "You will ensure all merchandise rails, shelves and/or islands are fully filled and merchandised in accordance with the prevailing marketing planogram for your store grade and profile." What this actually meant was simply: "Make sure there are no gaps on display when we let the punters in." The girls regarded this responsibility as a real chore, boring. Not the sort of thing they wanted to do when arriving tired after a big Friday night out.

So we changed it and introduced that value of fun. The same line from the job description now read: "Fashion is fun, remember that as you dive into the stock room and pull out your favourite, most exciting fashions. We want you to take your choices, the clothes you think customers should be wearing out tonight, on to the sales floor. Get them onto the racks, anywhere there are gaps, and get your choices noticed." When we trialled it, the effect was fantastic.

Because we had asked the girls to think for themselves – and who really is best placed to say what the trendiest clothes for 16 to 18-year-old girls are than a group of 16–18-year-old girls – they actually got excited by the task, even beginning to come in early to get the best picks. They also were competitive with each other and would jostle for space and monitor each other's selections like hawks. Very healthy stuff indeed with the unexpected side-effect that the girls also began to sell proactively. They would make sure every customer saw their personal picks and a constant supply of sizes and colours was always out on display. That's how a vision and a clear set of values can have a direct effect on the performance of the team.

Respect

Treat people how you yourself would wish to be treated. My nan used to say that to me – and, like a lot of the wisdom of her generation, it's absolutely on the money. In today's retail landscape, you have no option but to treat your people with respect.

A disrespectful market

I slightly wish Sir John Timpson, eponymous Chairman of Timpsons, was my dad (not really, dad!) because he is one of the nicest, most inspirational people in British retailing. He's very successful too, both strategically and operationally. For the former, he bravely moved Timpson from shoe retail to shoe repair. Had he obeyed only the trends, he wouldn't have put all his eggs in the repair market at a time when the trends said the world would only become more disposable. He has built his entire operational ethos on respect and trust. Trusting managers to set their own prices locally, trusting staff to be able to sort out complaints themselves and giving them the tools to do so. Respecting the ability of his people to make decisions like the grown-ups they are, and respecting ex-convicts' right to a chance of a return to normal life after serving their punishment.

10% of Timpson's staff have served time in prison, thanks to an initiative begun in 2003 by Sir John's son, James Timpson. The company now works with 70 prisons and operates 3 academies devoted to training ex-convicts, and ready preparing them to move into stores.

One more thing Timpson does that all retailers should is give everyone a customer service budget and then let them spend it however they see fit. Trust people, respect their honesty and ability and they will surprise you. In Timpson's case, Sir John claims that giving every person a £500 customer service budget has saved him "thousands and thousands over the long term".

Has it worked for Timpson? The business is very profitable, customer satisfaction is high, it is able to continue to expand and staff satisfaction is also very high. Shoe repair and key-cutting looks like an old-fashioned business, so perhaps it's fitting, then, that, as customer trends show customers beginning to crave experiences and products that are authentic and that reflect the human element, it turns out a business run on human values is so successful.

It is almost the received wisdom that life at an online business is work hard but play hard and that lots of bright young things get to run around playground offices drinking free Buzz Cola and napping in sleep pods. The slight disappointment comes when you discover that the vast majority of the top 50 online retailers are actually old-school, high-street ones. But among those that were originally, and this is the worst sort of jargon, "pure play" online businesses, often the culture really is built on respect, free thinking and an encouragement of disruption from within. Traditional organisational models suggest that such attributes are essential during the initial years of any new business but that there comes a time when the business must grow up.

I suspect that isn't true when a market is in the flux that retailing is in, if my hypothesis is right. Then all retailers must hand over some of their remaining power to the people within the business most able to challenge received wisdom, to ask why and to be allowed to try new things. And to be allowed to repeatedly fail in those new things as they strive to find the new things that will work.

To be completely frank, I wonder if the grown-up phase is ever really the right thing for a retailer. I joined a head office retail team in 1988 that had just moved into its grown-up phase, having been a genuinely maverick and game-changing operation in its sector. That retailer is no longer with us. It went bust in 2012 after having never again found its former entrepreneurial and eccentric spirit. It went from a disruptive market-changing cheeky innovator to a me-too also-ran. It was sad and, joining at 19, I found all the wistful talk of the recent fun days very frustrating. Directors would tell incredible tales that would all finish with, "Of course, we've got to be a bit more sensible now." I would suggest history has now proven that to be wrong.

Can you change a culture?

It doesn't happen often, but you can change a culture. Switzerland's Hennes & Mauritz went from boring and safe to fun and innovative, even rebranding as H&M, though you could argue it is due for a shake-up again. It took some hard personnel changes to precipitate the change but, once done, the business returned to growth.

Top Shop went from a paternal, and possibly patronising, culture to one that is fast, good fun, sharply on trend and even a trend-maker at times. One person made that happen and she is a genius.

Perhaps the most remarkable transformation has been at electrical retailer Dixons Carphone. The ball was started rolling by John Browett, whose subsequent difficulties at Apple get more attention than either they or John deserve. He recognised that service could not be dictated centrally and that, instead, teams in stores should be given the tools, training and bonus structures that both nudged them towards delivering better service, and that made it more likely that they would want to do so.

After Browett left, Seb James accelerated the process, continuing to grow customer satisfaction, but also revenue and profit. There was a time in the last decade when it looked like Dixons might not survive. To go from that to the point where it was able to successfully merge with customer-focused Charles Dunstone's Carphone Warehouse is an incredibly impressive story.

Testing cultures

There is an easy test to find out what sort of culture is in play at a given retailer and that is to ask its employees what it's like to work there. You might hear some moans initially, especially in the UK. We love to complain, but look out for forms of the following phrases. If you hear these consistently across employees in different teams and stores, you'll know the employment experience is positive:

- We get treated with respect.
- I feel like I can make a difference.
- I'm trained so well that I never look stupid in front of customers.
- My ideas are worth something.
- I'm allowed, no I'm encouraged, to use my brain.
- It's made clear that I can have a proper career here, if I want one.

The 1980s retail legacy

Back in the 1980s, there was a surge in consumer spending. In the UK, this surge ran alongside unprecedented levels of unemployment – for some, everything was rosy and, for others, desperate. A group of UK retailers became incredibly successful off the back of the surge, but some chose to exploit their workforces, knowing that the threat of unemployment loomed large. With demand for fashion, food, homewares and consumer goods outstripping supply at times, leading stores were able to sell almost everything they could put on a shelf. The best of these looked after their staff well and saw background unemployment as a reason to be a good employer rather than a bad one. On the flip side were those retailers who saw people as disposable, an expendable resource to be bullied into line. Customers were blind to the effects of this as they scrambled over themselves to buy, buy, buy and so the bully-boy retailers got away with treating staff badly.

I started in-store in 1985 and witnessed the worst of this at first hand. A management style emerged, and it was called JFDI or (just flipping do it; we know I've had to change the second word). Senior field management would swoop into store and demand, bully and threaten JFDI was anti-respect. It was all about conformity and subservience. I first entered retailing in the middle of these years and it was mean at times. Nasty even. It was an atmosphere that chewed people up, burnt them out, took advantage of job insecurity and made some people's lives a horrid experience.

But come the early 1990s and the boom and bust cycle was beginning to flatten. With that flattening came a calming in the rabid consumerism and large reductions in levels of unemployment and a longer-term sustainable prosperity was established. And something happened in the way people, especially in the UK, shopped. They became more discerning, as if the hangover of the 1980s was accompanied by an understanding that spending for the sake of spending wasn't a great idea any more.

And customers appeared to begin to notice that those businesses run on the principles of JFDI weren't nice places to shop. Customers aren't stupid. They might not be able to define what it is that they notice in a JFDI-led store, but it does affect them.

This effect is just one very good reason to invest in and show respect for your staff. Forget even the straightforward cost benefits of keeping your staff longer. The simple reality is that teams built on respect and passion ultimately bring more profit into your business. Teams built on fear and unreasonable pressure often create short-term sales gains, but they always crack, and usually this happens very quickly. What is more, they leave customers feeling negative about their interaction with the brand and less inclined to ever come back again. In an age of real-time access to live sales numbers it can be easy to fall back under pressure into a JFDI management style. Don't. What your business gains today it will lose tomorrow and next week.

Worryingly, I have noticed over the last couple of years that some big UK and US retailers, mostly bricks and mortar retailers that are feeling the pinch, are quietly reverting back to JFDI cultures. Whenever I see a profitable business begin to do this, I get a little downhearted. It might look attractive on a balance sheet to steal away a benefit or two, but, in the long term, those businesses will damage customer experiences and I promise that the consequence will be that customers go elsewhere. I quoted Aditya Chakrabortty's incendiary article on Boots earlier and, if there is a blueprint for the problems that JFDI causes, then she has described it there.

The respect deal

Respect, thankfully, is a two-way street. You will still have to deal with under-performing colleagues and you might find yourself having to exit people from your business. That is always hard to do, but in a team that has been built on respect you will have worked hard with that person to make things right. The people in your team will know that and will support your decisions rather than becoming unsettled by them. For some great tips on how to build respect, read Chapter 9.

Become your customers

Back in 2005, Martin Butler interviewed the brilliant retailer Jane Shepherdson for his essential book on retailing, *People Don't Buy What You Sell (They Buy What You Stand For)*: "I have this thing about men in suits, you know. People who drone on about the principles of retail. What bollocks! There aren't any principles of retailing."

Top Shop is the British retailer born as a concession in a Sheffield department store in 1964. Gloriously, it has never held itself to be anything more than a store selling cheap and cheerful clothes to young women. Shepherdson took on the top job in 1999, Top Shop's 35th year, and transformed it utterly, not in terms of market position or, necessarily, the type of clothes it sells, but by making the store exciting, unpredictable, passionate and anti-marketing. By that, I mean that she drilled into her entire team that they must ignore the rules and do what feels natural instead. This was, at the time, a huge risk, a proper gamble.

Top Shop's Big Idea is brilliantly simple: be our own customers, forget the needs of the business. That's shocking, but it's an attitude, a revolution indeed, that has put Top Shop among the world's most high-profile and successful retailers.

Here's an example of how Shepherdson forced the rules to be broken by thinking like a customer: "I would go into meetings and say 'Yes, I know that's selling and it's selling 2,000 units, but

---

I don't care, it's awful and we're not going to buy awful things any more, regardless of whether or not they will sell.' If you're going to earn people's trust, you have to set a standard. That set the standard. All the buyers now know that, and all the buyers now stand by every single thing in their range. Compare this to 10 or 20 years ago when some buyers would sit there saying: 'Have you seen this, isn't it horrible? Guess how many we sold last week . . . isn't that great?' I thought it was outrageous. How could they do that? It's not right, there's no integrity."

How often have you dropped a profitable product because you don't think your customers should be buying it? Never, is the answer for most of us. What that kind of thinking has done at Top Shop, together, it has to be said, with modern just-in-time logistics allowing fast stock turn, is to create a store that feels utterly in tune with customers. It's risk that is at the heart of that transformation.

The power of standing for something, of building the retail business around that Big Idea, then living and breathing it, is the best-kept secret in retailing. It's a passionate, instinctive thing and at the heart of every successful retail business.

Ownership – the value of mistakes

Mistakes are great. Mistakes are brilliant – get on with making things happen, make mistakes and learn from them and try more stuff.

People make mistakes when you let them make decisions. They get a lot right too. Being as close as they are to where the action is, your team are absolutely the best people to be making more decisions for the business.

And yet, providing local decision-making tools to individual stores is something that fills many retail directors with horror. It is easy to see how senior central management can get scared about letting their web teams and store managers loose. But all the evidence tells us that this is wrong. Wherever proper decision-making power has been delegated down to individual customer teams it has led to increased sales and profit. It has also, sometimes, resulted in more mistakes being made, but mistakes are only unlearned lessons. You make one, you learn from it and you move on.

Maybe that sounds a little too much like a homespun philosophy, but it also happens to be true. Think about the early careers of people like Richard Branson, bankrupt in his teens. Or Ray Krok, the genius behind McDonald's, who had a string of mistakes, false starts and lean times behind him when, at 52, he spotted the potential for franchised fast food. Mistakes are made when you try something new, different or difficult. Sure, you reduce your errors down to zero if you never try anything, but just see what happens to your business when you do that.

Recognition

Recognition is the bit that happens when you are saying thank you to somebody you've caught doing good things. It is the single most powerful motivation tool in life, let alone in business. Teams used to receiving recognition give better customer service, work more happily together, are more efficient, are more stable, and they make life at work more enjoyable for all. That is because, when you recognise an employee's contribution, you send out a very strong message that says: "I'm glad you came to work today, you made a difference." There's more to motivation than just recognition but it is recognition that is most important.

Most people want to do the best job they can in any given situation. Recognition is the tool that tells them it has been worth making the effort. Recognition is self-reinforcing: people want to do a good job, you recognise them for it when they do, they feel good, so they repeat the recognised action because they like feeling good. Maybe this is a simplified representation of what actually goes on in our heads, but do you see how small moments of praise can escalate into improved performance?

Given that recognition is so powerful, why is it that retail managers are almost never trained in or assessed on their ability to effectively recognise? I believe there are some simple reasons, mostly relating to how hard it is to both measure recognition and to define a list of exact things that should be recognised. They might include such things as improving team spirit, giving exceptional customer service or going the extra mile. Recognition is less about direct sales numbers, although you will want to recognise contribution in that area too.

Recognition is free. It doesn't cost a penny and can drive performance, in stores especially, more effectively than almost any other management tool I have ever seen. You simply must use it.

Please don't make a fuss

One of the issues that makes recognition hard to do at first is a cultural one. The British are embarrassed by praise, we struggle to accept it. Indeed, the most common response among British workers to receiving praise is to blush and to break eye contact. The strange parallel to that praise response is that we, generally, do not have the same problem when receiving criticism. When on the receiving end of criticism, most British workers will listen, if not always graciously, but they will listen. We all tend to have a system for receiving criticism, maybe not always a positive system, but it is, nonetheless, a system. When it comes to receiving praise, although we really like the feeling, we are a little unsure of how to react.

There is also a crucial difference between the British delivery of praise and of criticism. We tend to be specific when criticising, but only general when praising. It is this lack of clarity, I believe, that makes Brits so bad at giving and receiving praise. We give usefully specific criticism, such as: "The budget you did isn't right, where are the print costs?" We know, to be exact, that it is the print costs that are a problem, whereas praise would be vague: "Nice work on the budget."

This is important because the whole point of praise and recognition is that we do it in such a way that recipients understand exactly what they did well so that they can repeat that behaviour. In the budget example above, the person who has been criticised knows they now have to go and sort out the print costs. The other person, praised with the nice work on the budget comment, has no idea why this budget was better than the last one, or what it was exactly that they ought to repeat to get some more praise next time. Better praise would have been: "I like how you've laid out the budget. That's going to make it easier for me to get it approved. Thanks."

"Doing" recognition

"Little and often" is a brilliant management maxim. It's absolutely perfect when applied to recognition. To make too much of a moment of praise can make everybody feel uncomfortable. It can even, sometimes, encourage resentment from the team towards whomever you have singled out for extra-double helpings of praise. You are not attempting to make an individual feel like they are God's gift to retail. If the thing they've done is really special, then, by all means, mention it at a team meeting. But for the rest of the time, the best way to "do" recognition is this: spot something good, mention it quickly, say thank you, be specific.

The bad recognition habits we managers get into, often because we're embarrassed by praise, include worrying about singling out individuals, delaying praise, over-blowing praise, concentrating on catching people getting it wrong, and the inability to be specific with our praise. Delaying praise reduces the effectiveness of recognition. Recognition works best when fresh.

Too many people build their management style around spotting staff making mistakes and then correcting the errors. If you are one of them, try catching people doing good things instead. Do that and you will quickly find that staff actively attempt to repeat those good things and that they look for more good things to do. Recognition taps into so many crucial psychological needs. The easy bit to accept is that recognition, done properly, makes people feel good.

Recognition taps into crucial psychological needs

It is nice also to link recognition to small rewards, but this isn't at all critical. Study after study shows that the part employees actually value is that moment where their manager, or a colleague, or a customer, says "Thank you for . . .".

Behaviours

Although a good recognition habit is all about being spontaneous, saying thank you whenever you see the need, it helps to have in mind a list of the sorts of things that you will be looking out for which to give praise. At the risk of sounding like I've been snacking on a jargon butty, what you should be basing your recognition on are "observable positive behaviours". Essentially, that's all the good stuff people do that you can spot them doing.

When you first decide to introduce a formal recognition process, putting together a list of these observable positive behaviours helps the whole team to get a handle on what it is that you are looking for. Doing this will give you a list of behaviours that you know, if observed, will be a strong indicator that good things are happening. Tell everyone what is on your list and explain why each behaviour is there. Give a copy to new starters, and use it as a basis for review meetings.

"Observable" is the key. It tells you that the behaviours you are looking for are those that you actually have to "see" happen. In stores, sales is not an observable positive behaviour because it is an activity that (a) you already measure closely in the performance numbers and (b) you will be discussing the sales action with each member of the team anyway. How a person makes a sale, though, could easily include a positive observable behaviour: going out of their way to find a bit of information for a customer, or selling an item that was right for the customer but that had a lower commission rate on it for the salesperson.

Those observable positive behaviours that relate to helping make customers happy are important. With any luck, such behaviour will show up as a sale but, even if it doesn't, that customer has left the store with a good feeling about your business. That is worth its weight in gold, but in a way that is very hard to see from looking just at the hard performance numbers.

An easy way to "do" recognition

This is an old favourite of mine that has always proven to be far more powerful than the effort required in order to make it happen. Since I first wrote about it more than a decade ago, I've found more and more retail businesses incorporating something similar into their general culture – that's a very positive change. Doing specific recognition needs to be learned, so don't be embarrassed that it might not be part of your current style. You will get there by practice. Equally, don't assume that, because you do often say thank you, you are getting recognition right. I'll lay down good money that, when you are honest with yourself, you will find that 90% of those thank you moments are non-specific.

In the years between the first edition and this one, loads of managers have fed back that this part of the book is the one they were most sceptical about, but that, once done, had been the most rewarding. I guess I'm saying, "Disconnect the cynicism for a bit and give this stuff a go – you'll be glad you did."

The 20-second ceremony

I'm assuming here that your company doesn't have a formal recognition process in place. So use a couple of team meetings to make up your team's list of "observable positive behaviours". A good way to get a great list together is to start with the Big Idea, the vision and values, and think about the kind of things you can do to support them.

Now make up some "thank you" notes. These should have space on for the recipient's name and a bigger space for you to write down why you are pleased enough to want to say thank you. Print out a bunch of these and keep some in your pocket at all times. Whenever you see an opportunity to say thank you, fill one out quickly and go and put it into the hand of the person you want to say it to. You don't even have to say it, if you don't feel you can. You don't have to make a song and dance of it, you don't even have to speak, if you feel uncomfortable. What is important is that the exchange of this note is something both of you understand. It tells the recipient that you have noticed and that you are pleased, nothing more, nothing less. Takes about 20 seconds to do.

Dish out blank "thank you" notes to the team as well and encourage everyone to use these notes. Workmates recognising each other's efforts has almost as much power as when you do it. You have really cracked it when you get customers to fill in the notes.

The 20-second ceremony works so well and is unobtrusive. It takes little time and I've seen this work successfully in a mad-busy tiny KFC that was processing 50,000 lunch transactions a week. People really do respond to it. The notes can feel a bit silly at first but that soon goes and the process of recognition becomes part of the everyday team culture. You will never find a cheaper or more effective way in which to transform your team's performance.

KFC
Learning 'thank you'

KFC transformed its business in the UK in the late 1990s and has strengthened its position ever since. One of the major transformations, focuses was on the way in which it treated its people. As part of that process, we helped it create and introduce a recognition programme based on observable positive behaviours and on the 20-second recognition ceremony.

A beautiful example of how this tiny, simple ceremony could affect the way people felt about themselves and their performance came to me at a post-launch regional meeting. A manager, Mike, told me what had happened when he went through the 20-second ceremony for the first time. In fact, he told me he'd made somebody cry doing it, so I thought we might be in trouble. Dawn had worked at her KFC outlet for nearly ten years and had seen managers come and go, but had never been keen to take on that sort of extra responsibility for herself. She liked being one of the team and that was that. Mike had been her manager for nearly six months.

One morning, Mike spotted Dawn showing a new member of staff how to "double-bag" a waste bin. Double-bagging means putting in two bin liners at a time so that, at lunch, when the bin is full, you only have to throw one bag of waste away and the bin already has its next liner in place. Now this is a tiny thing and saves maybe a minute at peak time. But Mike saw Dawn do this and it occurred to him that he had seen Dawn help new people learn the ropes on countless occasions. She didn't have to, it wasn't part of her job, she just liked to do it. So Mike decided to use one of his "thank you" notes. He wrote it out and ticked a box that said: "For making new members of the team feel welcome" and, in his own words, he shyly handed it to Dawn.

Dawn burst into tears. Mike reassured her that it wasn't a P45 he'd just given her and asked what the matter was. So she told him: "You've never said 'thank you' to me before." Mike became quite indignant and replied that he had, often, at shift meetings. Dawn put him right. "No, you've said 'thanks' to the team, and that's nice, but you've never come to me, looked me in the eye

▶

and made it so clear that something good I do has been noticed. And, actually, none of my managers over the years has, either."

Dawn felt great about that moment of recognition and that's why there were tears. Most people feel the same way. What's so nice about this approach is that its effect snowballs. Slowly, but surely, more people begin to repeat the good things they do more often, and that gently spreads throughout the business.

Why recognition works

Why does specific recognition like that work so powerfully? It's about clarity: you say to somebody: "Well done, good job today" and it feels good to that person for a bit, but, when they later ask themselves what they did differently that meant they got praise today, it's difficult to actually know for sure. When, instead, you say: "Well done, thanks – you've made that new person feel welcome and I appreciate it, it helps to bring us closer as a team", that staff member walks away knowing exactly what behaviours to repeat in order to get nice praise again.

Now
Things you can do now

- Review your vision statement.
- List the five values you most associate with the current customer experience. Then find the five that you believe should reflect the current customer experience.
- Test your culture by asking your staff what it's like to work for you.
- List five concrete ways in which you have recognised contribution in the last three months. Can you do more? If so, what steps from the recognition section in this chapter should you take?

Next
Strategic considerations for the longer term

- Using the Matt Davies Halfords model, review and reconstruct your vision statement and accompanying strategic programmes.
- Rewrite job descriptions to reflect the above.
- Consider the introduction of structured recognition programmes.

Chapter

9

"We can't use the word 'happy'," said the client, "I just don't think we could ever convincingly claim we could make our people happy. It's not a definite thing, is it? It's nice and all, but people don't come to work to be happy, do they?" It was all I could do to hold back from telling that client to stick their project, then walk out. Shopping is fun, being happy is nice – these things do go together.

How to get people to give a damn

In this chapter we explore

- how happy teams improve customer experiences
- the five elements of motivation and how they apply to retail people
- why team meetings aren't optional.

Happy teams, happy customers

The principles of this chapter apply to the whole business, but are especially useful should you find yourself managing in the field. They are all about your opportunities to persuade people to want to get out of bed and turn up for work.

Motivated staff are critical to great customer experiences. It really is people who make all the difference. We've already looked at employment experience and store cultures (the vision and values stuff) so now we're going to get a bit deeper into the nitty gritty of motivation. In particular, I'd like to suggest some practical things you can do to improve the motivation of your retail teams. This chapter is a combination of research and observation of the best retailers and their teams.

The components of motivation

Individuals are motivated by a combination of:

- financial reward
- implied sanction

- self-respect
- non-financial reward
- recognition of value contributed.

The importance of each motivating component will be different for different people. Factors such as age, personal circumstances and social considerations all have an impact. Most of these differences, with one exception, need only subtle changes in your approach. The big variance is among the younger members of your team who are often disproportionately motivated by cash. You might think that everyone is but, over the next few pages, I'll show you why that's not quite true.

Show me the money – financial reward

A common mistake we all make on motivation is to assume that financial rewards are the most important and most motivating thing we can offer. The truth is – and this might be hard to accept because it is counter-intuitive – that money has very little motivating effect beyond a certain point. So long as the wage is fair, anything over that, such as special bonuses or massive cash competitions, has very little additional impact on employee motivation. People love getting it, sure, but it can even be counter-productive because the payment of large bonuses tends to condition staff to only ever put in extra effort if they can see a wad of cash in it for themselves. Pay too little, however, and money becomes an astonishingly important demotivator.

Those retailers with the most motivated workforces have observed that offering significant cash rewards in exchange for performance improvements has three negative effects:

- It drives too much focus into short-term revenue generation at the cost of falls in customer service quality.
- It conditions employees to only go beyond the job description when they are offered a cash incentive to do so.
- Bonuses become absorbed quickly into the employee's general budgets and, as such, are not remembered over the longer term, thus losing motivational impact.

There is so much credible research that proves that cash triggers only very short-term satisfaction in the mind of the recipient. It boils down to cash being, by its nature, ephemeral – here today and gone tomorrow. I know you probably still don't believe me, but this effect has now been observed time and time again. Money is important, but it doesn't create long-term motivation. You might need just to trust me on this one.

Incidentally, you can measure employee motivation by looking at factors such as employee satisfaction, employee turnover rates and customer service quality scores.

The stick to your carrot – implied sanction

Implied sanction is the stick to your reward carrot. It is the rule-book. It's "implied" because you may never have to use it, but the team knows you would, if pressed. It is "sanction" because it's what happens when the list of minimum standards is not met. Implied sanction is a strong motivating factor, but one that requires significant skill to manage effectively. It takes a lot of common sense too, and certainly sympathy with the concept of treating others how you would like them to treat you.

A sales assistant, for example, needs to know that a drop in customer satisfaction will lead to a serious chat. Furthermore, they must know that the serious chat will generate a set of actions that, if not carried out, will cast serious doubt over their future in the team. That's the sanction part.

The team needs to know that sanction is possible, but, at the same time, they must not be working in an atmosphere of paralysing dread of that sanction. It's a tricky balancing act sometimes but much better than the alternative, which is to manage by fear. Management by fear generates lots of problems, such as decreases in service quality. Frightened staff don't work well with customers. Fear can also lead to increased employee turnover and even industrial disputes.

In the 1980s, hard-bastard macho managers dominated retail management. Fear was a powerful motivator then because unemployment hung over pretty much everyone all of the time, especially in Europe. Times have changed and there have been retail vacancies going unfilled in the UK for some years now. Management by fear is a poor technique but we must recognise that we're all human. A lack of sanction for those times when we let standards slip lets us become lazy. To motivate, you must ensure that the team knows you have set standards for a good reason and that you will maintain those standards vigorously.

Treat me like a grown-up – self-respect

The default position for the majority of workers is to do the best job we can. If you create the right conditions, most people will work hard to deliver a good result. What stands behind that reality is self-respect. I've already talked about how the best teams are built on respect, and self-respect is a crucial component of that. It's what makes people feel like it's worth making the effort.

The opposite is also true: put individuals into situations where they are robbed of their self-respect and they will react accordingly. People will steal and treat customers with contempt, and why not? If you take away a person's self-respect, how can you ever expect that person to, in turn, respect your customers?

Without wishing to get horribly political, I'd like to ask you to take a look at what poverty and unemployment do to communities. Take away jobs, put people in shoddy housing they don't own or ever could, then crime, drugs and malcontent flourish. The truth is that, if I don't respect myself, I'm not going to respect you. You can do such a lot as a retail leader to encourage self-respect to grow among the members of your teams.

Here are some of the things you can do to foster a respect culture.

- **Share information:** tell the team the confidential stuff such as the state of the cash flow, company health, costs, losses and profits. Show that you trust them with such sensitive numbers. Some of it will find its way to your competitors, but the losses will be vastly outweighed by the benefits.

- **Delegate power:** allow team members to make decisions for themselves, especially on customer-facing issues such as discounts and resolving service issues. Give people the confidence to make these decisions by ensuring that you have a good set of practical and sensible guidelines in place. Good procedures help people to make good decisions. I've seen the provision of customer-delight budgets doing powerful good work when placed in the hands of people on the earliest rungs of the retail ladder.

- **Delegate responsibility:** in stores, make members of the team responsible for the performance of specific departments. Responsibility is a powerful source of self-respect, especially when combined with a variable such as profitability or sales revenue. In service centres, make individuals and small teams responsible for the satisfaction of their customers.

- **Encourage training:** make sure everyone who wants it has access to all the training opportunities available. Do so from the part-time shop floor assistant to the most senior directors. Make a habit of promoting manufacturer-sponsored training and seminars too. These are often of a high quality and they make a welcome break from the usual company formats. Make sure directors and heads go on this training too – they will sulk and moan about the value of their time, but hands on the product, while in the company of colleagues responsible directly for selling it, is insanely valuable. You are saying to the team members who go on these courses: "I value you and I want to give you access to skills you'll find useful."

- **Share the good jobs:** make members of the team responsible for specific tasks, especially those "cushy" jobs managers often keep for themselves.

- **Muck in:** if you expect the team to polish and dust, do it yourself too. Show that it is not a job that's beneath you. Get out of head office and work in stores, call centres and distribution often – you will learn more here than in a week of consultant meetings and the people around you in those places will respect you more.

- **Listen to both sides:** when a customer complains, listen to both sides of the issue. If this is happening on the shop floor, don't blame the salesperson in front of the customer. You are responsible for service quality, so you make the apology. Then go and talk with the salesperson and, if there really is an issue, give them an opportunity to suggest ways in which to solve it.

- **Don't wash your dirty linen in public (even if you run a dry cleaner's):** never embarrass or dress-down a colleague in public. I once observed a frustrated manager in Sainsbury's having a go at a cleaner in front of customers. This cleaner *had* been skiving, but that didn't matter, the manager ended up looking like a bully. That reflected badly on the shop.

- **Consider the rulebook:** is there anything really daft in the rulebook that just forces people to do stupid things? If there is, then get rid of it.

- **Let others do the talking:** give everybody who wants to a chance to run team meetings. Encourage staff to present ideas at these meetings too. Go with the three-slide rule to prevent meetings becoming too competitive or boring: one to set up the "what it is", one to explain the "how it is" and a final slide to summarise "why it is".

- **Listen:** shut up and listen to what people are telling you before you go making up your mind. Ask questions and allow people to give you the whole story. People respond better when they feel they are being listened to.

- **Encourage every opportunity for feedback:** get and give feedback on ideas, interviews, worries, suggestions and concerns. Do this in an honest, active way. Take things on board. If the answer to an idea or issue is yes, then get on and do it. If the answer is don't know, go and find out what you need to know. If the answer is no, explain why. Offering a shrug and a "because it just is" is never acceptable. Always do these things within a short time frame. Anglo-French giant Kingfisher encourages a French employment tradition that it finds incredibly useful, which is to bring in new employees after three months and encourage them to give honest feedback – what doesn't work, what do they miss from their previous employer's culture, what do they feel is underrated?

- **Build people back up:** if you ever have to pull somebody up, discipline them or criticise their performance, then always build that person back up again afterwards. Leave people on a high. If, instead, you send them back into the fray feeling rubbish about themselves, that will show. Let them know that you believe they can fix whatever is under discussion, and that is the basis for making an effort to discuss it.

- **Don't badmouth people:** every time you say "So and so is an idiot" in front of your team, you send a negative message about your attitude to colleagues. Negative talk infects your team – just don't do it!

- **Recognise contribution:** learn to give specific praise as well as specific criticism. This is really very hard to do at first but is the most powerful motivating force of them all. Recognition is free and makes a real difference. By giving recognition you are giving person X a reason to feel that getting out of bed and coming to work today was worth it. The keys to recognition are to be specific, to do it as soon as you think about it, and to do it little and often.

- **Celebrate success:** absolutely essential to the strength of the team is making time, and plenty of it, to celebrate success. I don't mean the embarrassing forced stuff such as ringing a bell every time somebody makes a sale. Celebrating success means saying "Well done" to people. It means making a small fuss of good things in the daily team meetings. It means going off for a pizza or a beer together. Toasting a hard-won target feels great. It feels even better if you've talked one of your suppliers into paying for the beer. People need to know that the effort they've put into achieving something had a point to it. Celebrating success is one critical way in which you can do that. It says: "I'm proud of us, we took on a challenge and we beat it together." I cannot stress enough that you will gain many times more benefit from putting aside a proper budget for doing this.

- **Be ready to admit your own mistakes:** if you get it wrong, be honest about it and move on: "Okay, I got this wrong, now how can you help me to do this right next time?"

- **Put the customer at the centre:** show your people that you respect them by showing them that you're all working together for the same boss: the customer (because it really is the customer that we work for). They are the ones who pay our wages. Teams need to have focus and in retail the customer is the best target for that focus. Everything you do must be built around the notion of helping customers to love buying from you.

The fun that is non-financial rewards

"Non-financial rewards" is just a name for the fun stuff. They can include all sorts of things such as extra days off, flash cars for a month, long-term product loans, gift vouchers, freebies and holidays. Now there is a really fine line here between exciting and tacky. It's so easy to make rewards embarrassing. Worse, lots of retailers go for the big dramatic holiday-type incentives where only one person can win anything significant. Maybe the best-performing store manager gets to go to Bermuda for a fortnight.

I've often worked with clients, employing thousands of people, who have insisted on running these demotivating incentive structures. They launch huge incentive programmes worth big money but concentrated into maybe only five major prizes. Fantastic for the lucky five but really all this succeeds in doing is turning off the thousands who are pretty sure they won't win. Worse, out of the 200 who think they are in with a chance, 195 high-achievers are left feeling positively demotivated when they don't win that holiday.

When it comes to all motivating rewards, including cash bonuses, recognition and non-cash bonuses, little and often is best. In this case little because that means you can spread the budget much further and, in doing so, touch far more people. Often because it keeps things fresh and gives you lots of opportunities to boost performance without incentive programmes going stale.

It's how you use the little non-financial rewards that is critical. If you are an owner of an independent store or site or a chain-store manager you have lots of freedom to do what you think will work best. Buddy-up with the manufacturer's reps. Let them do some training at your site one evening and suggest they give the expense account a workout by taking the team for a curry afterwards. I'm always pleasantly pleased by how consistent manufacturers' reps are in this regard. They always agree to it eventually. If you're an owner you should be doing these things anyway, out of your own pocket. Incidentally, building in an ideas session before you eat is a good way of recouping the cost.

Don't overdo it

The wrong way to use non-cash rewards is to over-hype the reward or to use inappropriate rewards. So, for example, offering to give someone a £10 Burger King voucher for doing 200% of their target is an insult to you both. Wrong too would be to make a shy person stand on a chair to receive a commemorative "Top Person" plaque. Use your best judgement and knowledge of the individual – what works for one might well turn off another.

Buy the team a daft gift each at Christmas but hand-write a thank-you note on each package, or at least get each section head to do so. It reminds people that they are important to you. Always generously mark people's birthdays, weddings and new babies. Preferably do so out of your own pocket rather than via a staff whip-round.

Try to include your employee's partners on social invites. Partners have a massive influence on your people and on their view of you. A career in retail features strange and challenging hours that take people away from their families. Don't make that worse by extending this exclusion to the team's social occasions. Getting partners involved in idea generation can be very effective too.

In-store dodges

If you are running a store, a good tip is to save any freebies you receive as a manager and pass them on to the team rather than keep them for yourself. Some managers save up these goodies to use in one go. Others dish them out straightaway. Either way, you must ensure that you don't fall into either of the following traps:

- Only ever giving stuff to the loudest members of the team because they are the ones you notice.

- Showing favouritism to a person who the team could, conceivably, suspect you of having more than a professional interest in.

Here are two ways of avoiding these freebie pitfalls and at the same time bringing some fun to the proceedings.

Team ballot

Say you've been lucky enough to find yourself with four bottles of champagne, two boxes of Belgian chocolates and a stack of good promotional T-shirts. Over a week, you have the team agree to nominate a colleague each for a thank you. All they have to do is write down the other person's name and a line on why they should be thanked. The key to participation is that anyone who doesn't make a nomination is disqualified from winning a prize themselves.

Then you all pile down to the pub after close-of-play one evening. Get a round in, then read out the thank-you notes. Everyone who has been nominated gets to choose a random envelope. Try to make sure that everyone who should have been nominated *has* been nominated. Inside each envelope is a note telling them which of the freebies they've earned.

This is effective because the team sees that you could have held on to all the stuff yourself but preferred them to have it. People love that, they really do. This works all the way up the chain too. If you are the CEO and you choose to send the office junior to Ascot on your bank jolly, that sends a powerful message. Asking people to select worthy recipients gets people focused on their place in the team too. Team ballots are not heavy affairs but they really do work – aim to run one every six months or every quarter at a push.

Balloon day

This method of giving away all your freebies can be hilarious, great fun, nicely competitive and very motivating. I write about it here from a store perspective but it's easy to imagine how you could make this work in a call centre or order fulfilment team. On one of your busiest days, you fill your office with balloons. Each balloon contains confetti and a little envelope that has the name of a prize in it. To spice things up a little, I usually chuck in some envelopes with fivers in them and some with a token for something silly like a chocolate bar. Then you draw up a big chart with the names of all your team on it.

Now you need to set a challenge. Challenges can include such things as to sell a specific item or to gain an "excellent" score on a customer service questionnaire (do this as an exit survey, having someone stand at the door with a clipboard gathering answers).

Selling add-ons, scoring a point for every transaction that includes a legitimate add-on ("legitimate" meaning the add-on was actually something that the customer will have been glad to have been sold).

Each time a person completes a unit of the challenge they earn a "pop".

You can also award random "free pops" to members of the team, especially to anyone who isn't actively involved in selling. Do this whenever you observe a positive behaviour. Those positive behaviours could include such things as solving a customer complaint or helping out a colleague. Each time a person earns a "pop", they get a token. These tokens are sticky and you can encourage people to stick them on the poster as the day goes on.

At the end of the day, after the punters have gone home, everyone gathers outside your office. Maybe you open some refreshments to help get the team revved up for the popping to commence. Starting with the person who has earned most "pops" you let each person into the room to pop the number of balloons they've earned during the day. Then they get to keep whatever falls out of the balloons.

I've run this one many times and it always gets everybody going. It's nice too if you can make the balloon day coincide with a team night out afterwards too. There are lots of variations on this theme such as having the prizes in lockers or in a sandbox and so on. I'm sure you can think up some yourselves too.

I've probably lost all my consultant credibility for talking about balloon days. You probably think it's all a bit beneath us as professionals but it isn't, this stuff makes good things happen.

Recognition and motivation

Each of the motivating factors we've gone through does in itself also have a recognition component. Giving out prizes is recognition, trusting somebody to make decisions is recognition and bonuses are also a form of recognition.

Team meetings

You have seen how important communication, team-building, recognition, respect and trust are. One of the most useful opportunities to make things happen in these areas is your daily team meeting. I did say "daily" team meeting.

I recommend you hold a 5 to 15-minute team meeting every single day. You don't have to do this but all the best retailers do. It's hard to build a team spirit if the team never gets to stop to spend a few minutes focusing together. Equally, what better way is there to swap ideas, jump on to opportunities and share responsibilities?

Although all management levels should do daily team meetings, they are critical in stores and often the missing ingredient in many an otherwise great store manager's repertoire. If you are a store manager or owner, grab your store diary now and write five headings into tomorrow's date and run a meeting around those five things. Some of the items worth covering in team meetings include:

- customer service issues and how these were solved
- forthcoming events
- promotions
- new products just in
- bargains identified
- review competitor activity
- review new best-practice ideas identified
- discuss incentive schemes
- review any challenges
- introduce new employees
- review targets and performance
- celebrate success
- recognition
- consider improvement ideas – even if you can only do this one it will have been worth having the meeting.

Please do this daily. I don't mean to nag and I know shifts and part-timers and such mean you'll need to juggle a bit but the effect is hugely positive. You're a leader and you can only be that if you set down plans, review those plans and keep everyone bang up to date with what's going on and what's expected of them.

Now
Things you can do now

- Consider honestly how you personally use the five motivation components in your management style. Where are you strong? Where are you weak? How does your style filter through your management team?

- Review the list of actions under motivation and create a plan that ensures all of these are regular and normal occurrences.
- Run a team ballot or balloon day.
- Introduce daily team meetings throughout the business.

Next
Strategic considerations for the longer term

- Benchmark remuneration, reward and bonuses versus best practice. Do this with the strategic goal to improve customer satisfaction. Container Store would be a very good place to start.

Chapter 10

What's the point in doing things the same way time after time? Variety is not only the spice of life but trying different ways to solve the same problem eventually leads you to better solutions.

A little better every time

In this chapter we explore

- the value of small-increment change
- gathering ideas for improvement
- inherent risks of measurement
- improvement opportunity lists
- A/B testing.

Do we have any idea?

Ideas are the fuel for organisations. What you do with those ideas, and how you convert them into action and improvements, is what then makes the organisation grow and prosper. Space for improvement can be readily found in all areas, especially in technique, systems, presentation, recruitment and performance. All retailers can benefit from a culture of everyday performance improvement but few try to. Don Taylor and Jeanne Smalling Archer, authors of the very helpful *Up Against the Wal-Marts* call this *"kaizen"*, as does Julian Richer in his awesome book *The Richer Way*. Others use different names for the same thing. *Kaizen* is Japanese for "continuous improvement involving everyone" and is a pretty good summation of the challenge.

Improvement in this sense isn't necessarily about massive earth-shattering changes. What we are looking for are those everyday improvements: improvements in the ways in which we look after each other, our relationships with customers and the quality and relevance of our processes. A typical example might be the discovery that one piece of paperwork can be integrated with some other process rather than dealt with separately. Combining the two will save money and time – so that's an improvement. It could be the realisation that the rules of a promotion we've created can be simplified to the benefit of the customer, and that is an improvement too.

Gathering improvement ideas

You will need to have two things in place:

- a way to gather ideas
- an improvements slot on the agenda for discussion at team meetings.

If you were to look at just 1 task or process in each daily team meeting, you will have 7 improvements each week, 30 for the month and 365 over a year. That's awesome. Okay, so maybe you won't get into this every day but you will still generate a significant store of improvement ideas every month. Working in this way is easy. You are not attempting to change the world in a day, you are just looking to change one little thing at a time.

Do you currently change anything each month? Does change only ever happen dramatically once a year? Doing it a little better every time puts you in the driving seat of change. Your team becomes a valuable engine of change.

Statistics can make you go blind – the measurement trap

Plenty of otherwise sensible people believe that you cannot improve that which you cannot measure. That's dangerous, wrong even, and here's why: some of the most effective customer satisfaction-improving tools are unmeasurable in a conventional sense. Smiling at a customer turns out to be one of the most effective ways to make them feel better about you and your company. How do you measure the number of smiles your team gives out?

Here's something to think about. A number of aspects of sexual performance can be measured. Factors such as duration, the dimensions of various body parts, room temperature, heart beats per minute can all be easily recorded and measured (you might need somebody with a clipboard to come in and write this stuff down for you, though). But do any of these factors automatically add up to guaranteed great sex? Of course not, as there is a deeper set of emotional, compatibility elements, a sprinkle of chemistry and magic even.

Measuring the wrong things is a real trap. This is a grim example but it's worth telling. A US Army general noticed that the daily success of the Vietnam War was being measured by relative casualty rates. A measure as crude and unpleasant as "if we kill more of them than they do of us, then we must be winning". Convinced this measure did not convey a useful picture, this general, instead, created a set of metrics that, also took into account territory, specific objectives, political and economic cost.

It is what the general said about his reasons for doing this that is absolutely relevant to retailing. He said: "We are only making important that which we can easily measure when instead we should be measuring only that which is important." Just because you can measure unit sales easily, for example, does not make that the most important part of your business to concentrate your improvement efforts in. Customer satisfaction is harder to measure but far more important because it relates to unit sales made today, tomorrow and next year.

Coca-Cola
Missing the wider story

In the early 1980s, the Coca-Cola Company had become incredibly twitchy about the strengthening performance of Pepsi, its nearest rival. Pepsi had made big strides into Coke's market and one stat, in particular, had the execs at Coke sweating. In 1972, 18% of drinkers said they drank Coke exclusively against just 4% choosing Pepsi. By the start of the 1980s, this ratio had moved to 12% favouring Coke exclusively and 11% Pepsi.

And that's when Pepsi pulled its genius move and unleashed "The Pepsi Challenge". Pepsi targeted committed Coke drinkers and presented them with two small cups of cola, one marked "Q" and one marked "M". Almost without fail, drinkers

▶

would take a sip and choose "M", which would, of course, then be revealed as Pepsi.

Initially, the team at Coke attempted to claim that Pepsi's campaign was fixed. But when they then ran similar experiments themselves, they discovered a 53% to 47% split in favour of Pepsi. For the market leader, this was a bombshell – the impact of a six percentage point spread could be measured in millions of dollars in potential lost revenue.

The team were horrified and commissioned a slew of additional market research projects. Each came back with similar results and attempts to qualify the choice for Pepsi began to suggest that Americans had fallen out of love with Coke's distinct "bite". What was once described as "refreshing" became "harsh". The same tasters began to associate words like "smooth" and "rounded" with Pepsi and went on to suggest they preferred these attributes.

Roy Stout was the head of Coke's consumer marketing research team and is the man who made the connection between losing market share and product taste. He reasoned: "If we have twice as many vending machines, have more shelf space, spend more on advertising, and are competitively priced, why are we losing [market share]? You look at the Pepsi Challenge and you have to begin asking about taste."

This bombshell drove the board at Coke to make an extraordinary decision. It would change the hitherto sacred and world-famous secret Coke recipe to take account of the perceived change in America's cola preferences. And thus was born "New Coke", which had a lighter and sweeter taste, a taste more like Pepsi, in fact.

Early test results were good. New Coke pulled level with Pepsi on blind tasting preferences. A little more tinkering followed and New Coke began to pull out a persistent 6 to 8% lead. The board then took the decision to take it to market and launched a massive campaign behind the new formula.

All the research said New Coke would be a winner.

It failed and failed dramatically. Tens of thousands of Coke drinkers rose up in protest, sales of the new drink faltered and, cutting a long story short, the company was forced into a humiliating climbdown and reintroduced the original formula as Classic Coke. Very shortly afterwards, sales of New Coke all but evaporated.

Why? The flaw was, in hindsight, a very simple one. Coke has a predominantly citrusy-burst flavour whereas Pepsi has a more raisiny-vanilla taste. Take one or two sips of Coke and the experience is quite sharp, the bite is very strong. Do the same with a can of Pepsi and the first gulps are much smoother, sweeter and gentler on the palate.

But drink a whole can of either cola and the experience changes completely. And this is the flaw – Coke drinkers like the way a can of coke tastes but they don't entirely like the first few sips. Coke drinkers who prefer the first sips of Pepsi when tested blind often complain of a cloying sweetness when they then go on to drink the whole can.

New Coke is a fantastic example of an entire company both putting too much emphasis on the research and ignoring instinct and emotion. So what were the real reasons for Coke's slipping market share?

Consensus of opinion is that Coke had allowed its marketing spend to mature along with the product. It had failed to sell to the younger, hipper cola drinkers Pepsi had become so adept at communicating with. Coke's customers were leaching away to a preference for coffee and later bottled waters whereas Pepsi's were still enjoying rotting their teeth on "The Choice of a New Generation".

I'm not entirely discrediting management by numbers but stories like this one go a long way to proving that without the emotional context you don't have the full story.

Some specific statistics and background information here are sourced from the version of this case study related in Blink *by Malcolm Gladwell.*

Go with your gut feel

Use your gut feel and allow yourself to apply improvements, even to those processes, tasks and interactions to which you are unable to attach numbers. I'd like to ask you to consider valuing the power of your gut feel more highly. Gut feel isn't random. It's a guide, an instinct that tells you a certain path may be the right one to take. It is also that good sense that tells you not to do something. But it needs tuning. Books like this one exist to help you separate out correct gut feel judgements from other emotional factors such as fear or laziness.

Behavioural science is now beginning to come round to seeing gut feel as something real and valuable. There is a lot of credible recent research that suggests decisions made on gut feel are more often than not the carefully calculated result of our experience and knowledge and that instinctive gut feel decisions get better as we add new experiences and knowledge to our memories. Think of your gut feel as a potent business weapon, a weapon that is unique to you.

Again, it's worth reading Daniel Kahneman's *Thinking Fast and Slow* for more insight into this process.

Making improvement work for you

Let's do it a little better every time. As well as running through ways to apply this idea at team meetings, you will need to create an environment in which the team feels comfortable to try things and suggest things. If you are the kind of person who greets every new idea with "I'd love to change that but..." or "I can't see that working", then soon people will stop trying and suggesting. Equally, if members of the team feel that you are likely to discipline them for making mistakes, then no one is going to want to try anything new for fear of punishment.

Get the culture of improvement established. Allow your people to question how they do things and you will benefit enormously. Make that an everyday occurrence: little steps but lots of them, and you and your customers will feel those improvements take hold.

Room for improvement

The best retailers do not stand still when successful. They strive to keep the momentum, keep growing and keep moving forward. That growth and movement is inspired by tiny little everyday improvements just as much as it is by sweeping change.

Here are some of the categories in which you will always be able to find lots of opportunities to improve things. The

thoughts listed here are a deliberate mix of actual ideas and of pointers to get you looking in the right places for ideas of your own.

You might like to pick out a single line during daily team meetings and have the team come up with some thoughts and ideas on that theme.

Improvement and customers

- Consider everything from the customer's perspective.
- Encourage customers to tell you their complaints (the most cost-effective research you'll ever do).
- And listen to them sincerely when they do.
- Think about the type of people who use your app, visit your store or shop your site – who are you missing?
- What do customers prefer about your competitors (ask them)?
- Talk to customers all the time (ask staff to tell you one thing at each meeting that they've heard from a customer).
- Aim to improve average transaction values.
- Use eye contact more and look for opportunities to do the equivalent in virtual spaces.
- Regularly walk your site and store like a customer would.
- Get hold of former customers and ask them why they don't love you any more.
- Use social media to communicate with customers as it's cheap, powerful and very direct.
- Whenever you are resolving a customer complaint, ask customers how they would improve your service.
- Remember names.
- Think carefully about the integrity of your pricing.
- Send customers stuff they might actually like to see.
- Where can you add value to the customer experience?
- What can you promise today that is better than yesterday?
- Run surveys.
- List for yourselves the benefits of doing business with you and then tell customers about these benefits.

- What do other people do well that you really ought to be ripping off for yourselves?
- List all the things in your business that regularly delight customers, then think about how to double the list.
- Are you leading by example?
- Write down a list of all the processes that touch customers directly – all of them.
- Then do a list of all those that don't – can you strip any of these out?
- Make it easy for customers to give you feedback – use the internet, suggestion boxes, till receipt surveys, telephone aftercare calls, open evenings, and everything else you can think of.
- Get customer opinion on new products before you put those products into your range.
- Ask customers to tell you what's missing.
- Ask customers to tell you what they like about your store.

Improvement and you

- Read stuff.
- Get involved in the business community – if you are an owner or manager, join your street or shopping centre advisory committee or the Chamber of Commerce.
- Talk to your business neighbours.
- Ask people about your management style (and listen openly when they tell you).
- Learn from those below you as well as above you.
- Seek out examples of great retailers and learn from them.
- Sign up to every internet resource you can find. There are loads of great retail Twitter feeds; for example, mine is @TheseRetailDays. Have a look at who I follow and you might find some of those useful to follow too.
- Get a subscription to *Retail Week* and learn to read between the lines (why did so and so make that choice? Why is X thriving? Why is Y on its uppers?).
- What things do you do outside of work that might be useful inside?

- Make an honest list of your strengths.
- Then one of your weaknesses.
- Go on courses.
- Sign up to every training and seminar resource you can, initially, as the more you go on the better you will become at recognising which ones are going to be truly useful in future.
- Naff as it might seem, set life goals and then yearly goals for yourself. What do these goals tell you about the areas in which you will need to concentrate personal improvements?
- Listen to people more than talk to people.
- Open your eyes!
- Go shopping more often – do things your customers do.
- Read the trade press.
- Learn from competitors.
- Learn from people outside your sector.
- Maintain your standards.
- Get rid of the "yes" people and surround yourself with people who challenge and inspire you.
- If you are in-store, appoint an honest and strong assistant manager as they will soon let you know where you have room for improvement.
- Improve the balance of your life: you look after shops, shopping is fun, try to see it more that way.

Improvement and colleagues

- Reward people for improving things.
- Consider issues from your team's perspective.
- Don't get mad with people for trying.
- Let grown-ups think for themselves – empower people to make their own improvements.
- Encourage talk, talk and more talk – leave every feedback channel open all the time.
- Give people a look at these lists.
- Buy employees a copy of *Smart Retail* for Christmas – remember to wrap it up nicely, in fact, get your dad a copy too, and all your friends.

- Recognise people's contributions.
- Don't rip off your staff, especially in the UK as the National Living Wage takes effect.
- Never criticise employees in front of anyone else.
- Build a great culture founded on trust and respect.
- Tell people you are chuffed with them whenever they make you feel that way.
- Are your job descriptions jargon-filled nonsense? Rewrite them all in human language.
- Build friendships but never forget that you are the boss – keep a perspective.
- Encourage the team to be open about their mistakes.
- Have a laugh together.
- Always, always celebrate success.
- Be human in your relationships – if someone is going through a life crisis, help them cope with it.
- Share the numbers – let the team own them as much as you do.
- Pay a profit-related bonus.
- Pay a customer service-related bonus.
- Smile when you walk through the door every morning, even if you don't feel like it.
- Make sure everyone knows about all available courses and seminars.
- Put aside cash for training.
- Let good people go on courses you've been on – use training as a reward.
- Be specific with instructions.
- Sales assistants, social media monitors and call centre staff get closest to your customers – listen to what they tell you about those customers.
- Challenge people and encourage them to challenge themselves.
- Teach by example.
- Show people that the best way to do things is to consider solutions rather than dwell on problems.
- Get the team involved in all the big decisions.

- Help employees to see that it is customers, not you, who pay their wages.

- Hold regular one-to-one appraisals but be prepared to allow employees to tell you what they think of you, of your business and of the team too.

- Have a team meeting every single day – just 15 minutes' worth, but make those minutes count.

A/B testing

We are still in the early Wild West days of selling online. Nobody really knows all of the rules. Not even Amazon would make that claim. More than that, Amazon is never satisfied that it has all the answers, that it is the only one doing everything right – quite the opposite, in fact. Amazon makes extensive use of a technique called A/B testing and you should too.

At its simplest, A/B testing is a method for testing a variation on a current webpage, so customer X might see the usual A version but customer Y might see the B version. More dynamic versions of the tool may constantly offer even the same customer subtly different versions of the page as well as doing so across customers, types, territories and whatever other grouping metrics are useful. In both cases, you can quickly see if changing elements of the page change customer behaviours.

Things to test can be as small as the size of a specific button, to as big as a full redesign and all points in between. If yours is a large business, then your IT team will, almost certainly, be on top of this tool but, even if you are smaller, or even a one-off, then A/B testing is still available cost-effectively for you too. There are loads of third-party consultants and some platforms even build it in. Explore your options and get testing.

Online taken off

Even in physical stores, you can operate a version of A/B testing and this isn't done often enough. Take an area such as the entranceway and play with versions of it across small numbers of stores. Test variation A across three stores versus three similar B control stores. Then swap back to the original in the test stores and put variation A into the three control stores. Measure footfall, conversion and ATV. You should be testing small variations such as these pretty much all the time and then rolling the learning into the wider estate. To make this easier, make sure your shopfitters and retail designers have considered modular fixtures in their format development. Modular means you can play with combinations at low cost and low risk.

A/B testing golden rule

There is one golden rule, and it should be obvious: A/B testing only works if you test just one change at a time. If your variation includes more than one difference, how will you know which one of those worked? Or worse, one might have worked but the others failed but you would only see the failure. So one change in colour on a page, one variation of a click box, one change of message. Online you can simultaneously test lots of those separately of course: 10,000 visitors, 2,000 see the original, 2,000 see variation one, 2,000 see variation two, etc.

Interpreting what constitutes one change in a physical environment can be trickier. Is one bit of POS enough of a change to test? Does it mean a whole display? I tend to believe in physical spaces; one family change counts as one thing: swapping all of one type of POS to a different colour or changing one display unit.

Now
Things you can do now

- Put improvement on the team meeting agenda.
- Review the lists for improvement. Select five items to tackle this month. Identify all the other items you feel could or should be tackled this year.

Next
Strategic considerations for the longer term

- Review your major KPIs within your performance management environment and check that they line up with improving outcomes for customers.
- Find five candidates for A/B testing.

Chapter

11

Customer service is talked about as if it's something that
is added value; it isn't, it is the basic currency
of the new retail landscape.

Love shopping!

In this chapter we explore

- where great customer service comes from
- the four rules of performance improvement
- why driving up average transaction values is your best improvement strategy.

We love shopping here!

Give customers the best possible experience whenever they buy from you, be that in-store or online – that's how you'll make more money.

There – the most blindingly obvious sentence in the whole book. Of course, such things as cost control, the basics of margin and pricing have to be right too but the starting point for everything we do in retail is the customer, how they feel about us, what they want from our stores and how we meet those needs. Sending customers out of your stores, or away from your sites, with a big smile on their faces, a smile that lasts through getting their new stuff home and using it, is your absolute priority. So, how do we paste that smile on their happy chops?

Happy customers: happy tills

Great customer service

I often talk about how customer service isn't an add-on activity and that great service quality comes from everything you do as a retailer. That word "experience" is important here: great customer service is made up of lots of individual customer experiences and

I much prefer using the word "experience" rather than "service". It's not a daft nod towards consultant blether. I reckon it's easier to understand how to improve things if you think at the individual level: what can I do for each individual customer? How can I make their specific experience of my business a great one? But when you talk about service, it feels like a nebulous thing. It's general and non-specific.

First and foremost, it's worth talking about why most initiatives focused on service quality fail. Sometimes, a marketing team will take a look at their list of "things to do" and one of the bullet points will read "Make customers love us again" and they'll commission an agency to come in and create some sort of "service event" for staff. They'll then have jolly good fun taking this event around the business and into the store estate and they'll say to people, "We order you, albeit in a nice way, to smile at customers and be their friends and love them so they will love us."

And these one-off initiatives do often deliver big early uplifts in customer satisfaction, but then those gains die off, usually quickly, and, before long, everything returns to normal. That's because the focus always moves on. No matter how committed a retailer is to raising customer service quality, there is always another issue waiting in the wings to occupy the minds of management and teams.

Permanent improvements in standards of customer care have to be earned from the ground up – you can't change things by layering initiatives on to unstable foundations. Building from the ground up is harder work but, ultimately, more satisfying because gains become self-sustaining and permanent. Dieting is a good analogy. Crash-dieting creates instant weight loss but almost always results in a net weight gain once the focus slips. Changing eating behaviours, seeking support, changing attitudes to food and learning about nutrition means slower weight loss but, for most, permanent and self-sustaining success.

"Self-sustaining" is the key phrase. A successful assault on changing the behaviours and relationships that lead employees to *want* to deliver great customer experiences becomes a positive viral thing. Changes feel good, staff get more from their employment experience and customers get more from shopping the business. Even better, these changes reinforce each other in a virtuous circle:

Happier staff → better customer experience → happier customers → better interaction with staff → happier staff . . . and round and round

Better still, that loop delivers gains in revenue and profit and draws in improvements in employee retention and contributes to reductions in employment costs. It is an absolute win-win.

Do what?

Here's a bunch of things you can do to make sure that you and your team are delivering great customer experiences and that you send your customers away delighted. These thoughts must be taken in the context of the seven secrets of retail. There is a huge amount there that sets the service experience context. They are the basics of creating great experiences.

- **Employee satisfaction:** I've probably gone on a bit about this, but it's worth saying again: put into practice the stuff in the "Team" section of this book. The most effective way to ensure your team are delivering better experiences is to improve the satisfaction of your staff. Having a reward and bonus programme based around customer satisfaction scores can be really effective too. It helps your team to make a direct link between how they look after customers and what goes into their own pockets.

- **Simplify:** be simple and straightforward for customers. Make promotions easy to understand and simple to redeem. Use plain language in your advertising and communications and be clear about what you can and can't do. Set up as something recognisably positive and then be that.

- **Deliver on the promise of your Big Idea:** whatever that Big Idea is, it is also a promise to your customers that you will be what you say you are. If a customer is coming to your business expecting you to be X, then make sure that you really are X and keep looking out for all those things you could be doing that serve to support and emphasise that.

- **Meet the fundamental discovery need:** all shopping is about discovery, so help your customers to make those great discoveries. Surprise, delight, inspire and wow them. Be proud of your stock, make heroes out of the amazing and brilliant and, above all, make sure your people are knowledgeable, that they, themselves, have access to your product and that they are open-minded enough to listen to customers' real needs and then to find great ways to meet those. Celebrating the hero products applies just as much online as in-store, so make sure your web store is full of accessible ways in, dotted with stand-out products, and that it doesn't become an illustrated spreadsheet.

- **Be consistent:** make sure your team are on top every day – make sure you exceed company standards, stay on top of your game. And across the company ensure that the experience is great, in every store, on every site, through your apps and into every order, every time. Easy to say, but consistency is something that appears near the top when researching customer likes.

- **Fix problems directly:** Any one of us could end up on *Watchdog* one day with Anne Robinson's curiously wonky face looming as she tells us that we are the devil incarnate. That's just the way the world is, but we can reduce our chances of this happening by accepting that we will make mistakes sometimes and then by getting on and fixing those problems quickly, fairly and with a smile.

- **Feedback:** making it easy for customers to give feedback to you is critical in improving service quality. If you haven't got a customer complaint process, one that's easy for customers to use, create one. Give customers quality surveys that they can fill in and send back to you. Give them pre-paid envelopes to make it even easier for them to do that. Give out your personal email address and watch for social media mentions. Encourage complaints and think of them as free market research. Some customers *will* rant and rage but at the heart of almost every complaint is a truth that, once learned, will help you make your business better. Oh, and it's far better that customers complain to you, and that you resolve their complaints, than it is for them to complain about you to their friends instead. On social media, where those complaints are public, get in early, be generous and decisive. There are a number of open tools available that aggregate your social media mentions and that can be useful to build a picture of positive/negative sentiment; one good one is www.socialmention.com.

- **Be honest and open:** if you don't know the answer to something, say so and then find out. Be ready to admit your mistakes and involve your team and your customers in fixing things and in improving the business. Have an open mind in all situations. Make sure you set the culture where your people feel safe to follow your lead in admitting mistakes and admitting they need help. Customers will benefit.

- **Don't pay sales commission:** put your people on individual sales commissions and some of them will shark your customers, especially in-store. That's simple, straightforward human nature. The best service organisations pay people bonuses based on customer satisfaction combined with something reflecting overall store profit performance. Or just be a great employer and give your front-line people good salaries. Some of the happiest, most satisfied customers in the USA are customers of the Container Store: "Our salespeople do not work on commission; instead, they're either salaried or paid by the hour with wages far above the retail industry norm. Therefore, they often work together in teams to find that complete solution for the customer, which allows them to spend as much time as necessary to help customers find what they need." That's smart retail right there.

- **Smile and be nice:** okay, I'm not talking the rictus grins of the retail damned, but do try to put your troubles to one side when dealing with your team and your customers. Use the great opportunity you have as a retailer to talk to people, enjoy their company and appreciate the fact that you're not stuck in an office staring at the same ten faces all day every day and fearing your turn on the tea run. Retail is ace like that. For every mean-spirited or rude customer, you'll work with a hundred who are good fun, who are loving spending their money. Shopping is fun – have fun yourself, you old misery.

- **Respect your people and they'll respect your customers:** treat people how you yourself would like to be treated. Be nice, be respectful, give the benefit of the doubt and remember that your people are grown-ups. Treat your team that way and they'll do the same with your customers.

- **Living and breathing it:** Every decision you make must be in the context of will it be good for customers. Every person you hire must be someone you think customers will enjoy being served by and every process, promotion and event you choose must be for the benefit and delight of customers. Delivering great customer experiences is not a bolt-on activity – it is the only activity. Every word in this book is written in the context of great customer service.

The four rules of performance improvement

If we are looking at customer experiences, it is also important to consider why we might be keen to deliver such good ones. It's because we want to take more money. If you don't agree, then you've spent too long listening to new-age consultants who will break your business faster than you can. So we're looking for performance improvements, but where do those actually come from?

There is no secret to performance improvement. The techniques can all be learned. It's about getting the details right and paying attention to the fundamentals, checking you're consistently hitting the right line.

The rules of performance improvement are beautifully simple and there are only four of them:

- Sell to new customers.
- Sell more in each transaction.
- Persuade existing customers to return to your business more often.
- Improve margin by cutting overheads and improving sales quality.

This is another of those "it's not rocket science" moments. The challenge is, of course, in understanding how best to apply each rule. *Smart Retail* deals with those things you can do to produce direct results from applying these rules to your customers. People, site and store issues also have a part to play in the successful application of these rules, but it is what you can do directly for the customer that has the most significant impact.

If I was forced to choose just one of the four rules of performance improvement over all others, the one I would pick is the second one: sell more in each transaction. Driving up average transaction values is all about maximising every opportunity. That in itself is a powerful business improvement philosophy. Making the very best of every customer who clicks on you or walks into your store is your absolute priority.

Transaction values is about maximising every opportunity

All of the tools I've written about in the secrets sections will have an effect on average transaction values, but it's worth pulling a few thoughts out quickly.

People

First and foremost, you must look above the budgets when weighing strategy. So many bricks and mortar retailers cut back on that expensive budget line labelled "Staff" during the 2000s only to discover too late that they had mostly succeeded in eroding the reward part of shopping in stores, just as the internet had arrived to make reward critical for their survival. Without great staff creating great experiences, you very much limit your opportunity to make customers feel that you are worth anything more than a basic spend.

That's the first useful bit of advice in this area: great shopping experiences make customers feel like spending. A customer who trusts you and enjoys shopping with you is much more likely to want to accept your advice when you recommend adding product B to their purchase of product A.

Build the solution

So, great advice is powerful and think about how Container Store is able to find ways to prove to customers that its help leads to better problem-solving. Can your people, not just on the shop floor but on Twitter, Facebook, in the call centre and on the help desk find ways to add value to the shopping process? I bet they can. Container Store sees customers buying an average of 8 items when they talk to a person, versus 1.2 when they self-serve. Remember that Container Store can only do that because it hires great people on higher than normal wages, trains them deeply, treats them like the grown-ups they are, and rewards customer satisfaction and profit rather than sales.

Building the solution means taking a base item and thinking about how that fits with a customer's various need states. Is it something that works best when used, worn or enjoyed with other things in the range? Should staff be talking about accessories that can add to the overall fun, effectiveness and benefit?

Think carefully too about how your sales process or your online merchandising focuses initial customer interest. If it's towards a product from which it is hard to sell up, or hard to add other product to, then you need to reconsider. I was looking recently at a client's sales process that they had centred around a very good core body product but that was just one element of an effective package of cosmetic, scent and lifestyle products. It is finding it hard to add those additional products to a purchase of the core one and, though there are other issues, one issue that jumped out was that the core body product was at least £2 cheaper than all the related products. Though the accepted pitch in that industry is from this core product outwards, either we need to challenge that received wisdom or juggle pricing because convincing a customer that an £8 item is essential and then trying to get a customer to add a £10 one and another £12.50 one is extremely tough psychologically. Those two price points are another band away from the £8 starter.

Adjacencies

Adjacencies then take on massive importance. Getting these right isn't science, it's an art. One of the best places to experience that art in action is IKEA. Every room set places distinct grab-me-now pieces into the space so something spotted in context will then pop up again in the marketplace, reinforcing it in the psyche. Place things together that go together, put low-cost impulse add-ons into piles and on strips alongside their showcased core products.

Pricing

IKEA is an enthusiastic user of round-number pricing. So am I, though William Poundstone disagrees in his otherwise superb book on pricing *Priceless*. I mention Poundstone because his book really is essential reading for retailers, but we disagree on this one thing. He reports on testing that appears to prove the .99 pricing strategy is the right one, but he only looks at experiments with single items. I strongly suspect that our mind is working differently when considering buying more than one thing together. My hypothesis, and feel free to test it for me and then let me lazily claim the credit, is that round-number pricing is simply easier maths and so makes calculating the value/affordability of a purchase an instant process rather than a complex one.

A £7 thing and a £3 thing together are £10. Not only is that an easy number to understand, it is also a unit of money with which we are instantly familiar. Even when we pay electronically, it is incredibly easy to visualise and decide to spend a tenner.

On the other hand, with a thing that is £6.99, the research sort of proves that we see it as costing £6 not £7. But a thing that is £6.99 and a thing that is £2.99 together are a harder calculation. It might take only a half second to come up with £9.98, but to do so requires conscious maths. Worse, £9.98 is abstract where £10 is not: 9.98 is a complex number.

UK music retailer Fopp, ruined by over-extension at the wrong moment, used adjacencies and round-number pricing to drive very healthy average transaction values and an items per basket that was well above two. The store was merchandised in such a way that you almost always ended up spending in blocks: £10 in the form of two £5 CDs, or you might arrive at the till clutching a £7 CD and find there a £3 bargain that was not only a punt but that was an easy £10 block to visualise spending. Good to see Fopp regaining a bit of strength too; it has a new store opening here in Oxford soon.

We all know, for now, what a tenner, a twenty-dollar bill or a ten euro note is and we can easily think in multiples of these. That feels psychologically important to me; let me know your experiences.

Make selection easy by curating choice

Helping customers to find the thing that meets their need states the best is critical and that extends to impulse buys. Don't crowd the tills; pick out a small number of products that are easy to say yes to as an add-on to their main purchase.

A nudge in the right direction

Use calls to action, such as limited availability, when-it's-gone-it's-gone deals, exclusive colour options for a season, and so on. These must be honest deals and they must be of obvious intrinsic value.

Now
Things you can do now

- Review the list of customer service improving things. List all the evidence you can find for these things already happening within the business. Then identify opportunities to spread good practice from one part of the business to another. Look for gaps and consider how these can be addressed.

- List all the measures you are currently taking in each of the four areas of performance improvement.

Next
Strategic considerations for the longer term

- Instigate an average transaction value performance improvement programme – consider the techniques listed here.

- Review all customer service initiatives and programmes either current or recently completed – review each in the light of this chapter. Are or have these programmes contributed to culture change and thus to long-lasting improvement in the customer experience? If the answer is no, consider appointing a specialist team to tackle a ground-up culture change.

Chapter

12

"He knows the price of everything and
the value of nothing."

Price and value

In this chapter we explore

- the triumph of honest pricing

- sources of genuine premium

- the continuing starring role of the bargain.

Options are narrowing

The retail textbooks you might have seen at university talk of a number of different price positioning strategies. In the essential *Retailing an Introduction*, Roger Cox and Paul Brittain offer up choices between cost-oriented pricing, demand-oriented pricing, competition-oriented pricing and a mix of these that they call multi-stage pricing. Each idea is valid and, at one time, each could happily co-exist in the splendid isolation of a hard-to-compare pre-internet world.

But now there is just one pricing strategy that makes any sense and I call it honest pricing. It is a process whereby the pricing reflects friction, reward and value. If a shirt is of the same cotton grade and same stitching quality, is a similar fit and pattern but is twice the price, there must be a good reason for that premium. That good reason has to come from the reward delivered to need states related to the process of buying and owning it. That can come from brand, it can come from all those wonderful marketed elements of the premium experience, but it still has to be committed and honest. A thin veil of premium positioning doesn't hold water any longer. It's the difference between Paul Smith's or Ted Baker's superb retail presence and the growing irrelevance of moment-in-time £30/$40 T-shirt hawking fashion brands that come and go (desperate to name a couple, but prevented from doing so for obvious legal reasons).

At the other end, being cheap is not enough on its own. Friction must be managed too – customers are less inclined to work too hard for a bargain unless that process is either fun (T.K. and T.J. Maxx) or extremely rewarding (Nordstrom Rack, Target). So where poundshops, five and dimes and cheap food stores were once authentically tatty they now must be clean, well merchandised, relevant and where the quality counts (see Aldi, Netto and Lidl for great examples of that last point, especially): a good balance of friction and reward.

I love poundshops. The new wave of British poundshops and value retailers are especially good – Poundland, B&M, The Range, Home Bargains and Guess How Much! are fun and honest, they stock things lots of people like and they offer them without pretention in nicely fitted stores, often with parking and always on easy bus routes. It's another form of honest pricing.

So, honest pricing could be described as the sum of your friction/reward indexing with an acceptable additional margin on top. It's neither cheap nor premium, but it is what is possible as a calculation of variables that may place you at an everyday low price, or at a premium or points in between, but the honest equation rules.

John Lewis' honest pricing

A great example of honest pricing is found at John Lewis where customers would certainly not describe the store as cheap but would say they trust it and they feel the value is good. Partly, John Lewis has achieved that through a price promise that can easily be mistaken for a price positioning that reads "Never knowingly undersold". It's a slogan that has been at the heart of

John Lewis since 1925 and is probably the most famous retailing motto in the UK. What it says is simple: we will try to make sure that we are always selling to you at the fair price. That's about honesty, not going out to source the cheapest example of a given product.

Honest pricing has won – on the internet, showrooming, coming cost-equalisation era. No retailer can afford to hike prices without hiking reward. Customers will not stand for it. There is a place for premium, as we will explore, but that place is found firmly in the context of high levels of customer reward.

Patagonia
Sustainable premium

Patagonia's red-brick Boston store is lovely to look at on the outside and stunning inside. There's history and strength here and I like it very much. But when I first looked at the clothes, I was surprised. At this point, I knew Patagonia only by its reputation for environmentally and sustainably sound clothing for "silent" sports (skiing, hiking, surfing; no motors or crowds) and technical casuals, but these clothes here seemed ordinary to me. Ordinary but pricey. Then I looked at a label and it said "Made in China". Immediately, my prejudices kicked in and I wondered how any apparel made in China could be made sustainably and without cheap labour.

So I took a checked shirt over to a member of staff and asked him about the $80 price tag on a Chinese-made shirt. His patient answer was a credit to the business. He said he understood my concerns and then told me all about the specific factory: how it participates in the Fair Labor Association, about schools built for workers' families and about the work Patagonia does to verify good conditions and pay fair prices. He then told the story of Patagonia's move away from chemical-drenched cotton to organic and how they build longevity into

▶

each product. He smilingly justified the value of the premium and, suddenly, I felt that my levels of reward for shopping at Patagonia were much higher than I realised. By choosing this company's products, I would be supporting considerate consumption and could feel even better about meeting my need states in this case, this way.

I love the realism at Patagonia, too. The business doesn't claim to be completely sustainable or completely good. In fact, it even says so on it's website: "We can't pose Patagonia as the model of a responsible company. We don't do everything a responsible company can do, nor does anyone else we know. But we can tell you how we came to realize our environmental and social responsibilities, and then began to act on them. Like other things in human life, it began with one step that led to another."

That honesty makes the customer feel included on that journey, it is authentic and engaging, it says that we're not perfect and we're just trying to be better and, in doing so, makes Patagonia accessible and easy to like.

Its premium price positioning is supported by significant levels of reward, beyond those I've already mentioned. The technical wear offers clear benefits, strongly defined and does so wrapped in the idea that buying these is a sustainable and earth-friendly choice.

Watch this video for one of their $80 fishing shirts for a masterclass in relating technical benefits: https://youtu.be/sGZFKpumN8U.

As an aside, I'd like to highly recommend you look at Patagonia's website. It is a fantastic model for curated selection and guided buying. The layout is engaging and varied, products look special and individual product pages are far from the boring standard template, but remain engaging and commercial. Each page also includes a photo and description of the place in which it was made – transparency that is reassuring, but that also makes the product feel more thought-through, more complete somehow.

Clean up your bargains act

We retailers sometimes sniff at bargains, the "manager's special" has a slightly tainted aura to us, which is a shame because customers – rich, poor, all points in-between – love bargains. A bargain is us, as customers, beating the system, as T.K. Maxx once said, "Get a buzz from a bargain" and, wow, do we ever get a buzz.

Strolling the Miracle Mile, birthplace of Chicago's world-famous retail history, I visited a Nordstrom that was so quiet I thought I was interrupting something sombre by walking through it. But then I left, walked around the block and to a separate entrance to Nordstrom's dedicated T.J. Maxx-alike bargain-rails store. Nordstrom Rack. From the bottom of the steep escalator leading up to the entrance proper. I could hear a faint rumble. Then, as I ascended. the rumble got louder until, at the top, it was a wall of noise coming from customers in a branded-clothing feeding frenzy. There were people going nuts everywhere: "Got to git me them barguns!" Profiling the customers on sight is always a dangerous game, but it felt like the mix was egalitarian, from tracksuit-clad youngsters to branded middle-aged and middle-class. It was brilliant and the surest indicator that the psychology of bargains might be interesting.

Back in 2007, I got this nice note from Irish book retailer Lyn Denny: "I'm the owner of a small independent bookshop in Ireland. We've been open a year and things are going great. I bought your book in September and haven't looked back. We immediately introduced a bargains table and it has been the fastest selling area of my store ever since. We are delighted with it and so are our customers." Lyn's store isn't some downmarket discount shop: Bookstór is a quality independent in a country that values literature highly. People love bargains and they work in almost any store. More than a decade later, Lyn's passionate and inspirational bookshop is still going strong.

I suspect one of the reasons we feel awkward about bargains is because bargains are hard to manage. They are ephemeral by their nature (end of line, special buys) or they are not quite to spec., last year's model, slightly off, and so on. They require an additional level of attention to detail above range reviews and they require nimble buyers and category managers with a commercial sensibility beyond new stock.

Pulling together the bargains is hard work. You must be inventive, on top of your inventory and ready to act fast. The work is worth it. You will drive customers into your business and the combination of honest pricing and real bargains will boost your reputation and your sales. Bargains give you competitive advantage because they are part of a rewarding customer experience.

The costs of consumption

While we're on the subject of pricing, this is a good place to talk about the flip side of the price-driven consumption frenzy. I'm one of those people who grew up in the 1970s and 1980s in a world that believed consumption at any rate could be sustained for ever. Too young to be bothered by the early 1970s oil shocks and too old to really "get it" when, late in the 1990s, environmental concerns began to break mainstream ground. Nearly two decades on and even people like me have been forced to confront the reality that the blue and green ball upon which we stand isn't going to last, if we keep kicking the crap out of it.

As retailers, we are in the vanguard of consumption and we have got some serious thinking to do. Here and now I need to say that I am an unashamed liberal capitalist and I believe strongly that the creation of wealth is a force for common good in the world. I believe we need to create wealth and then share it, support each other and improve living standards, not least because we also build our customers' spending power that way.

So how does that square with the need for sustainability? Being one of the world's biggest sources of employment is a pretty good start. Everyone is entitled to opportunity, dignity and the chance to earn a decent wage. Retail provides that and, time and time again, it is proved that those retailers that treat their staff with respect and that provide support and opportunities for self-fulfilment are the ones that customers prefer to shop with. On the customer side, growing awareness of the need for sustainable living is leading a revolution, with our customers taking more and more of their spend to those retailers whose practices have the least negative impact on the planet.

We're really good, as an industry, at moving minds and influencing consumer behaviour. I believe the most forward-thinking retailers have an opportunity here to move customers even faster towards truly sustainable consumption. Why wait for consumer trends and government regulation to push us? Let's drive that change ourselves, not just because doing so on a human level is a feel-good thing, but also because we can drive our business's success by doing so.

Making these moves is a good community choice and a great human one too. Of course, the usual caveats apply. Choose your position carefully, communicate it well and, above all, be authentic. If you say you have a commitment to X, then you must genuinely believe that commitment to be right or you run the risk of being found out.

Whole Foods Market
Standing for more than consumption

A key event in the early days of Whole Foods Market set the tone for the way in which this innovative food retailer sees itself as an integral part of the communities it serves. In 1981, a flood devastated Austin, Texas and, among the businesses ruined, was the company's then one and only store. The damage ran to $400,000 and, without insurance, they looked doomed. Incredibly, customers and neighbours volunteered to join staff in clearing up the mess and in repairing the store – creditors and suppliers too provided breathing space for the business to get back on its feet and, less than a month after the disaster, the store was up and trading again. Many people not employed by the company or financially dependent on it nevertheless felt they had a stake in the success of the business. If your local Jumbo, Wawa or Sainsbury's suffered a flood, would you be there bailing out and mopping up?

Right from the start, Whole Foods had a clear vision that the food it sells should be grown responsibly, that local supply was preferable to the established mass-production model, and that

▶

employees and the community should be closely involved in the decision making driving the business. It has a snappy line to sum up the way the business feels about its offer: "Whole Foods – "Whole People – Whole Planet".

What makes Whole Foods Market special is that it has made direct positive connections between doing the right thing and making money. Just one small example of that is that it offers financial support to employees who choose to do voluntary community service – and it knows that doing so makes both the employee and the community feel good. It also knows that a happy, motivated employee helps the business make more money and that an involvement with the community increases customer awareness. There is no cynicism in this. The top team want to be proud of the way in which they do business: they want to go to bed at night knowing that their working day has resulted in gain for everyone and in the right way.

What looked novel at Whole Foods Market, even five years ago, has rapidly become more normal: food provenance, authenticity in diet and sustainability are suddenly at the heart of consumer concerns and, by association, ours too.

Now
Things you can do now

- Describe your price positioning, think about it relative to competitors and to other ways in which customers might use the same budget.

- Wherever you are at a premium position, describe in detail your justifications. Are these really credible?

Next
Strategic considerations for the longer term

- Review your overarching price proposition in the context of the new retail fundamentals.

- As part of ongoing corporate social responsibility, consider how your customer fits within choices made.

Chapter

13

People in marketing often talk about the "personality" of a given product. A biscuit might be "reassuring and sensual"; a brand of shoe may exhibit "anarchic yet inquisitive" tendencies. Marketers have built their world view on such thinking, despite it being precisely the sort of babble a madman might come up with following years alone in an isolated cottage, during which time he falls in love with a fork and decides the light bulbs are conspiring against him.

Charlie Brooker, *The Guardian*

Cutting through
the marketing

In this chapter we explore

- a possible shift from aspiration to an expectation culture

- leveraging your voice

- extremely simple database marketing.

Retailers, customers, horsecrap

We hate hipsters, don't we? Just take a quick look at any clickbait aggregator and you'll find a hundred lists, such as:

- Ten ways hipsters have ruined food.

- Twenty-seven photos that prove hipsters are ridiculous.

- Barefoot hipsters stinking out your favourite stores.

And I think the moment a Glasgow restaurant served fish and chips in a galvanised steel bin lid marked peak hipster. Or maybe it was when British footballers began to look like 1930s Canadian lumberjacks? Possibly, we knew that the world had gone utterly mental when a café opened in London selling nothing but breakfast cereal.

So, yeah, hipsters: ridiculous people with their small-batch, slow-cooked, bicycling to light up their authentic-tools-only workshop, hand-pulled, analogue ways. And, yet, I've come to believe that, in fact, the hipster movement is simply the most extreme expression of a fundamental shift in Western consumption. I believe we have moved from an aspiration culture to an expectation culture. We used to aspire to owning Lamborghinis and Rolex watches and, for many, those things still represent a particular type of reflection of their success and achievements. But, in an era when Facebook's founder Mark Zuckerberg decides to follow Bill Gates' lead and give away the vast bulk of his fortune, and ultra-capitalist Warren Buffett persuades a dozen billionaires to join him in committing to give away at least half of their wealth, you know that something is happening in the West to conspicuous wealth.

The trend data certainly supports the notion that there has been a shift from consumers wanting ownership of "things" to participation in experiences instead and that this trend is only getting stronger. As retailers, we need to be aware of that experiences part especially, even if we are still selling "things". We can use the former, experiences, to create a different expectation for the latter.

The return of real

People are craving real experiences again, those that are tactile and sensual, and that should not be a surprise. First comes the disruption from a new technology and then comes the normalisation in which the beneficial parts of formally disruptive ideas are absorbed and the ephemera discarded. Take e-books, for example. After a period of intense Kindlefication of reading, e-book sales are stagnating and physical book sales are strengthening. Across global bookselling, bookshops are reporting customers returning and sales gently strengthening. E-books haven't failed, far from it, but they have found their place.

Knitting, baking, the maker movement – real is returning, where technology is enhancing the experience. So the bread is real and made by the consumer, but the recipe and a video on kneading techniques are playing on a tablet on the worktop, while artisanal flour has arrived from a tiny mill nobody would have heard of before the internet. The knitters are sourcing their yarns from great online suppliers or via links on knitting blogs; they get together in online forums but meet in cafés and the cafés start to link up with wool shops. Real experiences, social sharing and the pleasure of expectation returning. The trend for mindfulness is part of this too. Being aware of the impact on your mind and wellbeing through slowing down and enjoying real experiences. I find all this extremely optimistic and empowering: real and digital working together to make life easier to enjoy.

Authentic and artisanal

Even brands on the bling scale, such as Grey Goose, aren't launched conventionally any more. Its creators used early social media and word of mouth to create an idea that a night out in which the Grey Goose flows is a particular kind of experience. Looking forward to a "Grey Goose kinda night" isn't about aspiring to drink or own bottles of Grey Goose, but a shorthand for the expectation that a particular kind of experience will be had. That doesn't stop the bottles of Grey Goose on the table in the VIP area from being flaunted as aspirational status symbols, but the initial impetus is for the experience and how that satisfies a complex set of need states, including some that encompass the need for status.

When, in 2013, Grey Goose's owners Bacardi decided it needed to throw some conventional marketing effort behind the brand, two of the words it used to describe what it wanted to convey to drinkers were "authentic" and "craftsmanship". Words straight out of the hipster product manual and the advertising that followed played on the idea that Grey Goose was the product of a mythical rural French town, all patisserie, boulangerie and pre-war bars. Moving the product again to a slightly different expectation positioning, this time one that suggests what you get, is an incredibly authentic taste created by artisans.

Aspiration culture becomes expectation culture

Expectation appears to play a very important role in how a person experiences a particular scenario. It also now appears that implanting false memories to then have an impact on preferences is almost trivially easy. Could the way we talk about products and experiences before a sale also have an impact on how a customer feels about those things when finally using them? I am convinced it can and that our marketing communications are an essential part of setting up exactly that process.

Sorry, what? Did I just keep on going after dropping that bomb-shell on false memories? Prof. Giuliana Mazzoni at Hull University has shown how false memories can change people's behaviours. In one experiment, she plants a memory of having been sick when eating turkey sandwiches. (Her test subjects have been pre-screened and identified as having a particular fondness for turkey and so would be expected to eat and enjoy turkey sandwiches.) Having planted the false memories, subjects are invited back two weeks later for an experiment that they believe is unrelated and asked to eat and rate certain sandwiches. Consistently, the subjects eat far less of the turkey option from a platter of three and then rate the turkey poorly on taste. In a further experiment, they are asked about their history of turkey, with the subjects then self-suggesting a former bad experience with eating turkey.

A bad experience that didn't exist before the implantation of the false memory.

The implantation process is incredibly easy. At an initial interview, subjects are told that they have been entered into a computer programme that has suggested things that are likely to have happened to them when they were children. The first suggestions are small and extremely likely to have happened to most people, such as they liked chocolate and visited the seaside. Then a much less likely one is introduced, that they were sick after eating turkey, which is then followed up with what feels very much like a version of cold reading where the interviewer talks in confirming language, such as "You can remember the aftertaste that lingers for a few days, can't you?", and so on. Subjects are shown fake news stories from around the time they were children that talk about contaminated turkey meat making many people ill.

This idea is so powerful–doesn't it say so much about how we can influence customers' preferences and choices in positive ways? Plant those ideas that you are great to shop, be specific about why, reinforce positive ideas with confirming language. Possibly draw the line at inventing old news stories about how great you are but how important does it now become that, after a customer has a great experience, you reinforce that and stop being shy to remind them of those brilliant experiences?

BrewDog
Leveraging your marketing by being disruptive

The BrewDog model is an excellent one to follow – never advertised, but it has a point of view, it shouts about it, defends it, champions it and everything it does is in the context of an incredible commitment to great craft beer. The founders weren't afraid to make characters of themselves. They make a noise and tell the authorities where to get off when they think it gets in the customer's way. They make extensive use of digital media to connect with customers and they do so without nonsense or marketing speak. They position themselves as what they are: a bunch of people who love good beer, want to make good beer and who want to sell it to you and for you to love drinking it. *Remember that last sentence, as it is the most important piece of advice I can give you in this chapter.*

They also aren't afraid to manufacture their own controversy, such as the time founder James Watt was challenged by the drinks industry body The Portman Group over a high-strength 18% beer by the name of Tokyo Imperial Stout. The Portman Group had received complaints and thus had to act, demanding withdrawal of a beer that contravened voluntary beer industry codes of practice. It ruled that if BrewDog did not withdraw the beer, then retailers would be ordered to remove it from their shelves. Watt told them to sod off and soon the story reached the media. BrewDog, still largely unknown at the time, suddenly became, for the tabloids, purveyors of a drunken Britain but, at the same time, unwittingly, the media gave Watt an opportunity to explain what the brewery was really all about and to showcase BrewDog's craft credentials.

What the Portman Group didn't know was that BrewDog had only made 500 bottles of Tokyo, had no intention of making any more and had already sold the lot, mostly to overseas customers. A few months after the scrap, it was revealed that Portman had received just one complaint about Tokyo Imperial Stout and that it had come from a Mr J. Watt.

▶

What is essential is that at no point did BrewDog allow its credentials to slip. It might have brewed an irresponsibly strong beer but it had good reasons for having done so and could convincingly make the case as a maker of something different and special in an identikit UK beer landscape. Suddenly, BrewDog stood out, people wanted to try the beers and an expectation had been created.

For further study, enjoy this splendidly potty-mouthed 2014 apology issued by BrewDog again to the Portman Group: http://goo.gl/w2Rr7P.

In 2016, James Watt told *The Guardian* that traditional advertising is dead and, in any case, unaffordable for a small company. He added that new media was the place to shout your message and claimed that people: "want genuine, they want quality, they want passionate, they want real, they want integrity". In Watt's view: "The only way to build a brand is to live that brand. You have to live the values and the mission, then let the customer decide."

I think he is right. Whatever you sell, if you have got your Big Idea right, then you too can use these techniques to make big and authentic noises for your product and for your business. You can be passionate and brave and take on the world without feeling a poor relation to the big-spending advertisers on TV.

Your voice, get ready to use it

For the remainder of this chapter and the next, I'm going to talk about the practical things retailers can do to interpret what we've just discussed. If you're running a big retail business with a clever marketing team champing at the bit to get on with doing their thing, it's probably not for you but, if you're running a small chain or an indie, you'll find this part very useful.

Despite my reporting of the false memory hocus pocus above, marketing itself is not a mythical black art, it is nothing more, or less, than a common sense framework: a framework into which your activity can be fitted. Marketing theory is very simple. The skill, especially in the case of retail, is not in cleverly executing the practice of marketing but rather, it is in trusting your gut feel to keep things simple. Marketing is about under-standing who your customers are, where they can be found, what they need, and how much they will pay to satisfy those needs. That's really kind of it.

This sets up a series of questions. Who are we selling to? How do we tell them about our product? What will they pay for it? Notice how these questions form a chain? The answer to the first informs the second which, in turn, sets up the third. Answering these questions can help you to make better decisions on promo-tions and on advertising.

Questions chain:

1. Who might want to shop at a store like ours?

2. What might they like about us?

3. Which products would excite them?

4. What kind of promotions do they like?

5. Where can I find these people?

6. What should I tell them?

Each customer type looked at will create a slightly different thread. Use what you learn to select target audiences to talk to. The follow-ing pages list some of your options for reaching those audiences.

Social media

Unfortunately, it is really easy to get some rotten advice on the use of social media as a marketing tool for retailers, and it's easy to waste a ton of cash on that advice. I don't want to add to that, especially if you are reading this book a couple of years after pub-lication when the platforms and opportunities will have changed.

What I will do, though, is suggest some useful ground rules that have been consistent in best-practice over, at least, the last few years.

- **Tone of voice:** create a voice for the business and be consistent in using it.

- **Be active:** do not fall into the "if we build it, they will come" trap. Go and count the number of dead Facebook pages for retailers that get no attention whatsoever. You have to actively manage and engage.

- **Have something interesting to say:** content is king, so you have to have something to say that people are engaged by and keen to respond to. Don't update for the sake of it, be authentic and relevant.

- **The Google Algorithm:** read everything you can find on the Google Algorithm (and keep reading, as the algorithm is constantly updated), understanding as best you can because much of the detail is hidden, which signals that Google is listening for, and what it appears to be prioritising can be, the difference between your business appearing on page 1 of a search and page 100. Here's a good archive of the Algorithm: https://goo.gl/YraEdX.

- **Court bloggers:** create good relationships with relevant bloggers, vloggers and special interest groups relevant to you. A respected fashion blogger loving your new shoe model because you've worked with them will generate more sales than a month of telly adverts.

- **Get mentioned:** paying for celebrity tweet mentions, Instagram photos and the like is tacky as hell, but shifts product like little else. If you can get those for free by courting relationships and being a compelling partner to relevant people, then all the better.

- **Get ready for the platform that will kill the one you are on:** do not stand still on one platform. What's gaining attention and users' time today may not tomorrow. See, for example, Tumblr and Flickr that have faded somewhat in recent years as Medium and Instagram have surpassed them; and the same will happen to Medium and Instagram. The kids might be on Snapchat today, but tomorrow it'll be something else. Right now, Slack is a mostly corporate tool but has the possibility to develop into a discrete recommendations engine soon. (As soon as I submitted this manuscript, Instagram reported a fall in user numbers.)

- **Learn about chatbots:** start looking at chatbots right now – Google it and get involved. You've got four years to exploit the hell out of these. If you've no idea what one is, go and look at

Microsoft's Domino's chatbot that monitors a chatroom and will order you a pizza by you asking it to.

- **Sell on Amazon and eBay:** labour-intensive but even big online retailers such as Wiggle.com are using Amazon Marketplace to leverage their exposure. The system is superb on both platforms and gives you another shot beyond Google to be discovered in search. Both, obviously, shortcut your opportunity to show your hand before the order (other than by earned customer reputation) and so price sensitivity is high, but there is still useful revenue and stock-turn to be had.

- **Make lots of videos:** make product videos, reviews and how-tos and really commit to it and make sure everything is in your consistent voice. Remind customers of why buying from you is so good. Video is great because it is you talking – you the human face of the business and, if people like you, they will like the business.

- **Keep learning:** last, but not least, constantly, and I mean every day, find an example of best practice on a given platform. Who is using Pinterest to generate sales? What are they doing differently?

Reaching customers – traditional methods

Radio

If you feel you really must make adverts, then radio is still a great medium. It's very cost-effective and you can paint any image you want with words. Often big and shouty words work best. Plenty of stations will help you create your advert. Each station will also be able to give you profiles of their listeners for each of their shows. This means you can choose to advertise only on those stations, and only during those shows, listened to by people who might actually want to shop with you. There are also lots of resources available for do-it-yourself radio advertisers, and that helps makes the medium attractive.

Print

Clear bold messages work best. Don't do national if you are local. Don't be seduced by glamorous but vague graphics. A bold typographical treatment highlighting a great promotion accompanied by an illustration that relates to the experience you claim to be selling works well. And the old maxim of "less is more" absolutely applies. But, again, you must absolutely ensure your advert is consistent with your voice and that it sets up an expectation that you absolutely can deliver.

Posters

Traditional large-format posters can act like a second storefront, but they are expensive. These days, the sites available for placing an advert on are almost without limit: everything from posters in pub toilets to the handles of petrol pumps. JCDecaux is the largest independent outdoor media owner in the UK and worth talking to if you are interested in exploring posters.

Catalogues

A catalogue can be a single flyer or a 32-page colour extravaganza. Never underestimate the power of catalogues. They provide you with huge scope to tell people about your great products and, at the same time, talk about why your store is a nice place to visit and to do business with. Much missed US retail consultant George Whalin used to say: "If you have one item and just one page, that's a catalog, start from there and build it over time."

Never underestimate the power of catalogues.

Catalogues are exciting because there is so much you can do with them. You can hand them out as flyers, you can put them into the local free papers, you can mail them to your customer database and you can give them out to visitors to your store.

Consider how you might distribute your catalogue. Piles in the store are fine, but a stand outside is better. Having a colleague hand them out in the car park or up and down the street is always worth doing. Paying a delivery person to distribute catalogues door-to-door is useful too. Of course, this is also dependent on the type of catalogue you have gone for. If yours is thick, heavy and expensive, then distribution will have to be more limited. Similarly, if you know that your customer falls into a very narrow interest group, then you should consider distributing your catalogue directly to them – so a baby goods store might want to have its catalogue in the waiting area of the local maternity ward.

Banner advertising and Google adwords

The current consensus on banner advertising, now around long enough to be considered traditional, is that click-through and click-through to sale are miniscule. Your ad needs to be served a staggeringly high number of times to generate meaningful return. But, by the time you read this, things may have changed again.

Adwords campaigns can be extremely expensive, but can be extremely effective. I'm not going to give you advice here on how best to run an adwords campaign, because I'm far from the best person. Luckily, the internet, including Google, is full of pages of good DIY advice in this area. I would certainly, at least, recommend experimenting with adwords and always make full use of the extremely good analysis tools Google provides, whether you pay for clicks or not.

Easy ABC database marketing

Every store, physical or online, can, and must, build a customer database. Used sensibly, they drive customers to your site like few other direct advertising tools can. You don't need complex software to run them: any database program, such as Microsoft's Access, will do, though specialist services, such as MailChimp, can be very effective.

Here's how to do email database marketing really well:

- Always get permission, as customers hate email spam and junk mail – it irritates them. They respond much better to expected messages, so long as these are relevant.

- Make sure you actually have something to say, such as an exclusive offer, hard-to-get item here in stock now, end-of-line special bargain, one-off event or exciting new line due in on date X.

- Start the email with all your headings – just titles with no additional body text, for example: "Buy-one-get-one-free on all paperback fiction this weekend only", "New Dan Brown arrives in-store here on 11 June – reserve your copy now", or "David Beckham here signing his new autobiography on 1 July".

- Remember, time limits on offers always help to drive customers into action.

- Then, in the body of the email, below these headlines, you can expand on each subject. Try to keep words to a minimum, just tell the story and then get out. For example, "Buy one-get-one-free on all paperback fiction this weekend only". Or "Choose any two from our huge range of great titles and you get the cheapest free; that includes all of our current best-sellers as well as the full selection of classic fiction. Saturday and Sunday only – we're looking forward to seeing you!"

- Sign it! Customers appreciate a personal touch.

- Remember the rules: tell me what it is, tell me why I might want one, tell me how to get it.

The Data Protection Act

In the UK, if you are going to hold customers' data in a database, you must comply with the Data Protection Act 1998. Most retailers have notified that they wish to be registered under the Act. If you have done so, you are likely to be entitled also to use the data you hold for database marketing purposes. You must check, though, before moving on.

One of the key aspects of the Data Protection Act is permission. When you ask for someone's details, you must tell them that you will be holding these details in a database. You must also get their permission to send them things. Check on the www.gov.uk/data-protection/the-data-protection-act site for the latest advice on what to say and how to say it. Getting permission is good practice anyway, as there is little point in taking someone's address only to send them things they don't want to see.

Keeping track – measurement

Any direct activity needs to be made measurable. You can do this easily by adding coded coupons to printed materials and by using separate trackable URLs for digital marketing. Google Analytics is an incredibly powerful chunk of free support you can then leverage to see exactly where sales and visitors are coming from.

In many situations, it is useful to set up a basic Microsoft Excel spreadsheet to make tracking easy. Literally, just a few columns for the dates and then a few rows for the various promotions you are running. Then record the number of people responding, the total value of their purchases and the margin earned on each transaction. At the end of each week, work out the total profit accounted for by your promotions. Then deduct from that the cost of the activity you ran. So long as you capture every relevant sale, then this is a crude, but perfectly acceptable, way to track how well each promotion is working for you.

You also need to take account of the discounts you gave to normal customers, those people who would have bought from you, regardless of the promotion. That is quite tricky and will often be down to your instinctive judgement. All the same, it is important because this number helps you to realistically appraise returns from your efforts.

Now
Things you can do now

- List ways in which shopping your business delivers a distinct experience.
- How convincing and credible are your maker credentials?
- List all the ways you currently tell customers why they are so right to have chosen to shop with you. How are you reinforcing their choices?
- Run the questions-chain exercise.
- Identify three forthcoming items that could stand up to a database campaign.

Next
Strategic considerations for the longer term

- Consider the authenticity of your positioning and communications.
- Use the output from the above and from the questions-chain exercise as a basis for a new communications brief.

Chapter 14

The squeaky wheel gets the oil.

Promote or die

In this chapter we explore

- thirty ways to promote the business and an analysis of their impact on the four rules of performance improvement

- how to build a down and dirty 12-month promotions planner.

But I can just do it in social media

In the previous chapter, I talked a little bit about the use of social media to build customer awareness for your retail business. This chapter should give you some ideas on the sort of promotional content you might want to fuel that social media activity with. Carefully considered promotions are important because they create interest and surprise and, in conjunction with honest pricing, are essential performance improvement tools. There are, of course, those other factors we've talked about to consider – promotions in isolation from great customer experiences or attention to employee needs are near worthless. Poor, aggressive or sneaky promotions may bolster sales short-term, but unhappy customers will rarely come back.

Thirty promotions

I have listed most of the popular promotion options. I've included a table that makes it easy to see which promotions are good for achieving better performance under each of the four improvement rules. Finally, the promotions planner that follows after will help you to see what promotions are right for you and when to run them. This is very much a practical chapter and probably most useful for small chains or indie retailers, so fill your boots, plucky challengers!

Pop-up shops

With the emergence of space-brokers, such as the superb Appear Here (UK) www.appearhere.co.uk, We Are Pop Up (UK and some NYC) www.wearepopup.com and Republic Spaces (USA) www.republicspaces.com, the pop-up shop is now an affordable opportunity for any retailer, large or small, online or off, to extend their physical presence. The range of stuff you can do is as broad as your imagination. Just a few examples would include:

- Test a new location.
- Test a new product.
- Bring an online business into a physical selling space.
- Bring a new product to life.
- Reach a group of customers outside your existing audience.
- Test parts of a new format.
- Gain research data.
- Retail activation for manufacturers or brands[*].
- Pre-launch for PR or soft-launch new idea.
- Set up near a sporting or cultural event.
- Gain media exposure.
- Try something risky under a temporary branding.
- Intensify your sales space for peak season.
- Collaborative project.

In early 2016, Appear Here, for example, was brokering space in Top Shop's super-busy flagship Oxford Street store for just £150 a day. The power of a weeks pop-up inside a store like this could break your business into the mainstream. A month in an area of your city where you're currently not represented might bring you a whole new customer base. Bringing your online start-up into physical selling space might just give you the cashflow booster that sees you through to next month. Pop-ups are intense, fun,

---

[*]Idiotically, referring to these types of pop-ups as "brand activations" is now a thing, so watch out for that.

creative and very powerful. Again, Appear Here and the like can help you to understand and make the best of the spaces they offer and are, generally, delighted to give advice.

Infrastructure providers such as Square (payments) and Shopify (POS) mean even a market stall can now offer full payment options and can help you manage your inventory, pricing, pretty much everything. Both are further examples of how technology is setting free retail creativity. I did my first 'pop-up aged 13 in 1983 in a field in Peterborough where we'd grudgingly accept credit cards and use a gigantic sort of bicep-exerciser machine to physically imprint a card onto complex multi-part paper vouchers, which would then be signed and distributed to customer, accountant and the bank. I loved that first introduction to retail, red in tooth and claw – selling hard and having the best fun looking after big hairy bikers (genuinely among the nicest people in the world). Now? You can offer contactless at a pop-up market on a mountaintop using your phone. It's brilliant.

When planning your pop-up, remember your retail disciplines. Think through the objective, consider why people might care, be aware of the practical issues. I would strongly advise you to read through at least Secrets 3, 4 and 5 too, and think about how those principles would apply to a pop-up.

A fantastic checklist on pop-ups can be found on Shopify's website: https://goo.gl/SoZAjD.

Collaboration

When two brands are better than one, could you bring a known designer in to provide you with something exclusive? Is there a retailer you admire in another sector that might be open to work with you to create a collaborative range of products? In fashion, collaborations have become something of a staple. Right back in 2004, Karl Lagerfeld created a capsule collection for H&M that sold out within minutes of stores opening their doors, setting the template for the modern designer/fashion retailer collaboration. Earlier still, Target built its homewares reputation on the strength of a collaboration with Martha Stewart. They can be very productive – volume sales for the designer and loads of noise and premium margins for the retailer.

Sponsorship and community events

Don't dismiss requests for sponsorship right out of hand. Sometimes, a sensible sponsorship can be a very effective way to show your commitment to local communities, who will often return the favour later. Businesses located at the centre of smaller communities gain most benefit from this form of promotion. Sponsoring events, such as the town fun run or village fete, makes a very strong statement about your commitment to the community. Many retailers have reported that the goodwill this creates does translate into sales.

Adverts in changing rooms

Cheap, easy and brilliant. Put adverts in your changing rooms. Your customer is absolutely captive when they are in there and they have plenty of time to read. Think about featuring deals on accessories, especially – customers who bite will be helping to push up your average transaction values.

Children's competitions

Maybe we are just a nation of soppy souls, but children's competitions always work well. These can be very simple colouring competitions or letter writing. Perhaps themed "draw or write a letter about your mum for Mother's Day". Local papers love this sort of thing. You have a good chance of getting a photo of the winner in your store printed in the paper. Easy to run online, especially.

Tip sheets

No matter what your product, you can easily produce useful tip sheets. A sheet of tips might seem a little uninspiring, perhaps, but time and again retailers tell me that customers go nuts for these, often citing the tip sheets as the reason why customers come back. You can write tip sheets yourself or have a well-known expert do them for you at a cost. Formats can be anything from a full-colour booklet to a small card fixed to a shelf edge. My favourite format in stores is loose A5 so that customers can take the tip sheets away with them. Online you can do cool interactive things, add video, guided help and "pick lists" that link to all the product required.

Here are some examples of tip sheets:

- Recipes in a grocer's.

- Recommendations and explanations in a wine merchant's.

- How to automate home elements.

- Improvement projects in a DIY store.

- Ideal kit recommendation at a cycle retailer.

- How to furnish a kid's bedroom.

Loyalty programmes

I don't believe that customers are ever loyal to the over-hyped special offers, magazines or bits of tinsel that most loyalty programmes consist of. I've written about loyalty in general in the Secrets section of the book and you'll note that I'm pretty unconvinced, but there are useful options.

The kind of loyalty programmes that do work are those that feel more immediate and are usually much simpler. Maybe a coffee shop gives you a little card that they stamp each time you visit, and that entitles you to your sixth coffee free. Or a pizza company offers a loyalty bonus that allows you to get any pizza you want for free if you have saved up four receipts from previous orders. Those kinds of loyalty programmes are unobtrusive and relatively low cost and customers really like them.

If you've read anything on "nudge" theory, you'll know to create cards that already have two boxes pre-stamped. We daft humans are persuaded by those two pre-printed and stamped boxes that our mission to get the free burrito is closer and easier, even though the burrito place just put ten boxes on the card rather than the eight they actually calculated the promotion on.

Customer-get-customer

You could offer existing customers a gift, store vouchers perhaps, if they recommend your store to a friend who then makes a purchase. Customer-get-customer is especially easy to do online and your infrastructure provider may even have a simple voucher code generator available off the shelf.

In-store, if you don't have an electronic solution, all you need is a printed coupon, which you give to every customer with their till receipt. The customer can fill in this coupon and give it to their friend. The friend brings in the coupon and it has the original customer's details still written on it so you can send them their reward.

If you are confident that people like you enough to recommend your store to friends, this is an effective way in which to make it easy for them to do exactly that.

Buy one, get one free (or two-for-one, three-for-two)

In the early 2000s, this was the UK's most popular promotional mechanic. If you can afford to run them, run them. Promote such offers heavily. Talk to your suppliers about funding either the offer, the advertising or both! If you can run a steady stream of good offers over a long period, then this becomes even more effective because customers begin to pop in just to see what you've got on "special".

Sampler clubs

In some ways, this is an extension of the tip sheet idea, but with a chance for customers to actually try the product out. You take a group of your customers and sign them up to a hands-on sampling club. In that cycling kit tip sheet example earlier you could hold regular demonstration days out on the road just for members, hold set-up lessons with an expert, make pre-ordering on limited edition products available to the members first, and run exclusive offers. Online cycle retailer Wiggle.com run an uber version of this by sponsoring sportives at which they then preview product, provide ride set-up services and give demonstrations and advice – all strengthening their credentials among riders.

Percentage off

Exactly what it says, you run either a day where everything is 10% off, or you reduce a selection of lines for a limited period of time. It has become very hard to make such events really work, though. The DIY sheds, especially, have trained customers to think that anything less than a 25% discount isn't worth their while. Percentage-off promotions also make a negative statement about your usual prices. The Gap, for example, has suffered in 2016 as a result of heavy discounting throughout the previous three years – customers have come to resent paying full price there.

Special nights

Inviting selected customers to join you in the store for an exclusive evening of demonstrations and offers can be very effective. Provide refreshments and snacks and, if appropriate, bring in a relevant speaker, and entertainment too. Try to pick a theme or a special reason for doing it because that can help you to more effectively promote the night. A sports shop, for example, could invite customers in to celebrate the England football manager's birthday. It's frivolous, sure, but gives you a hook too. This is another one that can get you coverage in the local paper.

Surveys

You should be asking customers for their views anyway, but surveys can also be used as promotional tools. Create an online survey, using a tool such as www.surveymonkey.com and then send a link to members of your database. Include a thank-you voucher for a discount in-store or online. It reminds customers you are there, it tells them customer satisfaction is important to you and it gives them a reason to come and shop with you.

Celebrity visit

Getting a celebrity into your store for a PA (public appearance) can be fantastic for generating traffic. They are not always as expensive as you might think, either. TV actors, especially if they live locally, can be a bargain. You can find the contact details of almost all British-based actors in a book called Spotlight. Your town library will have a copy. Make sure you tell customers and the local paper that this is happening. A virtual version is easy to run, though needs tight moderating – online, you should pick somebody with direct relevance to your product. You can run these online as webinar-style sessions or as simple Q&A.

Book signings

You don't have to be a bookshop to hold book signings. A fishing tackle shop can get just as much benefit from having the captain of the British course fishing team in to sign their new book. In fact, it's sometimes a good way for a non-bookseller to get a celebrity in without having to pay them. Heavily promoting the event is key to making a book signing really work for you. If you run a café, get a local comedian in to sell their new book via a reading, or even to give it a second launch party.

Lunch at the store

People are so busy today that lunchtime often becomes a trade-off between eating and shopping. An idea from the USA is to help your customers to do both. Think about putting on a simple open-packaged lunch for every customer who visits you on one day or one week of lunchtimes. Obviously it's worth avoiding greasy or staining food. Leafleting local offices is the best way to promote these events. Word is that they are really very effective at getting new people into your store but I've been talking about this idea since 2007 and still we Brits are reluctant to try it!

Seminars, how-tos and in-store events

These are absolutely essential, whatever your business. Get local traders, designers and even manufacturers' reps in to show off your products and demonstrate what to do with them. Construct a series of seminars, how-tos, and in-store events and then give every customer a calendar with these marked on it. Seminars attract customers and they help customers to decide to spend more money. How-to demonstrations and events such as fashion shows bring theatre and drama into your store. That excites customers and helps to make their experience of your store a much more enjoyable and interesting one. Seminars attract customers and they help customers decide to spend more money. Most of these can be replicated online and, in both cases, consider approaching popular bloggers to be involved – their opinions and advice can be highly valued by customers.

Meeting place

If you have a training room or large office that is not fully utilised, consider offering it to local businesses as an outside meeting space. This creates massive goodwill and hardly anyone currently does it, which will mean you will stand out. Maybe invest in a coffee maker and a lick of paint to make the place attractive. Check your insurance terms, just in case.

Charity giving

An honest charity promotion is a winner in many sectors. The usual format would be to partner with a particular charity and then agree to donate a stated percentage of profits earned during a specific special charity day or series of events.

Local radio outside broadcasts

If you have got the space, offer to let the local radio station come and do an OB (outside broadcast) from your car park or store. Make it coincide with a strong event and you'll find the stations quite keen to be involved. Yes, local radio still exists.

Banded product

This is a cousin of the buy-one-get-one-free offers. Banding is usually applied to fast-moving lines and means either attaching a different product to another for free, or putting two products together as a package deal. It's a good way to move a slower line out with a more popular one and to please the customer at the same time.

Discount off future purchase

I am a big fan of this technique, also sometimes called "delayed discount". Every customer buying on the promotional day gets a money-off voucher that they can use in the store or online on another day. Usually, the value of the voucher depends on the value of the original spend, so a typical offer might look like this:

- Spend £20, get a £5 voucher off next purchase.
- Spend £50, get a £12 voucher off next purchase.
- Spend £100, get a £30 voucher off next purchase.

You can afford to be quite generous because a high proportion of the vouchers you give out will never be redeemed. Incidentally, make sure that whatever you use is secure and that it has an expiry date and a 0.0001p cash equivalent mark on it. Online redemption generally will be higher than in-store, so plan carefully.

Promote it on the day with lots of bold signs, or a bespoke site headline, and make sure you have told all your database contacts to come and visit. This promotion type makes a great story for social media sharing – people love to do each other favours and sharing details of a promotion such as this one feels like a nice thing to do.

Gift certificate promotions

This is very similar to the discount-off-future-purchase offer, except redeemed using normal store gift certificates, which can be used at any time. Customers treat gift certificates more like money, so redemption rates, and cost, will be much higher.

Buy now, pay later

A credit-based promotion and very popular among big-ticket retailers because it enables customers to fulfil tomorrow's desires today. Actually, they are a good deal for both punter and retailer. Like the storecard I'll mention in a bit, do be careful to make this a good, honest offer rather than something that ties people in debt they can't cope with.

Interest-free credit

A very powerful promotion that enables customers to buy your product and pay for it in instalments without them incurring any credit interest. Various deals are available to suit independent retailers and are worth serious consideration if you are aiming to move big-ticket items. The same considerations as above apply.

Storecard

Storecards earn us retailers a lot of money, and they can be very convenient for some customers. I struggle with storecards, though, from an ethical standpoint. This is a very expensive form of credit with interest rates that are way above those for ordinary credit cards or for personal loans. Lots of good ordinary people, our customers, get caught out by storecards and they run up huge debts with awful consequences. Retail is a people business, so I don't believe we should be responsible for making anyone's life more difficult. So, for that reason, I cannot recommend running a storecard.

Time-limited

Examples of these promotions include: at 4pm, all bread rolls free with soup for half an hour; every Monday, shoes are 20% off; on the hour, every hour, this Saturday we will offer a different item in limited stock at a crazy price. These are great for creating instant interest and PR. The countdown is another popular version of the time-limited promotion. In the last examples, if the stock is too limited, then you do risk annoying customers. Amazon.co.uk's 2010 "Black Friday" promotion of this type generated masses of bad press, as offers sold out fast, often in under a second. And, then again, in 2014, in the UK "Black Friday" in-store promotions, particularly those at large grocers, led to hideous scenes of customers fighting and staff being assaulted. So use with care!

Bargains (price promotions)

The most powerful promotion of all: the humble bargain. Scour your price lists, badger your suppliers, pester the marketing team, gather up end of lines or last season's stock and go mad for your customers. Bargains bring people in: they make them spend more and they bring them back again.

Displays in empty stores

I need to credit brilliant retail speaker Rick Segel with this great idea: find the landlords of an empty local retail unit and offer to put a display in the window. It makes the unit look more appealing for the landlord trying to find permanent tenants and provides you with an excellent advertising space. I first mentioned this in 2003 when it was super-rare. You see it a lot now and it seems to work well for everyone involved. So these aren't quite pop-ups as they're static but they are still very much worthwhile as drivers of additional awareness.

Joint activity

Look for promotions you can share with either manufacturers or other retailers in your association or street. The obvious benefit is that you can pool costs and then afford to promote the activity more aggressively. An example of retailers engaging in joint activity might be a "fun day" held within your shopping centre. A manufacturer and retailer joint activity could include manufacturer-supplied demonstrators, linked to a customer promotion and a manufacturer-funded staff incentive.

Promotions and the rules of performance improvement at a glance

The scale runs 0 to 10
 0 = No effect
 5 = Neutral effect
10 = Very powerful effect

1 Sell to new customers
2 Sell more in each transaction
3 Persuade existing customers to return to your store more often
4 Improve margin by cutting overheads and improving sales quality

	1	**2**	**3**	**4**
1 Pop-ups	10	2	8	0
2 Collaborations	10	7	10	8
3 Sponsorship and community events	4	0	10	4
4 Adverts in changing rooms	0	10	6	6
5 Children's competitions	0	5	7	5
6 Tip sheets	8	6	8	9
7 Loyalty programmes	0	5	10	3
8 Customer-get-customer	8	5	6	5
9 Buy one, get one free	8	7	10	2
10 Sampler clubs	1	5	10	7
11 Percentage off	6	7	6	3
12 Special nights	6	7	7	5
13 Surveys	6	0	8	6
14 Celebrity visit	10	0 or 10*	8	2
15 Book signings	8	0 or 10*	8	8
16 Lunch at the store	7	0	8	5
17 Seminars and how-to events	8	10	10	6
18 Meeting place	7	0	8	6
19 Charity giving	6	0	6	3
20 Local radio outside broadcasts	6	0	6	8
21 Banded product	8	5	8	7
22 Discount off future purchase	7	7	10	5
23 Gift certificate promotions	8	5	10	5
24 Buy now, pay later	7	5	7	4
25 Interest-free credit	8	6	8	5
26 Storecard	2	8	7	10
27 Time-limited	10	4	4	1
28 Bargains	10	10	10	5
29 Displays in empty stores	5	0	5	8
30 Joint activity	7	3	1	8

*A celebrity or author who is expert in the same field as the store can lead customers into buying all sorts of extras to go with a base purchase. However, a non-related one can't!

Promotions planner

Putting together a promotions planner is simple but essential. You need to know when you're doing things and, more importantly, why you're doing them. This is a very basic way to pull one together but it is a useful start.

1. Start with 12 sheets of A4, one for each month of the year.
2. Write in all the things you can predict will be happening, for example a January sale.
3. Then write down all the predictable quiet times for your business – summer holidays might be one.
4. Then write in all the predictable mad times, such as Christmas.
5. Add any product launches that you know of.
6. Write in any major events that could offer some good promotion links, the Olympics or a blockbuster movie, perhaps.
7. Now you will have a good idea where you have either dead zones to fill or mad times to avoid or strengthen, and you can see where some themed promotions might work well.

Choosing the right promotions is an art, but this information can really help you. For example, if your business is quiet during August because of summer holidays and most people being away, it might be sensible to run promotions that maximise transaction values to pull more cash in from the few customers you do have at that time.

Now
Things you can do now

- Select three promotions to run within the next quarter.
- Create a down and dirty 12-month promotions planner.

Next
Strategic considerations for the longer term

- Commission a wider review of promotional activity, and be especially careful to align this with whatever you have discovered from friction/reward indexing: who needs to be promoted to and why?

The Grands Magasins du Bonmarché; the world's first proper department store and an object lesson in theatre!

Source: Royal Institute of British Architects Picture Archives

Chapter

15

You'll learn more retail theatre in five minutes around
an old-school street market than you'll learn
in a month of store observations.

The great big theatre of shop

In this chapter we explore

- the essential need for movement in retail display, both physical and online
- best practice retail theatre
- use of ceremonies to create wow moments.

Movement and energy

You hear the expression "retail theatre" a lot but then ask the person saying what they mean by it and you'll hear a dozen different answers. It's just not that well-defined. Retail theatre is one of those things that everyone is aware is important but is not entirely confident in recognising or creating it. Perhaps that's why really good and consistent examples of retail theatre are quite hard to find but, as physical retail becomes ever more an entertainment, as customers demand more reward from visiting stores, then retail theatre becomes incredibly important and useful.

For me, retail theatre is everything that animates a store. I've always seen the shop floor as a stage and on it stories are told and narratives played out – theatre is the "thing" that brings those stories alive. It's the market stallholder barking their wares to the noisy party at Selfridges and all things in between that create movement, sound, smells and that demand to be touched or interacted with.

This is the one part of the book where I believe a real differentiation between virtual and physical stores has to be made. Theatre is a live thing, it lives in the physical space. Online, animation is critical, online performance and prodding of the senses are persuasive and important, but theatre is for the world of direct human interaction and direct triggering of emotion.

We will take a look at the problem and opportunity that comes from the poor quality of our eyesight in a moment and then, after that, I'll run through some of my favourite examples of retail theatre in action.

Hotel Chocolat's bit of theatre

Fabulous and authentic British chocolatier Hotel Chocolat handing round a silver tray of samples is supreme retail theatre. It doesn't care that you buy that particular chocolate, it just wants you to see, smell and taste chocolate and, when the assistant describes what they are offering, "This is our purest/sweetest/awesome/delicious X", it wants you to hear the words of good chocolate. You are in the store, you're thinking chocolate and now you are tasting and experiencing that chocolate and the result is you want more.

Why theatre?

Because bringing the store to life brings your customers to life too. Your biggest challenge is to get customers to pick up stuff and interact with it and with staff – get that happening and you sell more things. If that interaction is done inside a great, animated and exciting store, then you get the Stew Leonard's effect: a humble dairy becomes a sales machine and customers love it.

Us, the moles and the bats

Human sight is really poor when compared to many other mammals. In particular, our low-resolution eyes coupled to our face-pattern-recognising and motion-obsessed brains make seeing static things difficult. It is physiologically hard for people to pick out one thing from another if those things are static, such as cans of food on a fixture, a row of TVs on display or books packed in on shelves.

Worse, we don't even see colour in our peripheral vision (something to do with the angle at which light enters and then hits the retina) and what we think we're seeing isn't real time. That second is a gigantic head scrambler – there's quite a substantial delay in processing terms between a thing we are watching and our brain registering and dealing with seeing it. Gets crazy when you consider a task such as catching a ball where your brain applies an automatic compensation in its instructions to your arms for the fact that the ball you think you are seeing is actually physically closer to you than your eyes suggest. That's exactly why I dropped the one catching chance I ever got when playing for my brother's village cricket team. At least that's my story.

Let me put on the lab coat and explain. What we think we see is, in reality, the image after it's been mucked about with by our brain. Our brain applies two visual processes in particular that are great for survival of the species but rubbish for retailing. The first relates to faces: our big juicy brains are constantly looking to recognise faces so we can either defend ourselves from a competitive human, or mate with a willing one. So aggressively does our brain look for faces that it'll make them out of almost anything: patterns in wallpaper, shapes made by shadows or a gravy stain on a shirt. This process is exactly why people report seeing the face of Bowie in slices of toast or dead relatives in the shape of clouds. The more challenging process is the one that refuses to concentrate on static things and instead scans peripheral vision for movement, because, in the past bigger things were often trying to eat us and they tended to do so successfully by sneaking up in the periphery without being noticed until it was too late.

Let's talk about that in a retail situation. You'll have experienced what I'm about to describe as we all have. You're standing in the soup aisle in a supermarket facing the dozens of cans of soup. You want chicken noodle and you're staring and staring but you just can't see the one you want. And then, suddenly, 'Bang!' you finally spot the tin and it's been right in front of you all the time. You didn't see it at first because your brain was paying attention to somebody on your left taking a can down off the shelf, and to a trolley being pushed along to your right, and to a sign moving in the air-conditioning breeze above you. You found the chicken noodle in the end because your brain kicked in two different processes. First pattern and shape recognition and then a different process called "reading", forcing you to read labels, which is slower than looking for pictures and patterns.

Movement

Applying one part of retail theatre can solve these issues at a stroke. Picking stuff up and moving it around attracts customers' attention. You pick up a tin of soup and wave it about and suddenly it's the easiest thing in the world to see – everyone in that aisle can pick it out. Now, maybe that's not practical in Tesco but it is almost everywhere else. Let me give you an example and a case study.

Impulse cakes

The example is one you can observe for yourself and it involves the express queue in a typical urban M&S Simply Food. If you're there and you see a member of staff re-stocking the racks of small cakes and treats that are usually stationed at the point where the queue-guide turns . . . watch what happens . . . of the next ten people in the queue, eight of them will at least pick up a cake and, of those, most will buy it. Then contrast that with the rest of the time when the fixture isn't being re-stocked. You'll see maybe 1 in 30 customers picking up a cake. I'm not exaggerating these numbers. Observe it for yourself and have a think about an area of your store that might be boosted by movement, by taking something out of stasis and giving it energy.

Giving product a kinetic kick

A client of ours, a chain of bookstores, made one small change that boosted sales by up to 20% per store. And it was such a tiny change too. They had asked us to find a way to schedule shelf-stocking so that it could be done away from customers – the logic

---

being "get the book trolley off the shop floor before we get busy". I asked why this was a problem and they reckoned that it looked scruffy stocking shelves and that "as soon as you put something on the shelf, a customer will take it off again".

Now, then, I hope you're ahead of me right now. That client was seeing it as an unprofessional irritation, but you're already seeing an opportunity, aren't you? What was happening is that the books, which when static are nothing more than shapes with colours on them, had been given a boost of kinetic energy and customers were drawn to them. So, instead, we created a routine in which books would be shelved at the busiest periods, and we told staff that they were welcome to take all day to do it, provided the delay was because they were having conversations about books with customers who were drawn to the movement. And they did exactly this.

We even did things like taking all the books off one table, putting them on the floor near a different table, then taking the books off the second table and putting them on the first, finishing the job by picking up the original books off the floor and putting them on the now clear second table. Of course, we let the staff in on the gag, explaining that what looked like a nonsense job was actually generating movement and attracting customers. They loved it because it seemed to break a small barrier between them and customers. It seemed easier to start conversations as this process went on.

A round-up of great theatre

I've picked the following examples as a great cross-section of retail theatre. I'm not suggesting that each of these retailers is exploiting everything possible but there are elements of best practice that are worth using for inspiration. Or stealing wholesale, you decide.

Alfred Dunhill (UK and China)

Specifically, I'm looking here at Bourdon House (London) and Twin Villas (Shanghai). These magnificent houses are used as living film sets and are decorated such that it feels like a mysterious group of quintessential 1930s Englishman have maintained the residences as time portals to now. Every sense is triggered: smell the vetiver, juniper and tobacco; feel the handcrafted leathers and polished marble; hear the confident chatter of a chap instructing his tailor; taste beautiful morsels of food at the bar while sipping a Tom Collins; and see icons of gentlemen's classic style laid out before you for your leisurely perusal. Personally, I don't have the breeding for such places and invariably drop a drink on myself, say something that gives away the fact that I buy my socks by the kilo at Primark or just fall over, but for those in the target audience, this is theatre writ large – a place they can go to that lives up to the expectations they have of a life they feel comfortable living.

MAC (Canada)

Walk in and it's all girls at their dressing tables being pampered by other girls in a theatrical blur of brushes, eyeliners and kohl. The interiors are dark, loud and broody and customers are stylish and confident – the combination is theatre. It is active and positive, compelling and young.

Apple Store (USA)

Crowds are good theatre and the best way to attract a crowd, by the way, is to be crowded – already if the store is quiet, gather the team and start expansively demonstrating something. Do that in the eyeline of passing customers and, pretty soon, like meerkats, one or two will notice and wander over and then more will follow.

Apple manages crowds quite brilliantly – stand outside and watch an Apple crowd queuing for a new product launch. They. Are. Insane. Staff, with the zeal of happy cultists, will whoop, cheer and otherwise cajole the assembled throng into a near religious fervour where salvation is a slightly different phone than the one already in their pockets. It's brilliant, creating desire and expectation and reinforcing the sense that the products inside these stores are essential slices of life that must be had new and fresh.

Selfridges (UK)

Dull as ditchwater through the 1980s and 1990s until, in 1996, one of the kings of retail theatre, Vittorio Radice, swept in, ripped out the dark central escalator tower and opened up the store, spending £10m on the building in the process. Selfridges today has come full circle – back to the principles of wonder, entertainment and fun that the eponymous H. Gordon Selfridge founded the store with in 1909 – under the inspired creative leadership of Alannah Weston, who took over from Radice in 2004 and has continued to ramp up the energy and theatre in the store. Weston constantly improved the store both architecturally and theatrically, in particular through the use of strongly themed campaigns she calls "retail activism" that tackle current issues in engaging and often fun ways. Claiming not to be a retailer, Weston always had a keen eye for the numbers but perhaps coming to Selfridges from a world coloured by art, design and creativity is what has helped her to make this one of the most vibrant and exciting retail destinations on the planet.

Stew Leonard's (USA)

The entire store, all four of them, is packed with theatre. From the outside, one of the first things you see is the faux grain tower. It's a small thing, but it begins setting the stage for a dairy, farm-shop narrative. Then, inside, a single path takes you on a winding yellow-brick-road show through the product. At every step there are samples being flourished with smiles, animated products abound, literally in the form of animatronic milk cartons and a joke-telling cow's head, and a webcam live from the milkshed tells the story of freshness. On busy days, there are even people dressed as fruit dancing around the place. It's all active theatre and it's brilliant – please do make the effort to visit one.

Liberty (UK)

Here, it is the building itself that is a dramatic example of retail theatre. Built in 1924 from the black and white timbers of two British warships, Liberty's London home is a character in and of itself. It tells customers lots of the story of its proposition before they even enter. Under the inspirational leadership of Ed Burstell, Liberty has returned to its roots as a theatrical destination, much in the manner of Selfridges, but because of the scale of the building and its interior, Burstell has chosen to tell a more intimate story. It's a retail narrative that has brought Liberty right back into the consciousness of Londoners and is a great example of how a retailer can use the limitations of space to create positive results.

IKEA (Sweden)

In furniture retailing, room sets have always been a staple feature, but it was IKEA that turned them into a procession of interactive plays, each representing a possible lifestyle. The store layout moves every visitor past every room, and every room is a more complete stage set than was traditional in the sector. There are walls, lighting, false ceilings, facsimile windows, rugs and detail – to the extent that it is easy to imagine all the things in that room set in your own home. It's another form of retail narrative, one that makes it incredibly easy for customers to put themselves into.

Kiehl's (US)

Looking like somebody's idea of an apothecary fit for an episode of Seinfeld, Keihl's interiors are straight out of a TV studio, but manage to, at the same time, feel authentic and honest. That's because the people working the film set are superbly well selected and trained and offer such an engaging service. The customer experience is full of little ceremonies of theatre, from the way staff can have a customer seated and sampling in seconds to the freebie sachets of product that are presented at the end with a friendly flourish. I love the Kiehl's customer experience and highly recommend all retailers to study it. There's theatre and engagement in spades here.

Digging out the moments

A good way to introduce theatre into your store is to break down everything you do into small "ceremonies", little routines that create a bit of difference, done with a flourish. It can be something as simple as presenting the bag in a particular way at the end of a sale, the way your people greet customers, the steps in a demonstration, and so on. Any routine element of the customer journey can be made into a ceremony, from attracting attention to taking the money.

Sony's moment of theatre

I once taught Sony's in-store demonstrators to "flourish" a remote control in such a way that it would attract customers. A tiny moment of theatre that, at first, the team were distrustful of. It involved holding the remote down at the hip at arm's length, then circling it out to the side and then out front and wind-milling the other arm over to press a button, then as the button was pressed making a startled "wow" gesture. It sounds nuts, and the way some of them performed the move it looked nuts but, after a while, they began to enjoy the silliness and expression of the thing. The magic bit, though, was out in stores where most of them discovered that this daft bit of movement and theatre could draw a crowd faster than the 23-hour Greggs in Newcastle giving out free pies*. Before they knew it, an intrigued potential customer would be at their shoulder wondering what the fuss was. That's theatre from ceremony.

---

*This is, of course, a lie as nothing draws a crowd faster than free pies in any Greggs. The Sony crowds did form fast, though.

At hotel chain Malmaison, it packs these theatrical ceremonies into everything. Look at the way it deals with a dinner order for a glass of port. Instead of bringing you a glass of port, they bring a clean, empty glass and their port decanter. Your glass is checked, given a little extra polish, placed down and the port is poured there in front of you. It's a process that adds very little to the time it takes to serve a glass of port, but it looks fantastic to the customer – the lovely liquid appetisingly pouring out, the gently pleasing glass-filling sound and the rich colour of a generously filled decanter, the delicious odour rising as molecules are jumbled into the glass – expectation and anticipation go through the roof. There's very little efficiency cost to this, either. The port would still need pouring and the waiter would still need to have come to the table and returned back to the kitchen.

Lovely boutique French jewellery brand Les Néréides fills its sales journey with lots of ceremonies that add up to a deliciously satisfying customer experience. It starts with a visually reinforcing store layout: everything is fresh, collections are given room to breathe and staff are dressed in sweet summery clothes that match well with the design ethos of the jewellery. That's theatre too – it's the equivalent of great set and costumes. As soon as customers interact with the habitually happy and approachable staff, the ceremonies kick in. Lots of drawers of product are removed and placed upon the counter, but in a set way so that only the items that are currently "in play" are visible.

You'll see women, buying for themselves, given mirrors and encouraging comment, and you'll see assistants trying on necklaces to help people buy gifts for female partners. It's incredibly human and involving. Then purchases are wrapped in paper and the paper sprayed with the house scent, then dropped with a deliberate flourish into nicely designed gift bags that seem modern and classic all at the same time (much like the jewellery) and, finally, the bag is tied ostentatiously with a pretty bow. The whole process is full of ceremonies and it makes the experience feel very special indeed, especially given this is costume jewellery selling at a very reasonable price.

Fundamentals of retail theatre

For our next journey into retail theatre we're going out on to the street – we'll maybe even learn about other parts of the puzzle too. That's because the best lesson on the fundamentals of retail you could ever have is to be found at traditional street markets. I don't mean the cool new-wave artisan street markets either, but the honest cut-throat ones. In particular, the fruit and veg stalls on those markets. Right there is where you will see the most efficient, simple and effective principles all in action – not because somebody spent a year studying at the London School of Economics but, instead, because those principles have been passed down over the generations. From father to son, from mother to daughter – because they work.

Seriously, I can't recommend strongly enough that you go and quietly observe the dynamics of a busy street market.

Traders calling out to punters can be exhilarating to watch and listen to, especially when it's done well. What you can learn from listening to these calls (called "barking") is a sense of what really turns customers on. The lines shouted out have been passed down from trader to trader and adapted over generations. Traders still use them because they make customers react. Go beyond the old-time vocal theatricals and you can see some incredible promotional instinct at work. In particular, fruit and veg sellers do two things when they bark:

- They bark the promotions: "two for a pound".
- But listen closely to the words they use when describing the produce – it's not just "cherry, strawberry, apples, oranges, pineapples". You'll hear "Sweet cherry!", "Lovely ripe strawberry!", "Get your fresh apples!" and "Juicy golden pineapple!"

The adjectives – fresh, delicious, ripe, sweet, rosy-red, juicy – are part of the performance and they materially affect the way passing customers feel about what's being sold. If you're even vaguely craving sugar and you hear "sweet and delicious red cherry!" you'll start picturing them in your subconscious, you'll be imagining what they might taste like. There's a chance that your mouth may even be watering right now. Incredible stuff! Remember the Warby Parker example earlier – these words mean things, they're important, they trigger a response and, when spoken, have a visceral effect on us.

As part of building theatre in-store (and when writing about product online), you need to encourage your team to use adjectives like these whenever they're talking about the products they love: awesome colours, fantastic fit, stunning design, superb taste.

This does two things: it engages customers, but, even better, it also gives them the words they will use later to describe how pleased they are with whatever it is they've bought: "Yeah, I got these new jeans, they're a fantastic fit."

There are merchandising lessons there too

Fruit and veg on a stall tends to be laid out pitched at an angle up off the table, with orders then being fulfilled from produce behind the angled crates. This arrangement makes it look like there is more food there than perhaps there really is – this is important because we animals are reassured when we see what we perceive to be plenty. You didn't think we were influenced by that stuff, maybe? We are, all of us. We had a convenience store client in Kazakhstan once where fear of shortage had been directly passed down from the Soviet era to people born after independence. Retailers overfilled shelves and over-fronted everything as a direct result.

Look at the way colours are arranged on a fruit and veg stall too. Rather than blending harmoniously from red to orange to yellow and so on, contrasting colours are put next to each other. This is to help our poor eyes pick one thing out from another but also because, when you walk past this arrangement, it flickers in your peripheral vision where you are seeing it in high-contrast monochrome. That flickering attracts our attention and makes passers-by almost involuntarily glance over.

Stage managing for effect

Managing perceptions is another aspect of great retail theatre and here, again, the fruit and veg sellers can do interesting things. When I originally wrote Smart Retail, I would often need to walk down the Whitechapel Road and past the permanent street-market there. The market contains six greengrocers' stalls, each offering similar products. One morning, I noticed lychees had arrived; these are a big draw for the greengrocers there. On five of the stalls, lychees were all presented at the front in a sort of hot-spot visible to all customers.

But, on the sixth stall, they weren't even on the table. This greengrocer hadn't even had time to get his lychee stock on to a shelf because it was still all on his delivery trolley and customers were pulling boxes of lychees straight from his trolley. Next day, the lychees were again right out front on their delivery trolley . . . and the next . . . something didn't seem right.

I asked the stallholder, Dinesh, why he did this. Dinesh said that customers who saw the lychees tended to believe his were extra fresh because they hadn't been around long enough to be taken off the delivery trolley. "How fresh are they?" I asked. "Three days, these ones." "Do your customers really believe your lychees are fresher than everyone else's because you've not even been able to get them onto the stall?" "Yeah, they do."

Suspending disbelief, helping customers to feel a positive thing. These are theatrical tools and you'll find ways to apply them to your business too.

Why shopping channel presenters are unheralded geniuses

One easy way to get a bit of performance and movement into the store is to do lots of demonstrations. Again, watch market stall-holders: they handle the product constantly, rotating stock, shifting clothes, rearranging sizes or colours, juggling sweets, playing music, sparking up toys, cooking spices on their hotplates. If a stall is momentarily quiet, the stallholder will do their equivalent of my crazy remote control flourish, fishing for customers until they get a new bite. Almost every trader you see will hold a bag of product in his hand as he barks out the deal on that item. A tiny detail but, again, it's done because it's useful in attracting customers.

Another great training ground for learning demonstration skills, and I am serious, is the shopping channels on telly. Watch the guest presenters, especially. These are the people from the product manufacturers who get to come on and plug their wares. These men and women are often brilliant instinctive performers who talk and demonstrate benefit after benefit. Now, I'm like everyone else who gets a bit annoyed when these presenters are talking up something obviously shoddy, but the techniques are still valid. Imagine applying it to your best stuff, to product you genuinely believe to be great. Online, these are the people you need making product videos for you. Have a look at AO.com from the UK for its benefit-driven videos and at the superb review videos at US motorcycle retailer RevZilla. This one is a good example: https://goo.gl/1PJzos. I should mention that the jacket he's rightly cheering on there is made by our family business and it's brilliant. Buy one!

What I'm suggesting you do here is to tap into the power of everyday performance. The demonstrating and playing with stock. Customers really are drawn to products when they see life and action around them. Helping customers to more easily imagine your product actually working for them is very powerful.

Dunkin' v Krispy Kreme
Prodding every sense all at the same time

At the height of its success, Krispy Kreme (KK) stores were taking three times more money than similarly sized Dunkin' Donuts stores. Broadly the same product (although KK reckons its recipe delivers a better texture), same sort of locations, maybe Krispy Kreme had a little bit more of an authentic brand heritage, but that's marginal.

So how come it sells so many lovely, lovely doughnuts?

Scott Livengood is the man who took the business from $200m to $1.2bn revenues in just three years. His big innovation? The introduction of a big bit of retail theatre. Just like fashion, doughnuts are best when hot and fresh in-store. Livengood's moment of genius was to connect the childhood delight of hanging around the kitchen when mum or dad were baking with the process of buying a doughnut.

Up until Livengood's arrival, fresh Krispy Kreme doughnuts arrived at customers through an anonymous hatch in the wall so that the machinery of cooking that doughnut was kept well out of view. Livengood recognised that watching your doughnut being cooked fresh in front of you, taking in the wonderful cooking aroma, would heighten anticipation and spike desire for the product. Stores were then redesigned to make the most of what became "doughnut theatres" and cooking times were changed from early morning to times that matched the optimum desire times – lunchtime and late afternoon – with the aromas then pumped out into the street.

Livengood also decided that free hot doughnuts should be given out to waiting customers during cook times. His finance team said this would halve sales at best, customers coming in for two doughnuts would only buy one and get the other free. What Livengood knew instinctively was that many new customers would come just because there was the possibility of a fresh hot free doughnut and would buy more while there.

A tiny moment of truth: during a store visit, Scott witnessed a staff member wave to a child from inside the "doughnut theatre". It made the kid's day and it appeared the staff member felt good about the interaction too. Scott says that was the moment he realised that he'd done something special.

There is a sting in this particular tale that goes back to Big Idea. The USA is waking up to the need to eat more healthily, which is, potentially, the distant death knell for the doughnut. Krispy Kreme has failed to adapt to this change in the market and is suffering as a result.

Dunkin' Donuts, on the other hand, has moved itself towards a coffee positioning. It has significantly improved the coffee itself, installed proper Italian coffee machines and is now using the advertising slogan "America Runs on Dunkin". It's clever: Dunkin' is now telling customers, "Hey, we're the real American coffee place and we have the finest American snack to go with your coffee." The result is that Dunkin' now serves more cups of coffee per year in the USA than Starbucks, doughnuts have become a small percentage of the sales mix and profitability has gone through the roof.

Now
Things you can do now

- Identify five sources of animation in your merchandising. Can any of these be broadened into other parts of the offer?
- Find three things in the list of great retail theatre examples that could be adapted to your business.
- Find three opportunities to demonstrate product.

Next
Strategic considerations for the longer term

- Find every opportunity through the complete customer journey to define ceremonies – instigate a programme to create these.
- Ensure that theatre, movement and opportunities to demonstrate are at the heart of your next format development process.

Chapter

16

At the end of the day, it's a game of two halves
and, erm, one of those halves will
always be a shop.

Detail, detail, detail – the store environment

In this chapter we explore

- the job of the store
- positioning key fixtures and fittings
- creating great windows
- the value of clear sight-lines.

Using the space

Finally, a chapter just for physical stores. This chapter is an overview of the most critical components of a store and is, essentially, here for indie retailers. It's mostly common sense but is also the stuff I get asked for most often by indie operators and, if it's useful, then I'm delighted to be able to put it here.

There are some useful general principles in this but the detail specific to you is something you are going to have to work out for yourself, based on those principles. It's not as tricky as that might suggest, however. If you know what you are (your Big Idea), if you've worked out how you are going to deliver discovery and if you've identified your opportunities to create some theatre, then you are a good distance towards understanding how to make the physical aspect of the store work properly.

At its simplest, the store fixtures and fittings, signage, colours and windows are there to do a very simple set of things:

- To tell customers the story of what you are and how they will benefit from visiting.
- To tempt them to come in.

- To display products so that customers want to touch and pick them up.
- To showcase curation and promotion.
- To lead customers through the different ranges.
- To make it easy to select and pay for stuff.

If you can put a tick next to each one of those things and say, "Yep, what we've got does all of those", then you're on the money already. Go at each with a lot of honest vigour, though – walk through each as if you were a customer. Retail guru Martin Butler has a great expression: "Spend an hour in your customer's moccasins each day." He's right too, do this and you'll see things differently.

Look and feel

It's relatively easy these days to create knockout gorgeous stores at a sensible cost. Especially as manufacturers are often keen to supply retailers with great-looking free, or part-sponsored, display systems. But, even if you're spending your own money, you must match that spend to your Big Idea. A poundshop doesn't need the same level of quality or design as, perhaps, a boutique jeweller. Equally, stores such as Hotel Chocolat prove that you can achieve classy results on relatively modest budgets (go and have a closer look at the fixtures and fittings – it has managed to adapt some pretty standard kit and make it look amazing – that's clever retailing).

Windows

Your windows are your outside communicators and they must be made to work hard for you. So many retailers seem to think this either means filling them with meaningless piles of stock or filling them with a billion confusing messages, neither of which are any use to you.

A good window display is critical. It must be welcoming: it must give passers-by new reasons to come in and it has to be readable in three seconds. New products are great as window features. When I asked the owner of a successful hardware store how he promoted his hot new items he said, "I put them in the window with a bloody great sign on them that says 'bargain' and 'brilliant' on it. Customers notice the sign. I know they do because they ask me about these new products and then they buy them." And, of course, seasonal or special-occasion activity must be celebrated in your windows too.

The easiest mistake to make with windows is poor lighting, so go brighter than you think. Dull and subdued might be classy, but nobody will even notice you even have a window if they can't immediately see into it. Good stage footlights are an excellent solution, but use LEDs to reduce heat build up, especially in smaller stores.

Broadly, your windows can do three things, either individually or in combination. They can do the following.

Intrigue

These are abstract but sharply focused images that pique customers' interest. AllSaints launched as a new brand using this technique with main windows that featured rows and rows of old sewing machines. It is a theatrical intrigue, makes people want to know what's going on, and has the psychological bonus that in customers' subconscious it suggests tailoring, hand-making and quality, all of which helped support AllSaints' premium positioning.

Inform

Use simple and sharp messages often accompanied by a single product: "Sale Now On", "Our Best Ever Jacket £99", "New Stock Preview". Vinyl lettering is incredibly cheap now, easy to apply and easy to remove. You can change the message every week, if you want to.

Inspire

Design a window display that gets customers thinking about the store and its contents. Gap had a terrific one recently: three fun spring dresses in the window with a great typographical treatment that just said: "Flirty Dresses are the Key to Spring". That's inspiring – it instantly has the customer thinking about ditching the winter blues and jumping into a fun spring wardrobe.

PetSmart's windows

Walk up to PetSmart's Broadway store and you'll usually see a little crowd of people peering into the window. You might even stop to stare too – for one part of that window looks directly in on their pet-grooming room. You'll see pampered pooches having their coats trimmed, their claws nipped and all manner of other crazy pet nonsense. New Yorkers love it and it's a brilliant example of a window that both intrigues and inspires – it makes you look and it tells you that PetSmart loves your pets.

Baskets

If yours is a store where customers ever need to pick up more than one item, then you must offer baskets. Customers who pick up a basket nearly always buy something and very often buy more than customers who don't have a basket. Stores always benefit from having baskets available invitingly on the side edges of the transition zone.

Put the baskets higher up, at waist height, not on the floor. Perching baskets on a table makes it very easy for your customers to just dangle an arm down and almost absent-mindedly pick up a basket. Doing so will increase sales and average transaction values.

Transition zone

This is the area near the door that transfers customers from the outside into the store. You have an opportunity here to make or break the customer experience. If the zone is too empty, customers can feel exposed and then reluctant to move further into the store. If it's too cluttered, that's off-putting too. Instead, it should be clear and easy but with things of interest in it to draw people in gently.

You also need to be aware throughout the store, but here especially, of what retail anthropologist Paco Underhill calls the

My all-time favourite window is also one of the simplest I've ever seen: it's an understated and fun masterpiece – you can't see the shoes. Almost everyone walks over to have a look.

These
shoes
are
rather
nice,
aren'
they?

Source: Koworld

"butt-brush factor". He noticed that customers hate standing anywhere that puts them at risk of other customers constantly brushing past them. In the transition zone, this effect can be useful because it keeps people moving forward into the store. In front of displays, though, it can be a problem because you want customers to linger in those areas. When they do linger, they tend to buy more often. Take a look at all the customer flows in your store, from the entrance and back out again, to see where you can make improvements.

Hot-spots and dead spots

Working with BP, one of the questions they asked us was about the best location for hot offers. Traditionally, these were displayed on an end-fixture facing customers directly as they walked in. We suspected this might actually be a dead zone rather than hot retail promotional space. We ran an observational study across a number of sites that involved tracking customers' gaze as they walked in. We noticed two things:

- Nearly three quarters of all customers turned directly left on entry (BP shops tend to have their door on the far right when viewed from the forecourt), without even looking at that first fixture.

- More than half of all customers (including some in the group above) did an incredible thing when they entered the shop, relating to their main reason for visiting the forecourt, which was to buy fuel. I bet you've already guessed what they did. Some 53% of all customers would step into the shop and immediately look back over their left shoulder to check their pump number as they moved into the store. These people were never even aware there *was* a fixture, let alone looked at it.

So where are the hot-spots? Every store layout is different and, away from FMCG, you should be looking to make all parts of the store worth stopping and interacting with. Avoid high-traffic areas, but make it natural to go from one hot-spot to the next so that customers feel they are always engaged. I hate saying it, but outside of FMCG and variety stores it isn't quite true that "eye level is buy level". Here's the thing – if everything is displayed at eye level, it requires fixtures that are at least as tall, which obscures sightlines. People feel the most comfortable when they aren't hemmed in by aisles and you have a better opportunity to draw people around the store if they can see the things they want or are interested in over and through other displays.

Good promotional hot-spots

Creative use of promotions is essential. Fill the store with them, show people excellent value and then make it easy for them to take you up on your brilliant offers. Never allow a promotion spot to go empty. If you have run out of a line, even for just a few hours, get the promotion POS off the floor right now. If you don't, you will annoy customers who will feel you have let them down.

The ideal promotional hot-spots are:

- visible from the door
- well lit
- bristling with stock
- easy to linger in front of
- honestly presented
- clearly merchandised
- well signed
- surprising.

Promotional product can mean a lot of different things, remember, such as:

- price offers
- products we want to showcase because we love them
- new acquisitions
- seasonal favourites
- things that go together (preferably with a package price)
- new ideas
- products in the news
- hot trend items.

A good tip in a small store is to reserve a space that's in a customer's immediate eye-line when they come in through the front door, and use that to showcase a changing selection. Mark it as such, make it clear and both regulars and new customers alike will make it their first stop on each visit.

Back wall

Do you remember how record shops (now making a comeback in 2016) always used to feature the top 20 singles up on the back wall? That was so they could draw every customer right the way through the store. The really savvy stores would make it very easy for customers to walk through the middle of the shop to the back wall, so customers would all be flowing down that central aisle. Then, when a customer had found their chosen single, they would turn and look for the cash desk. This would be placed back up towards the doors. The customer couldn't easily walk back along the central aisle because it was full of people heading towards them, so they would zigzag through the displays to either side. This zigzagging was brilliant because it meant the customer was exposed to a whole succession of promotional hot-spots as they navigated their indirect course.

Cash desks

There are lots of arguments over where best to put cash desks. To be honest, all have their pros and cons. My preferred position is half-way down one side wall. You can see most of the store from there, queuing can be dealt with neatly and it doesn't eat into the best selling areas.

Here are the most popular options:

- Half-way down one side – my favourite.
- At the front to one side – makes it easy to greet customers walking in, but puts the desk right in the middle of important promotional space.
- In a centre island – although islands can break up sight-lines, this can work really well, especially if you are able to have two people working the desk most of the time because the pair can then watch half the store each, giving you full visual cover.
- On the back wall – popular really only because it usually puts staff near to back-of-house areas. It makes it hard to greet customers and is the shoplifters' favourite option because staff are so far from the door.

Impulse buys

Whatever you sell there will be products in your range that will make great cash-desk impulse purchases. In a newsagent's, chocolate is an obvious example. Hip clothing stores will put cheap toys and iconic trinkets on the counter. Anything that is attractive, low cost and that is physically small makes a great impulse purchase. Vary your selections a little and don't crowd the till area. A few well-chosen items can have a direct impact on increasing your average transaction values. Avoid, at all costs, the hideously uncomfortable joke of forcing your staff to actively sell these items. Staff at WHSmith are made to ask customers if they would like "Any half-price chocolate today, sir?" They hate having to do it and customers are made to feel uncomfortable. It's pushy and weird.

Sight-lines

Two considerations here are foremost:

- Can customers see their way around the store?
- Can you see them?

Customers like to be drawn through your space by the exciting and attractive products and promotions you put in their middle-distance forward vision, even as their brains fight to pay greater attention to the peripheral and to movement. They will often miss things that are right next to them, unless you lead them right to the spot.

Being able to see customers is important because it makes it easy for you and the team to acknowledge them. It is also vital in reducing shoplifting. If you can see the thief better, they are less able to steal – simple as that.

Signage

Always go for crisp and readable over complex, over-designed or wordy. Customers just do not have the time or inclination to decipher clever complicated messages. Promotional signage, especially, should convey a strong bold message in just a few seconds. Tatty signage does nothing for your store – if POS gets damaged, throw it away or replace it immediately.

Now
Things you can do now

- Go and stand across the street and watch customers and your store for a while. What do they see? What do they miss? Which customers go inside? What connects them?
- Check your store against the list under "Using your space". If any are missing, create a plan to fix this.
- Check your windows: do they intrigue, inform and/or inspire?
- Introduce baskets.
- Review your potential hot-spots.

Next
Strategic considerations for the longer term

- Review the plan for your windows versus the promotions planner mentioned in Chapter 14.
- Consider developing a new format that addresses every single point raised throughout *Smart Retail*. Don't worry, we can help, so give me a call :)

What did you think of this book?

We're really keen to hear from you about this book, so that we can make our publishing even better.

Please log on to the following website and leave us your feedback.

It will only take a few minutes and your thoughts are invaluable to us.

www.pearsoned.co.uk/bookfeedback

Epilogue – And we're done?

Wow, 92,000 words later and I hope we're still friends. This has been the biggest change to the book yet, massive shifts in the fundamentals of retailing made this one nearly a two-year writing job. New research and new ideas meant I'd scrap whole sections and start again in new directions. It's only been the last year when reliable patterns have begun to emerge that I've been able to keep things stable.

So it was hard work writing the book, but I sincerely hope that it's been useful reading it. People constantly email me their feedback and thoughts on previous versions and it is both humbling that you would take the time to do so and incredibly useful to read and absorb. *Smart Retail* gets better each time because it is ours: the content isn't my system or process, it's my distillation of your best practice.

Next steps

All of the tools, ideas and interventions I've written about are areas in which my team and I consult. We are a great first port of call should you want to shed light on these things. We've developed formats for global giants, provided customer insight to many of the most important retailers and we've constantly solved problems all along the retail spectrum, as well as helping a number of giant consumer brands better position their product at retail.

Typical consultancy projects for us include:

- finding the Big Idea
- customer-experience improvement
- friction/reward indexing
- retail activation
- store- and product-performance improvement

- format development
- retail troubleshooting
- "back to the floor" insight
- bespoke seminars
- expert assessment and strategy.

Further *Smart Retail*

Smart Retail speaking

Nothing brings this stuff to life like me turning up and passionately talking about it. I've got a set of cracking insight-filled, idea-packed and practical talks that send delegates away buzzing and motivated.

Smart Retail seminars

Practical, proven and very effective – my team and I deliver a set of superb training seminars. Our induction day is legendary and our Street Time Live day, in which we take your people structured-shopping, is one of the most powerful things I've ever been involved in. Always tailored to your business, market and objectives, these seminars are spot on.

My email: richard@smart-circle.com

Web: www.Smart-Circle.com

Twitter: @TheseRetailDays

Facebook: Smart Retail Book

Thank you for buying and reading *Smart Retail*.

All the best

Richard

Appendix I
Reading stores the practical way

I talk a lot in the book about experiencing your stores as customers do and here is a good way to do that. Regularly run this assessment of your own store but also of competitors and non-competitors alike. You'll uncover loads of ideas and possibilities each time you do. There are three areas to observe:

- the store
- the staff
- the customers.

The store

I'll bet good money that you already do this when you walk into a shop: you look around. You look at the fixtures, the offers, the dirt on the carpet and you spot the display gaps. You might even see those gaps and suck your teeth a bit and feel relieved that some other manager is under pressure for once.

Start outside the store – over the road, if possible:

- Watch people walking past.
- How many glance at the window?
- How do they react if they do?
- How do they move if they then come into the store?

Now find a place inside to stand still and observe:

- Watch where customers are going.
- Which part of each section do they enter first?
- Look at people's eyes. What do they see? What do they miss?

- What things do they touch? Which items do they pick up and from where? How long do customers linger over each display fixture?

- How many browsers at each display take something to the counter or to the changing room?

- What sorts of people are shopping at the store? Mums with pushchairs, office workers or mechanics? (This profile will be different at different times of the day.)

- Pay special regard to what happens in the transition zone, that area near the door that transfers customers from the outside and then into the store – how do people move through this area?

Most of us make a really basic mistake when we shop at our own store. We tend to look at it from back to front. We usually see the store from the back staff area or warehouse through the shop floor and out of the front doors. It's a natural mistake but incredibly unhelpful. We just aren't seeing the store in the way our customers do.

Then take a look at the basic store components, including:

- window displays
- promotions
- range
- pricing logic
- fixtures and fittings
- lighting layouts
- added-value ideas.

Make a special note of the bits of the store in which a lot of customers seem to be picking stuff up, as that physical interaction is one of your best starts to converting a browse into a sale. What is it that you've done in these areas that customers seem to be reacting to?

Go through this in your competitors' stores and in other stores that interest you too. I believe firms should not only encourage you to go out reading your competitors' stores but they should even give you a paid session, every week, to go off and do so. In fact, they should even give you a fiver to go and get a latte to slurp while you walk around improving your business through learning from your competitors and other retailers.

The staff

Talk to staff every time you go into a shop. An easy icebreaker is to ask, "What's it like working here?" You will usually get a plain answer along the lines of, "It's not too bad", which doesn't tell you much, but does give you a chance to then ask: "What do you like about it?" Nearly every time you ask that, the assistant will let slip a nugget of useful information:

- "There's a nice team spirit."
- "The pay is good."
- "It's a laugh."
- "We're treated with a bit of respect."
- "Every day is different."
- "I like customers."

Each of those answers allows you to unobtrusively ask further questions that help to get to specific employment practices in play at that store. Try to chat with the store manager too. Tell them what you do. Share some thoughts and ideas with them and they often will with you.

Most people do love to share their opinions – turn that to your advantage.

The customers

Listen. What do customers say to each other? What do they say to assistants? How are customers being approached?

Talking to customers in your own store is easy as you've got a badge on that says you are okay to talk to. Talking to customers elsewhere is a bit harder to do. Brits tend to be a little wary of strangers asking questions but it can be done without you appearing to be a nutter. Most people do love to share their opinions – turn that to your advantage.

In your own store you can ask lots of open questions, such as:

- "How well have we looked after you today?"
- "What do you think about how we've changed our displays?"
- "How easy was it to find what you were looking for?"
- "What do you think of these new products?"
- "How easy is it to shop in my store?"
- "What was the first thing you noticed when you came in today?"
- "What's your opinion on how I've set up my till area?"
- "What am I missing in my store, do you think?"
- "What sort of things do other shops like mine do that you really like?"

When I'm in my civvies and out in somebody else's store, I find the most successful question tends to be: "I run a store like this one, what do you like about this shop?" and I'll be asking that usually while waiting in a queue at the tills. Lots of other opportunities to open up a conversation usually present themselves while wandering around the store too.

If the customer starts to chat happily, be conversational and don't try to sound like you're doing a survey. People tend to respond along the lines of, "Oh, I like the way they do X but I really wish they would sort out that damn Y." Maybe we just like complaining, but I have found, over and over again, that these little chats can uncover a glaring problem for you to look out for in your own store. Of course, some customers will also happily give you a rundown of what it is that attracts them to the particular store you are in, and that's extra useful.

Appendix II
Street time

Street Time is the inspirational real-world-insight event that every retail team should experience. Each Street Time is structured around the clients' specific challenge or opportunity. The event then works to explore best practice, history, strategies and ideas relevant to that challenge and finishes with a tailored exercise in which teams compete to create the best solutions.

What do we do?

Usually run as a one-day event for small teams, Street Time puts delegates out onto the streets (and online) right into the best and worst customer experiences. It dissects and then shows, through practical experience, exactly why one retail idea works where another doesn't.

It's a great way to find inspiration in the following areas:

- Big Idea
- friction/reward
- discovery
- curation and narrative.

I've run Street Time for senior management teams from the likes of BP, Hotel Chocolat, Odeon, B&Q and Sony – through to mass events such as hosting 70 of Kingfisher's global brightest and best in Warsaw. We've run Street Time all over Europe, even once had Peter Jones live-review the results, and always been humbled and delighted by client feedback.It's a powerful session that brings Smart Retail alive.

Appendix III
Books for retailers

Decent books on retailing are few and far between, which is one of the reasons why I wrote this one. Of those rarities, the ones listed here are the best. Two of the titles are pretty hard to get hold of in the UK but are available at www.amazon.co.uk. Most bookshops may be able to order them for you too.

Visual Merchandising by Tony Morgan (Laurence King, 2016)

The most recent update keeps this book an essential read. It's the one book on visual merchandising (windows, signage, fixtures and fittings if you're wondering) that manages to be both incredibly strong on the loveliness of design and on the practical things that design is there to support. A really good companion to *Smart Retail*.

The Richer Way by Julian Richer (Richer Publishing, 5th edition, 2009)

Richer manages people better than anyone I have ever come across. This is the story of how he does that. Essential reading.

Made in America: My Story by Sam Walton with John Huey (Doubleday, 1992)

The story of how Sam Walton and his team built the world's biggest company: Walmart. This is a lot of fun, full of breathtaking daring, down-home philosophy and some great retail stories. An absolute must-read, even now so long after it was first published. I love this book.

Uncontainable: How Passion, Commitment, and Conscious Capitalism Built a Business Where Everyone Thrives by Kip Tindell, Casey Shilling and Paul Keegan (Grand Central Publishing, 2014)

Another founding story, this time of Container Store and this one is packed with insight you can use. The descriptions of how the business got from A to B on issues are fascinating and the whole thing is told in sparky and very readable dialogue. It's a great book about a fantastic retail business.

Thinking, Fast and Slow by Daniel Kahneman (Penguin, 2012)

Not specifically a retail book at all but it is definitely a book for retailers. It is the best explanation you'll find of why we make the choices we make and the ways in which those choices can easily be disrupted by simple changes in context. If you've ever struggled to understand why customers and colleagues make the decisions they make, then there's a very strong chance that you will find the answers in here.

Inside the Nudge Unit: How small changes can make a big difference by David Halpern (WH Allen, 2016)

Another one that isn't about retail but that all retailers will benefit from reading. Halpern is the behavioural scientist behind the UK Government's hugely successful Behavioural Insights Team. In this book Halpern brings to life lots of case studies that you'll have heard about and describes in detail the mechanisms that made them effective. Like Thinking Fast and Slow, there is massive insight here into what prompts us to make the choices we make.

Index